THE DEATH OF SOCRATES
AND
THE LIFE OF PHILOSOPHY

THE DEATH OF SOCRATES
AND
THE LIFE OF PHILOSOPHY

An Interpretation of Plato's *Phaedo*

Peter J. Ahrensdorf

State University of New York Press

Published by
State University of New York Press, Albany

For information, address State University of New York
Press, State University Plaza, Albany, NY 12246

Production by Diane Ganeles
Marketing by Theresa Abad Swierzowski

Library of Congress Cataloging-in-Publication Data

Ahrensdorf, Peter J., 1958–
    The death of Socrates and the life of philosophy : an
interpretation of Plato's Phaedo / Peter J. Ahrensdorf.
        p.   cm.
    Includes bibliographical references and index.
    ISBN 0-7914-2633-5 (alk. paper). — ISBN 0-7914-2634-3 (pbk. :
alk. paper)
    1. Plato.   Phaedo.   2. Rationalism.   3. Philosophy and religion.
I. Title.
B379.A87   1995
184—dc20   94-40812
                                                        CIP

10 9 8 7 6 5 4 3 2 1

To the memory of
Allan Bloom

Contents

Acknowledgments

The publication of this book gives me the welcome opportunity to acknowledge many debts. My work on the *Phaedo* began with my dissertation for the degree of Doctor of Philosophy in the Committee on Social Thought at the University of Chicago. Earlier versions of sections of chapters 1 and 12 can be found in "The Question of Historical Context and the Study of Plato," *Polity*, Fall 1994. I would like to thank the John M. Olin Foundation for its generous financial support. I thank, as well, Davidson College, especially Thomas Kazee and Dean Robert Williams, for their encouragement and support, and the State University of New York Press and its readers for their editorial assistance and helpful comments.

I also wish to express my deep gratitude to my mother and my late father, Victoria and Joachim Ahrensdorf, to my brother and sister, Ramon Valenzuela and Carmen Nakassis, and to Ursula Michaelis for their unstinting support of and faith in me.

My life has been blessed by the presence of many remarkable teachers and friends, and whatever merit this book may have should be attributed to them. Thomas Pangle introduced me to the study of Plato and has been a truly invaluable source of advice, encouragement, and inspiration throughout the many stages of my education and of this work. David Grene generously made available to me his immense classical learning; whatever knowledge I have of the ancient Greek language I owe primarily to him. Nathan Tarcov gave me the benefit of his always wise counsel, his uncannily perceptive questions and comments, and his own example as a scholar and a thinker. Through his writings, his classes, and his conversation, David Bolotin has taught me more than I can adequately acknowledge about the *Phaedo*, in particular, and the Socratic way of life as a whole.

Stephen Wirls, Fred Baumann, and Paul Stern assisted me enormously with their challenging questions, their fruitful suggestions, and their steadfast support. Alfred Mele graciously provided me with careful and constructive criticisms of portions of the manuscript, as well as always astute advice and friendly encouragement. Robert Bartlett read the entire manuscript with exceptional care, and his insistence that I clarify my thoughts has improved it in crucial ways.

To my friends, Richard Ruderman and Steven Kautz, I owe a special debt. The former read the manuscript with his characteristic sensitivity and intelligence and offered me the most rewarding insights and suggestions. The latter was unbelievably generous with his time and advice and offered me the most candid, the most timely, and the most beneficial criticisms. Both have provided me with encouragement and guidance throughout the many stages of this work and, indeed, throughout my adult life, and from them I have learned more than they can know.

My wife Alejandra always knew when to reassure, when to insist, and what to advise. Without her love, her patience, and her sound judgment, and without the inspiriting example of her own diligence and fortitude, I never could have brought this work to completion.

To Allan Bloom, my late teacher and friend, I owe more than I can say. I dedicate this book to his memory.

Peter J. Ahrensdorf

Introduction

While all of Plato's dialogues celebrate the philosophic life as a whole and the life of Socrates in particular, none does so more dramatically or more movingly than the *Phaedo*.[1] There we see the philosopher face death with a nobility which all must admire (see 58e3–59a1, 116c4–8). There we see him proclaim and defend his pious belief in the immortality of the soul even as his fellow citizens are executing him for impiety. Finally, there we see Socrates die as a victim of human prejudice and injustice and as a martyr for the truth. No other dialogue comes as close to evoking the tragic sentiments of pity and fear, and the tears that accompany such sentiments, as this one does. In no other dialogue do the actions presented come so close to overshadowing the argument as they do here. No other dialogue comes closer to being a true drama than does the *Phaedo*.

More than any other Platonic dialogue, the *Phaedo* invites its readers to revere the philosopher Socrates as a kind of hero. The dialogue virtually opens with Phaedo's praise of Socrates' extraordinary serenity and fearlessness in the face of death, and it closes with Phaedo's famous statement, on behalf of his friends, that Socrates was the best man they had ever known or tested and that he was especially the most wise and the most just. More importantly, our own experience of reading the dialogue, of being with Socrates on his last day, of hearing his final conversation with his friends, and of witnessing his death seems to confirm the justice of Phaedo's praise of Socrates and encourages us to admire him as Phaedo does. As Cicero says, Socrates at his death "spoke in language which made him seem not as one thrust out to die but as one ascending to the heavens."[2] And, as Jacques Maritain says of Socrates' actual death, it is "the most sublime death to which merely human wisdom can lead."[3]

Indeed, it is above all through the *Phaedo* that Plato secured for Socrates, and therewith for the philosopher as such, a place among the great heroes of what we now call Western civilization. Before Plato wrote, the philosopher, that is, the man who devotes his life to the quest for wisdom, was an object of ridicule, suspicion, and even of hatred, a subject

1

of comedy and not tragedy, and a man certainly not deemed comparable to the true models of human excellence to be found, for example, in the poems of Homer.[4] But through his dramatic portrayal of Socrates' life and especially through his portrayal of that man's death, Plato transformed the hitherto despised and scorned philosopher into an object of respect and even of admiration. As Nietzsche declares, "The *dying Socrates* became the new ideal, never seen before, of noble Greek youths."[5] And, as Voltaire states, "The death of this martyr was actually the apotheosis of philosophy."[6] From Plato's unforgettable account of Socrates' death, men learned to revere what they had hitherto ridiculed. They learned to look up to a kind of human being on whom they had previously looked down. They learned to see nobility and virtue where before they had seen only corruption and vice. Henceforth, the philosopher Socrates was to be repeatedly ranked among the most glorious of heroes and the most holy of martyrs. He was to be compared continuously with the warrior Alexander, the citizen Cato, and the divine Jesus.[7] And as a result of Plato's truly singular poetic achievement, the philosopher has, for some twenty-five hundred years, retained a largely unchallenged presence within our pantheon of heroes and our imaginings of human greatness.

Yet, while Plato's moving portrayal of the dying Socrates deliberately tempts us to regard that philosopher as a simply admirable human being, the *Phaedo* as a whole quietly but unmistakably encourages us to resist that temptation. For the *Phaedo* is primarily devoted, not to portraying the death of Socrates, but rather to presenting his *argument* for the goodness of the philosophic life. That argument takes the form of a defense speech, of an apology, and it is appropriately preceded and provoked by an indictment of the philosophic life (see 62c9–64a3, 69d7ff.; see also 95b7–e6). Indeed, the *Phaedo* is nothing less than a reenactment of the trial of Socrates, with the important difference that here, in contrast with his *Apology of Socrates*, Plato presents a detailed version of the prosecution's speech, and specifically of the impiety charge, against Socrates. Early in the dialogue, two of Socrates' most devoted companions accuse him and all philosophers of leading unwise, unjust, and impious lives. And Socrates takes this charge so seriously that he devotes the entirety of the last conversation of his life to defending himself and philosophy against that charge. In Socrates' companions' eyes and even in his own eyes, the philosopher's life-long attempt to discover the truth about things on his own and for himself is not self-evidently admirable or even good but is rather profoundly questionable and hence always stands in need of a defense. The *Phaedo* comes to sight as a eulogy for the philosopher Socrates, but it is, in fact, an apology of Socrates. It is Socrates' last apology, his final defense of the philosophic life before he was executed by the city of Athens for impiety.

Although it is true, then, that the *Phaedo*'s dramatic presentation of Socrates' death invites us to admire the philosopher, its presentation of both the impiety charge against Socrates and his defense against that charge encourages us to challenge, to doubt, and to question for ourselves the goodness of his philosophic life. It encourages us to take seriously the possibility that the human being who devotes his life to the pursuit of wisdom through reason alone is, in truth, an unwise, unjust, and impious human being. It encourages us to wonder whether Socrates was not justly condemned by the Athenians and even whether he will not be justly condemned by the gods or by God in an afterlife. Yet, by doing this, the *Phaedo* may not diminish but rather enhance our admiration for the philosophic way of life. For, by encouraging us to see and to feel for ourselves the strength of the case against philosophy, it may enable us to appreciate more deeply and more soundly than we could have otherwise the full strength of the case for philosophy. In this way, the *Phaedo* may point us toward a genuine admiration for the philosopher, one that comes from our minds as well as our hearts, and one that focuses not only on the philosopher's fearlessness or nobility but also, and above all, on his wisdom.

If we assume, as scholars generally do, that Socrates was a plain-spoken man who always said what he meant and meant what he said, and if we read his speeches in the *Phaedo* accordingly, then his defense of the philosophic life in that dialogue will appear to be quite straightforward. In response to his companions' charge that he and all philosophers lead unwise, unjust, and impious lives, Socrates claims that he and all genuine philosophers actually cherish throughout their lives the pious hope that, when they die, their souls will dwell with the gods forever (see 62c9–63c7, 63e8–64a9, 69c3–e2). And when one of his companions points out that the soul of a human being who has died may not continue to exist at all, Socrates proceeds to argue and even, as he claims, to demonstrate that the soul is, in truth, immortal (see 69e6–70b4, 77b1–d5). Socrates, then, attempts to vindicate the philosophic life in the *Phaedo* by attempting to prove to his friends that there is an afterlife in which the philosopher will be rewarded by the gods with everlasting happiness (see 80d5–81a10, 107c8–d5, 115d2–6). And the dialogue suggests that he succeeds in this attempt. For the dialogue ends with Phaedo's praise of Socrates, on behalf of his friends, as the best, the wisest, and the most just man they ever knew or tested. Yet, as Socrates himself seems to acknowledge in the dialogue and as ancient, modern, and contemporary commentators have observed, the arguments in the *Phaedo* fail to establish that the individual soul is immortal.[8] It appears, then, that Socrates' final defense of the philosophic life is, in truth, a failure. As David Bostock says of the final argument, it is "extremely disappointing," it is based on a "presumption of the conclusion," but "this is simply a mistake which we can do nothing to put right."[9]

R. Hackforth does suggest that "it is only if we allow that the appeal is to faith that we can avoid a feeling of deep disappointment in this matter, inasmuch as from the standpoint of logic the argument has petered out into futility."[10] And such scholars as John Burnet, A. E. Taylor, R. S. Bluck, and David White have also suggested that Socrates' argument for immortality, and therewith his defense of the life of reason, may be ultimately based on "faith" and "mysticism."[11] But, as David Gallop points out, "the bathos of an appeal to religious faith at the climax of a philosophically sophisticated argument would only deepen the disappointment. . . . The 'religious faith' interpretation simply undercuts the central enterprise of the dialogue."[12] Yet Gallop agrees with Hackforth that Socrates embraces the final argument without reservation.[13] The dialogue, then, seems to leave us wondering whether the philosopher, who ostensibly lives his life in strict accordance with reason, does not, in fact, live his life cherishing in his heart a noble but ultimately unreasonable hope for personal immortality and everlasting happiness (compare 63e8–64a9, 107a8–c4, 114c6–8 with 88b3–8, 95b8–e6).

Now, insofar as this reading of the dialogue leaves us in this state of perplexity, it encourages us to examine on our own and for ourselves the question of whether it truly is good for a human being to devote his life to the quest for wisdom. As Gallop puts it, "The work is not an exposition of his [Plato's] doctrines, but a meditation upon the issues it raises, and a stimulus to the reader to explore them for himself."[14] Yet the dialogue itself can positively assist us and even guide us in our investigation of this question if only we will return to it and study it with an appropriate care.[15] Before we embark on such a study, however, we must first reconsider our initial assumption that Socrates was a plain-spoken man who always spoke his mind to his interlocutors. For even though that assumption is commonly made by scholars, it is, in fact, a false assumption. Far from being a plain-spoken man, Socrates was, as we know from the dialogues themselves, a supremely ironic man.[16] And consequently, a reading of the *Phaedo* that is based on the assumption that Socrates always said what he meant and meant what he said is bound to be inadequate.[17] Before we turn to a more careful study of Socrates' speeches in the *Phaedo*, then, let us first consider the distinctive character of Socratic speech as such.

In that other apology of Socrates, namely, the defense speech he gave at his trial, Socrates suggests to his audience that he is speaking ironically to them.[18] He suggests, in other words, that he is not being altogether frank or truthful with his audience but that he is rather concealing from them his truest thoughts. And he thereby confirms what is said about him in a number of Platonic dialogues[19] and especially in that other famous praise of Socrates, namely, the one given by the altogether frank Alcibiades in the *Symposium* (222c1-3). For there Alcibiades says that Socrates spends his whole life being ironic with his fellow human beings (216e2-5; see also 218d5-6). In this way, he suggests that none of Socrates' speeches are simply straightforward, that none of them simply communicate his true thoughts, and hence that Socrates never simply speaks his mind to others. Yet Alcibiades also says in the *Symposium* that Socrates' speeches are the only ones that possess intelligence and that consequently it is fitting for the man who would become noble and good to examine them (221d7-222a6; see also 216e5-217a2). Alcibiades suggests, then, that, while Socrates' ironic speeches conceal the truth from many of those who listen to them, they also reveal the truth to those who study them with care and who are capable of learning (see 218a2-6). And Socrates himself seems to indicate in the *Symposium* that what Alcibiades says about his speeches is altogether true (see 214e4-215a1).

The suggestion that Socrates at times deliberately conceals the truth from his interlocutors is, to be sure, a controversial one. For example, while Gregory Vlastos acknowledges that "the intention to deceive, so alien to our word for irony, is normal in its Greek ancestor *eironeia, eiron, eironeuomai*," he nonetheless denies that Plato's Socrates ever deliberately deceived anyone on the grounds that such disingenuousness would have been incompatible with Plato's praise of Socrates in the *Phaedo* as "the most just man" he had ever known.[20] Yet in the *Republic* Socrates explicitly argues that it is sometimes just to deceive not only one's enemies but also one's friends (see 331c1–d3, 382c6-10; see also 414b8–415d5, 450d10–e1), and in the *Phaedo* he explicitly warns his friends that he may deceive them (91a1–c5). It would seem, then, that, at least according to Plato's Socrates, it is quite possible both to deceive human beings on occasion and to be a most just man.[21]

Now, if we assume that Socrates was not only a master of irony but also a man who sought to help others learn the truth, we arrive at the following conclusion regarding the character of his speeches: in his speeches, Socrates sought to intimate the truth to those "few who are capable of discovering [it] by themselves by means of slight indication" while at the same time concealing the truth from those who could not profit from it.[22] As Friedrich Schleiermacher says, "the real investigation is overdrawn with another, not like a veil, but, as it were, an adhesive skin, which conceals from the inattentive reader, and from him alone, the matter which is to be properly considered or discovered, while it only sharpens and clears the mind of an attentive one to perceive the inward connection."[23] Socratic speech, then, is, in a very precise sense, double talk:[24] it seeks to lead those who are able to benefit from the truth to grasp the truth, and it seeks to lead those who are not able to benefit from the truth to embrace opinions which, while perhaps not true, may nonetheless be beneficial to them. And consequently, when reading Socrates' speeches in defense of the philosophic life in the *Phaedo*, we cannot simply regard what he says on the surface as an expression of his true thoughts but must rather look beneath the surface.[25]

Yet, if we cannot accept what Socrates says at face value, how can we determine what he truly thought? How can we know, when burrowing beneath the surface, that what we unearth is his true thought? How can we know, when interpreting his speeches, that we are not simply reading into them our own assumptions or guesses about what Socrates must have truly thought? How, in sum, can we avoid all the dangers of arbitrary interpretation?

We can, I believe, avoid these dangers and discover what Socrates really thought but only if we begin by taking our bearing from his interlocutors. The Platonic dialogues, as we know, are dramas rather than treatises, and in them we never see Socrates, the hero of those dramas, giving a soliloquy. Instead, we always see him speaking to particular characters and addressing their particular questions and concerns. Accordingly, the only nonarbitrary beginning point for our reading of the dialogues is to begin from his interlocutors' particular concerns. We must try to identify what those concerns are, to see their importance, and to make them, or recognize them as, our own concerns. We must try, in other words, to see and to feel for ourselves what is at stake for Socrates' interlocutors in this particular conversation. And, most importantly, we must try to awaken in ourselves the desire to learn the truth about the matter being discussed (see 91b7–c5). This way of reading the dialogues will eventually lead us beyond the interlocutors. Our desire to know the truth will naturally lead us to examine whether Socrates adequately addresses their specific concerns and whether he adequately answers their specific questions and objections. Inevitably, we will be led to question assertions that they fail to question and to object to arguments that they find unobjectionable. And if we follow through on the interlocutors' own questions and concerns even more rigorously than they do, we may come to see Socrates' innermost thought even more clearly than they do, and we may even finally arrive at the center of his thought. But unless we begin from their concerns, unless, that is, we begin from the only starting point that the dialogue itself provides us with, we run the great risk of interpreting Socrates' speeches arbitrarily and of being led astray by our preconceived notions of what he really thought or by our imagination. Socrates' interlocutors in the *Phaedo*, then, are our natural stepping stones into the dialogue, and it is only by beginning from where they begin that we can hope to understand how

Socrates defended the philosophic life on the day of his death and whether he defended it adequately.

Kenneth Dorter and Ronna Burger have written books on the *Phaedo* which emphasize, as I do, the dramatic character of the dialogue and which contain, in my opinion, many extremely interesting and helpful observations. Nevertheless, it seems to me that they are unduly dismissive of the interlocutors' "emotional" concerns, that they are too quick to assume that Socrates speaks "over the heads of his interlocutors," and that consequently they tend to ignore what I regard as the only nonarbitrary beginning point for a study of Socrates' speeches to his interlocutors in the dialogue.[26] Paul Stern's excellent book on the *Phaedo* pays considerably more attention to the concerns of the interlocutors. Nevertheless, I am inclined to think that he departs too quickly from their pious perspective and consequently underestimates the degree to which Socrates' defense of the philosophic life in the dialogue is directed against the theoretical challenge posed to that way of life by piety.[27] Perhaps the most significant substantive difference between the interpretations of Dorter, Burger, and Stern and my own is that I believe that Socrates takes quite seriously the pious claim that the *individual* soul is immortal and that his defense of the philosophic life in the dialogue is based on an investigation of that claim.[28] The interpretation of the *Phaedo* which I have found to be the most helpful and to which I am most indebted is David Bolotin's article, "The Life of Philosophy and the Immortality of the Soul: An Introduction to Plato's *Phaedo*."

Chapter 1

The Context of Socrates' Defense of Philosophy

We cannot hope to understand Socrates' defense of the philosophic life in the *Phaedo* unless we understand the audience to which that defense is addressed. Only by discerning the distinctive character of his interlocutors and of their doubts about the philosophic life can we discern the distinctive character of the defense which Socrates presents to them. Only by seeing and feeling for ourselves the strength of their doubts can we determine how or whether Socrates answers those doubts.

We know from the other dialogues of Plato and from the Socratic works of Xenophon that the men who were with Socrates on the day of his death were among his most devoted followers.[1] We also know that a number of them went on to become founders of important schools of philosophy and authors of philosophic works.[2] But even though they have been persuaded by Socrates' speeches and moved by his example to live, or to try to live, the philosophic life, on the day of his death, they cannot help but wonder about the wisdom and goodness of that way of life (see 62c9–63b3). In order to understand the reason for their doubts, we must attempt to put ourselves in their shoes, to imagine ourselves in their world, and to see through their eyes the significance of the impending execution of Socrates.

I. The Persecution of the Philosophers

The execution of Socrates signifies more to these men than the loss of a teacher and a friend. For the conviction and condemnation of Socrates is part of a persistent pattern of persecution of philosophers in the Greek cities of their time, a pattern that has emerged most ominously in the most civilized of those cities, Athens. This hostility to philosophers renders the philosophic pursuit of wisdom an extremely dangerous activity. Since these companions of Socrates are devoted to philosophy, the execution of their companion must remind them that they, too, may be persecuted if they persist in their devotion (see 64a10–b6). In this way, the execution of Socrates must lead them to wonder whether, given the threat of persecution, the life devoted to the rational pursuit of wisdom is itself a wise or good way of life.

9

The conviction and subsequent execution of Socrates by Athens was not the only instance of a Greek city persecuting a philosopher.[3] Soon after the emergence of philosophy in Greece, philosophers began to suffer from the hostility of the politically powerful. Pythagoras and his followers had formidable enemies in Sicily. A large number of Pythagoreans were slain there, and, according to one account, Pythagoras himself was killed while fleeing from an angry mob.[4] Xenophanes was expelled from his native city, Colophon. And Zeno was put to death for plotting to overthrow the tyrant of Elea.[5]

But of greater importance than these instances was the plight of philosophers in Athens, the self-proclaimed school of Greece and the Greek city most open to philosophy.[6] Anaxagoras was the first philosopher to take up residence in Athens. There he became the adviser and friend of Pericles. But his friendship with Pericles did not prevent him from being imprisoned. He barely won release from prison and fled from the city.[7] Damon, a sophist and an associate of Pericles and Socrates, was ostracized.[8] Protagoras was expelled from Athens, and his books were burned in the agora.[9] The philosopher Diagoras was condemned to death and fled from Athens. The Athenians then announced that a talent of silver would be awarded to the man who killed him.[10] And Socrates himself was condemned to death and executed.

Philosophers and their associates, then, were frequently victims of severe persecution in Athens. It is true that philosophers appear to have been drawn to Athens by her reputation for openness. Other cities were also hostile to philosophy.[11] And Parmenides, Zeno, and Democritus appear to have passed through Athens without being harassed.[12] Nevertheless, the number and the prominence of the philosophers who were persecuted indicates that, by the end of the fifth century B.C., a clear pattern of persecution of philosophers by Athens had emerged.[13]

Nor did this hostility to philosophers abate soon after the execution of Socrates. Plato and his companions fled from Athens shortly after that execution. Aristotle later had to steal away from Athens for fear of imprisonment. Fifty years after Socrates' death, his execution was publicly cited with approval. And, at about the same time, Isocrates thought it necessary to make a defense of philosophy in response to the Athenians' strong opposition to it.[14] The Athenians' hostility to philosophy, then, was neither evanescent nor superficial but persistent and deep-seated.

II. The Philosophers and the Impiety Charge

But what was the cause of this hostility? Although the reasons varied from case to case, the principal cause of the hostility to the philosophers was the widely held opinion that they were impious. Anaxagoras, Protagoras, Diagoras, Socrates, and Aristotle were all accused and convicted of impiety.[15] In the *Apology* Socrates states that the standard charge against philosophers is atheism, and Plato has the Athenian Stranger repeat and elaborate on this statement in the *Laws*.[16] In the eyes of the people, their leaders, and their poets, the philosophers were atheists, and they corrupted the youth by turning them into atheists as well.[17]

The charge of impiety was an extremely grave charge in the cities of ancient Greece.[18] Religion was at the heart of family and political life in the ancient city. The Greeks claimed to derive their moral codes and their laws from the gods. To call into question the existence of the gods was tantamount to undermining the most fundamental moral beliefs and the legitimacy of the city's laws.[19] Accordingly, the Greeks took their piety most seriously. The Athenians, for example, showed themselves willing on a number of occasions to sacrifice political and military advantage for religious reasons. They attempted to arrest their outstanding general, Alcibiades, and then condemned him to death in absentia at a crucial moment in the Peloponnesian War because he had allegedly mocked his city's religion.[20] The general Nicias chose to risk the destruction of the Athenian army in Sicily rather than refuse to heed what he and most of the Athenians took to be a sign from the gods.[21] Finally, the Athenians put to death the admirals who had just led them to one of their city's greatest naval victories because they had chosen not to gather the bodies of the dead Athenian sailors—as required by religious custom—during a dangerous storm after their victory.[22] The Athenians were willing to court military disaster and to execute victorious generals in order to fulfill their religious duties.[23] They believed that to leave impiety unpunished was to commit impiety and thereby to provoke the anger of the gods.[24] Those who did not believe in their gods and who taught others not to believe in them were, then, peculiarly dangerous criminals and were to be treated accordingly.

But what was the basis of the charge that the philosophers were impious? Plutarch, in a key passage of his life of Nicias (23), sheds light on this important question:

> But just as all these things were ready [for the Athenian forces' retreat from Syracuse] and none of the enemy was on the watch, since they did not expect it, there was an eclipse of the moon by night, and a great fear entered Nicias and those of the rest who, because of their inexperience or superstition, were struck with terror at such things. For that the darkening of the sun at the end of the month was somehow caused by the moon was already understood even by the many. But what it was that the moon encountered and how, being full, she should suddenly lose her light and

emit all sorts of colors, this was not easy to grasp, but they believed it strange and a sign from a god in advance of certain great misfortunes. For the first man to set down in writing the clearest and boldest argument of all about the shining and shadowing of the moon was Anaxagoras. And neither was he ancient nor was the argument reputable, but it was still secret and proceeded among a few and with a certain caution or trust. For they [the many] did not abide the natural philosophers and the praters about the heavens, as they were called at that time, because they reduced the divine to unreasoning causes, improvident powers, and necessary properties. But even Protagoras went into exile, the imprisoned Anaxagoras was barely saved by Pericles, and Socrates, who did not concern himself with any of such things,[25] nevertheless died on account of philosophy. But later the reputation of Plato shone forth, on account of the life of the man and because he placed the natural necessities under the divine and more authoritative principles, and took away the slander against these arguments and gave a path to these studies to all men. At any rate, his companion Dion, although there was an eclipse of the moon at the time when he was about to set sail out of Zacynthe against Dionysius, was not at all disturbed but put to sea, and landing at Syracuse he expelled the tyrant.

Plutarch explains that the many were hostile to philosophers because they reduced what the many thought divine—the gods who cared for human beings and who were free to reward and punish them—to unreasoning causes, improvident powers, and necessary properties. In the eyes of the many, the philosophers reduced the divine to the natural, the religious to the scientific. The philosophers taught that eclipses are not signs of the gods' righteous anger but predictable natural phenomena. They showed that thunder and lightning are not divine punishments of the wicked but forces of uncaring nature. The philosophers revealed a universe that is deaf to man's demand for cosmic justice.[26] These discoveries shattered the Greeks' vision of a universe that supported and enforced their laws and their moral codes. The philosophers demystified the world, and this demystification threatened to delegitimize and demoralize the ancient city. By challenging, in particular, the belief in gods who reward the just and punish the unjust, the philosophers threatened to undermine the belief in the superiority of the just life to the unjust life and therewith the belief in the goodness of justice itself.[27] This "atheistical trend of early Greek philosophy," as one scholar has called it, seemed to lead to the conclusion that the gods do not exist, that there are no divine sanctions for morality, and therefore that everything is permitted to human beings.[28] Unwilling or unable to accept this conclusion, the cities of ancient Greece strove to quiet and even to silence the philosophers. And, in doing so, they understood themselves to be acting not only on behalf of themselves and their gods but on behalf of justice itself.

The religious persecution of the philosophers posed a grave threat to the very survival of philosophy in ancient Greece. The philosophers were defenseless in the face of the hostility of the Greek cities. The threat of imprisonment, exile, or even execution hung over their heads at all times.[29] Over time such persecution must have reduced philosophers to solitude, silence, and even to extinction.

It is true that, in the twentieth century, there have been some who have denied that philosophers in general and Socrates in particular were persecuted for religious reasons in ancient Greece. Most prominently, John Burnet claimed that Socrates was put to death not because he was believed to be impious but rather because of his criticism of the democracy and its leaders.[30] Since this claim has been repeated by such scholars as Taylor, G. M. A. Grube, and I. F. Stone, and since I believe it is mistaken, I wish to examine it in some detail.[31]

Burnet writes:

> We have now to ask why Sokrates was charged with irreligion and why he was put to death. We must at once put aside the idea that it was for not believing the stories about the gods. It is not likely that any educated man believed these, and uneducated people probably knew little about them. There was no church and no priesthood, and therefore the conception of religious orthodoxy did not exist. So far as mythology was concerned, you might take any liberty.

Burnet's claim that the impiety charge against Socrates was not the real charge against him is based, then, on the broader claim that Greek piety did not entail "belief in narratives of any kind." "No one," he goes on to say, "could be prosecuted for what we call religious opinions."[32] And earlier in this book he claims, "Speculative opinions . . . were no part of Greek religion, which consisted entirely in worship and not in theological affirmations or negations."[33] According to Burnet, the Greeks did not care whether or not men's opinions were pious—that is, whether or not they actually believed in the gods—so long as their actions were not impious.[34] And, since Socrates' actions were not impious, he could not have been condemned to death for impiety. Therefore, Burnet concludes, he must have been condemned for his association with the antidemocratic Critias and Alcibiades.[35]

Burnet's explanation of why Socrates was condemned is, however, contradicted by Plato's own words and by the historical evidence available to us from other ancient sources. Although Burnet says that "Plato indicates in the clearest possible manner that Sokrates really owed his death to his political attitude," Plato himself says in the *Seventh Letter*, which

Burnet regards as genuine, that Socrates was condemned to death for impiety *tout court* (325b1–c5).[36] And in the *Apology* (26a8–b7) and *Euthyphro* (2b12-3b4), Plato presents Socrates as saying that, by charging him with corrupting the youth, the Athenians were specifically charging him with teaching the youth not to believe in the gods of the city. Furthermore, according to Plato's Socrates and Athenian Stranger, the standard charge against philosophers was atheism, that is, the opinion that the gods do not exist.[37] Plato, then, indicates quite clearly that Socrates owed his condemnation primarily to the Athenians' opinion that he was impious.

Moreover, Burnet overlooks the fact that, in addition to being regarded as antidemocratic, Socrates' companions, Alcibiades and Critias, were also regarded as impious. Alcibiades was condemned to death for impiety, and Critias was a well known atheist.[38] Even the political hostility against Socrates, then, was connected with the belief that he and his companions were impious.[39]

Finally, in order to maintain his view that the Greeks did not prosecute men for their religious opinions, Burnet is compelled to give accounts of the impiety trials of the philosophers which are at odds with ancient accounts of those trials. He says that "even Diagoras, the typical atheist of those days, was not tried for his opinions, but for offences in language against the temples and festivals." But ancient writers state clearly that Diagoras was condemned for being an atheist, that is, for his opinion that the gods do not exist, and not merely for his language against temples and festivals or for his actions.[40] In his discussion of the impiety charge against Anaxagoras, Burnet implies that he was accused of impiety for political reasons. But Plato and Plutarch both indicate that he was brought to trial primarily for religious reasons.[41] Finally, Burnet claims that it is "highly improbable" that Protagoras was accused of impiety. He then remarks that, even if Protagoras did say, "With regard to the gods, I cannot feel sure that they are or that they are not. . . ." (Burnet's own translation), "There is surely nothing impious in these words from any point of view, and certainly none from the Greek." Yet ancient writers report that Protagoras was indeed accused of impiety, that he was forced to flee Athens, and that his books were burned in the Athenian agora precisely because of the very statement that Burnet cites.[42]

Burnet's remark about Protagoras is noteworthy because it indicates how he may have arrived at the conclusion that the Greeks never prosecuted anyone for his opinions about the gods. Burnet himself evidently believes that a man can be pious without being convinced that gods exist. And he evidently assumes that the Greeks must have shared this opinion and consequently must have tolerated any and all opinions about their gods. Therefore, he concludes, the Greeks never prosecuted anyone for his religious opinions. But Burnet's opinion about piety is not one which the Greeks held.[43] As I have tried to show, the conviction that gods exist—and, specifically, that gods who reward the righteous and punish the wicked exist—was, in the Greeks' view, the foundation not only of their religious life but of their political, moral, and family life as well. Accordingly, they regarded any challenge to that fundamental conviction as an intolerable challenge to their whole way of life.[44]

By claiming, then, that the Greeks never prosecuted philosophers or anyone else for their religious opinions, Burnet overlooks the relevant historical evidence. But I would suggest that Burnet fails to appreciate the gravity of the impiety charge against the philosophers above all because he fails to appreciate the gravity of the religious question as both the Greek many and the philosophers understood that question. He fails to appreciate the political importance of religion in the ancient city and hence fails to appreciate the illiberal character of the ancient city.[45] Consequently he fails to recognize the hostile context within which the Greek philosophers lived and, in Socrates' case, died.

III. The Doubts of Socrates' Companions

Philosophy at the time of Socrates' death was, then, an activity fraught with danger. A young man—as Socrates' principal interlocutors in the *Phaedo* all are at this time (see 89a3, d2-5)—would know that, by devoting himself to philosophy, he would be risking his good name, his well-being, and even his life. At best, his fellow citizens would regard him as ridiculous and contemptible. At worst, they would view him as a criminal who deserves to be punished by men and by gods.[46] And even sophisticated men would despise him as an unmanly man who is unable to defend himself against his enemies.[47]

On the day that Socrates' last conversation is to take place, his companions must be especially aware of the dangers that attend the philosophic life. During the preceding thirty days, they have gathered every morning in the courtroom where Socrates was convicted and condemned to death. They have then spent the day in prison conversing with their friend. Finally, they have left him in the evening wondering whether the next day would be his last (see 59d1–e7). Throughout this difficult period, Socrates' companions must have been wondering what fate they, too, might suffer if they persist in their devotion to the philosophic life.

Up until now, Socrates' companions have been willing to brave these dangers and have devoted themselves to the pursuit of wisdom in the company and under the guidance of their friend. But on the day that

Socrates is to be executed, their confidence in the wisdom and goodness of the philosophic life must be shaken. For how, they must wonder, can it be wise to engage in a pursuit which renders a man incapable of saving himself or his friends from the greatest of dangers?[48] And how can it be good to lead a life which exposes one to the threat of persecution by men and of punishment by the gods?

Socrates' two young Theban companions, Simmias and Cebes, may have additional reasons for wondering about the wisdom and the goodness of the philosophic life. As we know from the only other dialogue in which Plato mentions them together, the *Crito*, these two, along with Crito, were leaders of the plot to rescue Socrates from prison.[49] Simmias and Cebes know, then, that Socrates could have avoided his execution and that he deliberately chose not to do so. Socrates did explain to Crito that he was refusing to escape out of respect for the laws of Athens (50a6–54d1). And Crito probably repeated this conversation to Cebes and Simmias. But, being Thebans, Cebes and Simmias may not feel much respect for the laws of Athens and may not have been convinced by the arguments that Socrates made to the Athenian Crito. Moreover, insofar as they take Socrates' claim that the philosophic life is the best way of life more seriously than Crito does, they may doubt that Socrates would be willing to sacrifice his life out of respect for the laws of Athens unless he himself had come to despair of his philosophic life.[50] But, if Socrates himself is renouncing his claim that the philosophic life is the best way of life, how can they persist in believing that claim? It would seem, then, that Simmias and Cebes have especially strong reasons for questioning the goodness of the philosophic life on the day of Socrates' death. For this reason, it is perhaps appropriate that Socrates address his last defense of the philosophic life to them in particular.

Chapter 2

The Opening of the Dialogue

The *Phaedo* would seem to present the final victory of the city of Athens over the philosopher Socrates. After all, it is in that dialogue that the Athenians finally execute Socrates for not believing in their gods and for corrupting their young. And that execution would seem to demonstrate most clearly the power of the Athenians and, indeed, of any political community to silence not only this philosopher but any philosopher.

Yet, through the dramatic setting of the *Phaedo*, Plato suggests that, while the Athenians did succeed in killing Socrates, they failed in their efforts to silence him.[1] For, rather than presenting the last conversation and death of Socrates directly as, for example, he presents the defense speech of Socrates at his trial, Plato presents them through the account that Phaedo, a young friend of Socrates, gives a long time after Socrates' death to other friends of philosophy far away from Athens (see 57a1–b2). And through that account, Phaedo seems to inspire in his audience an admiration for Socrates and thereby seems to win new followers and friends for Socrates (see 88c8–89a8, 102a2-9). Plato underscores the importance of the fact that Phaedo is telling the story of Socrates' last day by naming the dialogue after him. For, while six Platonic dialogues are narrated by Socrates (*Republic, Protagoras, Euthydemus, Charmides, Lovers, Lysis*) and three are narrated by other men (*Symposium, Parmenides, Phaedo*), the *Phaedo* is the only dialogue that Plato names after the narrator. In this way, Plato suggests that, through followers like Phaedo (and, of course, like Plato himself) who will continue to recount the speeches of their teacher, Socrates will continue to inspire, to teach, and to "corrupt" the philosophic young.[2] Through the dramatic setting of this dialogue, then, Plato seems to anticipate what, in fact, actually took place, namely, that, despite the execution of that man at the hands of the Athenians, Socrates the philosopher and the teacher continued (and continues) to exert his influence on men and hence to live on, so to speak, through the accounts of his followers.[3]

Yet, precisely insofar as Socrates' philosophic activity led him to be persecuted and eventually to be executed by the Athenians, why did his young friends continue to devote themselves to him and to the philosophic life after his death? Why did they seek to persuade other men to admire and to follow the example of a man who was condemned and executed by his fellow citizens for the crime of impiety? Why did they not rather conclude that the philosophic life which Socrates led is an unwise and unjust way of life? In order to address these questions, let us consider the case of Phaedo more carefully.

In the opening scene of the *Phaedo*, Plato presents a conversation between Phaedo and Echecrates which takes place in Phlius, a town in the Peloponnesus, a long time after Socrates' death. Echecrates, who is a follower of the philosophers and who is acquainted, at least, with Socrates and his milieu,[4] first asks Phaedo whether he, himself, was present on the day that Socrates drank the poison. When Phaedo replies that he was indeed there, Echecrates asks him what Socrates said before he died and how he died and then goes on to urge him to explain as thoroughly, clearly, and precisely as he can, both to himself and to his companions, all that was said and done on that day (57a1-58d3).

Now, insofar as Echecrates is himself trying to live the philosophic life, it seems natural that he should be so eager to learn how the philosopher Socrates faced death. But one would think that recounting the last conversation and death of Socrates would be a painful task for Phaedo. For, by remembering that day, he would be remembering the day on which he saw his beloved teacher and friend suffer a seemingly terrible and pitiable fate and on which he himself suffered a terrible and pitiable loss (see 58e1-3, 116a4-7, 117c5–d1). Moreover, insofar as Phaedo not only loved Socrates as a friend but admired him as a singularly good, wise, and just man, he must be pained by the thought that the just are so weak in this world and that the unjust are so strong (see 118a15-17). Finally, and most simply, it would seem that the memory of Socrates' execution would be frightening to Phaedo. For, inasmuch as he was closely associated with that man and insofar as he himself is devoted to philosophy, he must fear that he, too, may suffer persecution. It would seem, then, that Phaedo would find the memory of Socrates' last day so dispiriting that he would be at least reluctant to relive that day by describing it to Echecrates.

Yet Phaedo says that remembering Socrates, both by speaking and listening to others, is always for him the most pleasant of all things (58d4-6). And he says this in response to Echecrates' request that he give a complete account of that man's death. Surprisingly, Phaedo enjoys remembering not only Socrates as a whole but also quite specifically the last conversation and death of that man.

Phaedo explains that, to his surprise, he did not feel pity for Socrates on the day of his death. For that man appeared to him to be happy, both in his bearing and in his speeches. And so fearlessly and nobly did he die that Phaedo felt assured that Socrates was not going to Hades without the blessing of the gods and that he would fare well there, if indeed anyone else ever had (58e1-59a2). Phaedo did not pity his friend on that day, then, both because Socrates seemed to him to feel confident that he would fare well in Hades and because Socrates persuaded him that his confidence was justified. And even though Phaedo does not appear to feel entirely certain that anyone ever does, in fact, fare well in Hades, he evidently does feel certain that, if anyone ever has, Socrates will as well. In other words, even though he may not have been entirely convinced by Socrates that everlasting happiness is available to any human being, it seems that Phaedo was entirely convinced by Socrates that the philosopher is so virtuous and so noble a human being that he deserves to be rewarded with an everlasting happiness. Socrates' bearing and speeches in the face of death, then, encouraged Phaedo to believe that, if there is any justice in the world, the philosopher will live on and fare well after death.[5]

Now, it seems to be because of this belief that Phaedo takes the pleasure he does in remembering the day of Socrates' death. For, in the light of that belief, Phaedo must remember that day, not so much as the day on which Socrates was executed by Athens, but rather as the day on which he was rewarded by the gods. Furthermore, and more importantly, it would seem to be above all because of this belief that Phaedo takes pleasure in remembering Socrates' life as a whole. For the belief that Socrates' philosophic life culminated with the divine reward of everlasting happiness would clearly vindicate the wisdom and the justice of his way of life, despite the Athenians' verdict that he was guilty of injustice and despite their execution of him (see 118a15-17).

On the other hand, insofar as Phaedo's memory of Socrates' last day must include the memory of his own loss of the man whom he cherished as a father and whom he admired above all others, the pleasure he takes in remembering that day, however great it may be, must be mixed with a certain feeling of pain.[6] Indeed, it may be because that pain is so great that Phaedo does not say that remembering Socrates in silence and in solitude is his greatest pleasure but rather that remembering him while speaking or listening to others is his greatest pleasure. For, when hearing Socrates' speeches, as they are spoken aloud by himself or by others, Phaedo may feel that Socrates is somehow still with him and may therefore feel less keenly the pain of his loss (see 115c6–d2).

The case of Phaedo suggests that Socrates' success in foiling the attempt of the Athenians to silence him depended on his success in persuading his companions that the soul is immortal and that the philosopher, in particular, will enjoy an everlasting happiness after death. For Phaedo's belief in the wisdom and justice of the philosophic life seems to depend on his belief that the philosopher will be rewarded by the gods after death. And it seems to be because of this belief that he persists in devoting himself to the Socratic way of life and that he encourages Echecrates and others to admire and to follow the example of that man who was condemned to death and executed for impiety.

In these ways, the case of Phaedo highlights the importance of Echecrates' question, how did Socrates die? For Phaedo suggests that it was through his seemingly happy, fearless, and noble death that Socrates persuaded him that he would be rewarded by the gods after death and thereby strengthened his belief in the wisdom and the goodness of Socrates' philosophic life. Yet, even and especially if we grant the accuracy of Phaedo's impression that Socrates died happily, fearlessly, and nobly, the question still remains, did he die wisely? Did he have sufficient reasons for facing death confidently and without fear? Or was his confidence based on unreasonable hopes? It is only by turning to Socrates' arguments on the day of his death that we can determine whether he had good reasons for dying, as Phaedo claims he died, without fear. It is only by turning to his speeches that we can know, in the fullest and most important sense, how Socrates died. It is only by turning to those speeches that we can know whether Phaedo's confidence in the wisdom and the justice of Socrates' philosophic life is warranted.

Chapter 3

The Opening of Socrates' Last Conversation

The opening of Socrates' last conversation with his friends culminates with the charge of Cebes and Simmias that he is guilty of impiety and
with their demand that he make an "apology" as though he were in a court
of law. By making this charge, they are, as Socrates suggests, repeating the
charge which the Athenians made against him at his trial (63b1-3). And by
agreeing to their demand, Socrates agrees to defend himself once again
against the charge that he is impious. We see, then, that the conversation
narrated in the *Phaedo* is a reenactment of the trial of Socrates. Yet the fact
that the impiety charge then made by the prejudiced and hostile Athenians
is now repeated by two of Socrates' most devoted companions would seem
to render that charge much more credible.[1] Moreover, the fact that Socrates devotes the last day of his life to defending himself against their impiety
charge, even though he is under no compulsion to do so, suggests that he
himself takes this charge most seriously. In these ways, then, the *Phaedo*
encourages us to take the impiety charge against Socrates seriously. By
presenting the impiety charge of his friends, the dialogue encourages us to
wonder whether Socrates was not justly accused and condemned by his
enemies. And by encouraging us to consider the possibility that the philosopher is impious, it encourages us to wonder whether he will not be justly
condemned by the gods after his death.[2]

I. The Philosopher's Readiness to Die

Phaedo tells his audience that, when he and his friends entered Socrates'
prison cell on the day he was to be executed, they found him with his wife,
Xanthippe, who was holding their baby in her arms. The Athenian prison
officials have evidently granted her the privilege of seeing her husband before
his friends were allowed to see him. In the eyes of the city, it seems, the ties
of matrimony and family deserve even greater respect than those of friendship.
When Xanthippe sees her husband's friends enter, she cries out and
says, "Socrates, this is the last time your friends will speak to you and you

to them." Now, the youthful Phaedo dismisses these words as a typical expression of female sentimentality (59e8-60a6). But what Xanthippe says here is actually quite surprising. Since her husband was famous for neglecting his family in order to spend time with his friends, we might expect her to feel little sympathy for these men.[3] We might also expect her to want to have her husband to herself on this day and hence to be displeased by the intrusion of his companions. Yet Xanthippe expresses pity here not for herself, as well she might,[4] nor for her husband alone, but also for his friends. She feels a pity for Socrates which Phaedo himself expects to feel on this day (58e1-3, 59a1-2; see also 84d5-7), and she feels a pity for his friends which they will feel for themselves throughout this day (76b10-12, 78a1-2, 116a5-7, 117c5–e4). In this, her only appearance in Plato's dialogues, Xanthippe reveals herself to be a strikingly sensitive and understanding woman.[5] Accordingly, Socrates' response to her is especially shocking. For he does not speak to her at all but simply tells Crito to have her removed and taken home.[6]

Socrates' dismissal of Xanthippe here seems simply to reflect his devotion to his friends and his indifference to his wife. In contrast to official Athens, it seems, friendship means more to him than family. Yet, upon closer examination, Socrates' dismissal of Xanthippe actually calls into question the depth of his devotion to his friends. For Socrates seems to dismiss not only his wife but also her expression of pity for him. He seems to dismiss her because she fails to understand that he is happy on this day and because he doubts that he can persuade her that he is happy (compare 60a3-6 with 58e1-59a1).[7] But Xanthippe believes that Socrates is sad on this day precisely because she believes that he loves his friends and consequently feels sad that he must leave them. And, if she is mistaken and he is dying happily and easily, how much can his friends really mean to him? How can he die happily and easily unless he loves his friends as little as he seems to love his wife (see 63a7-9)?

Once Xanthippe is removed from the cell, Socrates, who has just been released from his chains, sits up in bed and begins to rub his leg. As he is rubbing, he remarks to his companions on how strange a thing this is which human beings call pleasant. For the pleasant, he explains, is so strangely related by nature to what is thought to be its opposite, the painful, that, although the two of them are not willing to be present in a human being at the same time, if someone should pursue and catch one of the two, he is almost always compelled to catch the other as well. And, in Socrates' opinion, if the poet Aesop had reflected on these things, he would have composed a tale that the god wished to reconcile these two warring beings. But since the god was unable to do so, he fastened their heads together. And, for this reason, should one of the two be present in someone, the other will follow later. This, Socrates says, is probably what has just happened to him. First there was pain in his leg because of his chains. But now that his leg has been released, pleasure appears to have followed that pain (60a9–c7). And before long, he implies, this pleasure, too, will come to an end. As Socrates feels the pleasure of rubbing his leg, he evidently resists the temptation to believe that this pleasure, or any other pleasure he may feel on this day, will last for long.

Socrates here warns his companions against the natural human tendency to believe that, if we pursue pleasure and catch it, it will be ours forever. In almost all cases, he says, it is necessary that pain follow pleasure. And since this is so, he implies, we should resign ourselves to this natural necessity rather than struggle against it. Socrates, then, seems here to urge his companions to ignore his wife's lament that this is the last time he and they will enjoy the pleasure of conversing with one another and to accept manfully the necessity that this pleasure will, as all pleasures must, come to an end (see 59a1-7; compare 60a3-6, b4 with b3; see also 117d7–e2). And he also seems to suggest that, since he himself accepts this necessity, he will face his own death calmly, without hope of everlasting pleasure but also without fear of everlasting pain. Yet Socrates does not simply exhort his friends to deny, on this painful day, their longing for a pleasure which is not merely fleeting. For by saying that, when a man catches the pleasant, he is "*almost* always" compelled to catch the painful as well, Socrates leaves open the possibility, at least, that human beings may enjoy an everlasting pleasure after death.

Socrates' remarks prompt Cebes to speak up and to ask him why he has been composing poetry in prison—setting Aesop's fables to verse and composing a hymn to Apollo—when he never did such a thing before. Evenus, a sophist and poet, and a number of others have been asking Cebes this question and reasonably so (60c8–e1).[8] For Socrates, who was known to have believed that poetry aims at pleasing the passions rather than teaching what is true and hence that it is an enemy of philosophy, has now, since his trial, been composing poetry himself rather than dedicating himself exclusively to the philosophic pursuit of wisdom.[9] It would seem reasonable, then, to ask, have the unfavorable outcome of his trial and the ordeal of his imprisonment led Socrates to abandon his dedication to philosophy?[10] Furthermore, Socrates, who was condemned by the Athenians for not believing in the gods of the city, has now been composing a hymn to Apollo, the ancestral god of Athens.[11] Has Socrates, then, become afraid, as his death approaches, that the Athenians' judgment that he is guilty of impiety may be correct? Has he been seeking to appease the gods lest they inflict on him an everlasting pain in Hades?

Socrates' response to Cebes would seem to confirm the suspicion that, on the threshold of death, he has become afraid of the gods. For he attributes his composition of poetry in prison to his desire to purify himself of any impiety he may have committed and to his belief that it is "safer" not to die before he has purified himself (60d7–e3, 61a8–b1). In his first clear allusion in the dialogue to the afterlife, Socrates expresses a fear of punishment rather than a hope for rewards in Hades.

Socrates explains to Cebes that he has been composing poetry because he is concerned that he may have committed the specific impiety of disobeying the command of a dream that has often appeared to him in the course of his life. Socrates apparently believes that this dream is the revelation of a divine commandment.[12] And that commandment has always been the same: "Socrates, compose music and work [at it]." Now, Socrates reveals here that he has always striven to obey that divine commandment. His desire to be pious, he suggests, has not been awakened by his impending execution but has always animated him, at least since the time his dream first appeared to him.

However, despite his longstanding desire to obey the divine commandment, Socrates is not sure that he has succeeded in doing so, for he is not sure that he has correctly interpreted that commandment. While he used to believe that the god was commanding him to practice the greatest music—which, according to Socrates, is philosophy—and hence was encouraging him in his pursuit of wisdom, since his trial he has begun to wonder whether the god was not actually commanding him to practice popular or vulgar music—which consists, according to him, of hymns to the gods and tales (60e4–61b7). It seems, then, that Socrates now wonders whether, in his sincere attempt to obey the god, he was not, in fact, disobeying the god and hence committing impiety.

Socrates' doubts about his former interpretation of the god's commandment seem to be reasonable. For, by interpreting the commandment to "compose music and work [at it]" to mean "continue to philosophize," he does not interpret it according to the ordinary meaning of its words. Instead, he interprets it in the light of his own opinion that philosophy is the greatest music. But how does he know that the god shares his opinion about philosophy? How does he know that the god is not commanding him to compose music in the ordinary sense of composing hymns instead of philosophizing? Indeed, how does he know that the god, who first communicated with him only after Socrates had begun to philosophize (60e4–61a4), has not been sending this dream to him over and over again precisely in order to command him to stop trying to discover the truth about things on his own and for himself?

Yet Socrates' recent interpretation of his dream is also beset by difficulties. For how does he know that the words of the commandment in the dream ought to be interpreted in their ordinary—or vulgar—sense? Socrates himself admits that he is not sure that his recent interpretation of the dream is correct. He says twice that he is composing poetry only in case this is what the dream has been commanding him to do (60d8–e3, 61a4-8). In fact, what he says does not preclude the possibility that the dream does not come from a god at all. For he does not say that he is certain either that it does come from a god or that he has committed an impiety. Yet, given his doubts about the accuracy of his second interpretation of the dream, how does he now know that he is not in truth disobeying the god, and hence committing impiety, despite what might seem to be the most pious intentions?

The difficulties that beset Socrates' attempt to be pious may not be idiosyncratic but may rather constitute difficulties that beset any attempt to be pious. For, insofar as piety consists of obeying the commandments of the gods (compare 61c9-10, e5-6 with 62a1-7) and insofar as the gods reveal their commandments through religious experiences, such as dreams,[13] the question may inevitably arise, how can we know that the commandments we dream of are from a god and not products of our idle—or bedeviled—imaginations?[14] And even if we are certain that they are from a god, how can we be certain that we are interpreting them correctly? In sum, how can we be sure that, in our very effort to obey the gods, we are not inadvertently disobeying them and thereby exposing ourselves to their wrath?

Socrates' admission that his life-long devotion to philosophy may have been opposed by the gods would seem to be tantamount to an admission that he may, in fact, be guilty of impiety. And this admission, in turn, would seem to be tantamount to an admission that he may be punished for his disobedience to the gods in an afterlife. Socrates seems, then, to express to his companions here the gravest of doubts regarding the piety, the wisdom, and the justice of the philosophic life he has led and thereby seems to encourage them in their own doubts about that way of life. Yet he concludes his explanation of his music-making by saying that Evenus and, indeed, everyone who has a worthy share in philosophy will be willing and even eager to die as quickly as possible (61b7–c9). Despite his apparent uncertainty as to whether he is guilty of impiety, he displays an astonishing confidence that death is good for worthy philosophers and hence, presumably, good for himself. But how can Socrates both be uncertain that he is free of impiety and be confident that he will not be punished for impiety in an afterlife?

What Socrates says here about the philosopher's readiness to die would seem to dispel his companions' suspicions that he has been led by the unfavorable outcome of his trial to doubt the wisdom of his life-long devotion to philosophy. For, if he believes that the philosopher is positively eager to die, then he clearly must not believe that the threat of death by persecution calls into question the wisdom of the philosophic life. And if he himself is eager to die now, then, he must not fear at all the power of the Athenians to kill him. By suggesting, then, that the philosopher does not merely accept death as a natural necessity but rather regards death as good, Socrates emphatically denies that the persecution of men poses any threat to the happiness of the philosopher.

Yet Socrates' companions can hardly regard what he says here as a heartening affirmation of the wisdom of the philosophic life. Simmias, at any rate, is astonished by Socrates' words here and understandably so (61b7–c7). For Socrates seems to portray the philosopher as one who does not fear losing his life because he regards life itself as an evil. And how can a way of life which leads to such a bleak conclusion be wise or good for a human being?

Furthermore, by suggesting that the philosopher is eager to die as quickly as possible, Socrates may appear to be suggesting that the philosopher will put an end to his own life even though, as he goes on to point out, it is said that there is a divine prohibition against suicide (see 61c9-10, 62a1-7).[15] Socrates runs the risk, then, of appearing to portray the philosopher as a man who ignores the gods' commandments and hence as an impious man. Indeed, given his companions' awareness that he could have saved himself from execution but chose not to do so, Socrates may also appear to them to be admitting here that he himself has been impiously seeking to fulfill his own wish for death. And he may even seem to be encouraging his young companions to disregard the divine prohibition against suicide themselves. We see, then, that, in his attempt to reassure his companions that he is not distressed to be dying now and hence that the threat of death by persecution does not call into question the wisdom of his philosophic life, Socrates runs the risk of calling into question the piety, and therewith the justice as well as the wisdom, of his way of life.[16] Indeed, he runs the risk of vindicating the Athenians' charge that he is impious and that he corrupts the youth by teaching them to be impious as well.

II. Socrates' Argument Against Suicide

Accordingly, Socrates immediately tells his companions that, even though the philosopher wishes to die, "perhaps" he will not take his own life, "for they say that it is not lawful." In this way, Socrates reminds his companions of the divine prohibition against suicide and suggests that they should obey it (61c9-10).

Cebes now speaks up and asks Socrates what he means by saying both that it is unlawful to kill oneself and that the philosopher wishes to die. And when Socrates offers to explain what he means, Cebes asks more specifically, "Why in the world do they say that it is unlawful to kill oneself?" In contrast with his friend Simmias, what especially perplexes Cebes is not so much Socrates' claim that the philosopher wishes to die but rather the claim that this wish is opposed by a divine law (compare 61b7–c7 with e5-9). Indeed, Cebes feels a considerable sympathy for the philosopher's wish to die. For, as he explains, he was already interested in the question, why not suicide? when he was studying with the philosopher Philolaus in Thebes. And even though Philolaus and others as well have repeatedly told him that it is forbidden to kill oneself, Cebes has persisted in seeking for a clear reason for the allegedly divine law against suicide. But so far, he says, he has not found any (61c10–e9).

Cebes' persistent interest in the question of suicide indicates that he is rather unhappy with his own life. And, inasmuch as he has devoted his life up until now to philosophy, his interest in this question suggests that he has grave doubts regarding the goodness of the philosophic life. But why have his doubts about the goodness of this one way of life led him to doubt the goodness of life itself? Why haven't they led him to consider other ways of life? Cebes' apparent lack of interest in other ways of life suggests that he regards the philosophic life as the only possible life worth living. In other words, Cebes seems to take most seriously and even to be wholly convinced by the Socratic claim that the unexamined life is simply not worth living.[17] And, consequently, his suspicion or fear that even the philosophic life may not be worth living leads him, it seems, to despair of life itself and to think seriously about abandoning it altogether. Cebes' interest in suicide, then, seems to reflect both the depth of his devotion to the philosophic life and the depth of his disappointment with it.

Now, Cebes has, of course, been told that there is a divine law against suicide. And insofar as he has obeyed that law up till now, it would seem that he is a pious young man. Yet so serious is his interest in suicide that he dares to wonder whether that law is truly divine.

Socrates responds to Cebes' demand for a clear account of the divine law against suicide by encouraging him to exert himself in his quest for such an account. Nevertheless, he says, it will perhaps appear strange to Cebes if he should hear that, given the complexity of human affairs, this alone is simple, that it is never better for any human being to be dead than to be alive. And he goes on to say that it perhaps already appears strange to Cebes if those for whom it is better to be dead may not benefit themselves—by killing themselves—without committing impiety but must rather wait for someone else to benefit them. Cebes responds to this account of his doubts about the divine law by laughing gently in agreement (62a1-9).

This exchange suggests that it is Cebes' suspicion that death may sometimes be better for a human being than life that has led him to wonder whether the law against suicide is truly divine. He evidently accepts the pious claim or assumption that the gods are good rulers of human beings and consequently believes that a truly divine law must be good for human beings (compare 62d3-6 with b6-8). Yet Cebes makes the further assumption that it is possible for human beings not only to believe but to know that a divine law is good. And this assumption might seem objectionable, at least from the standpoint of piety. For it might seem that, insofar as the gods are said to be not only good but also mysterious beings, we should admit that it is not possible for us to understand in what sense their laws are good for us (see 62b2-6), that we should simply trust or have faith in the goodness of their laws, and hence that we should obey the divine laws even though we do not understand them. It might be objected, then, that Cebes' desire for a clear reason for the divine prohibition against suicide is a sign of his dogmatic refusal to accept any authority other than reason and hence a sign that he is not genuinely pious.[18]

Yet Cebes might reply by saying that he wants to understand the prohibition against suicide precisely because he wants to be pious. He might argue that, insofar as we know that the gods are good rulers of human beings—and hence that, to this extent, at least, they are not mysterious beings—we may legitimately conclude that they wish to reveal clearly to us what they demand of us. For it would seem to be unjust of the gods—and therefore incompatible with their goodness—to conceal from us what we ought to do in order to enjoy the blessings of their rule. Now, it is true that we are told that the gods demand that we refrain from killing ourselves. But we are told this, it seems, by human beings rather than by the gods themselves (see 61c10, e5-6). And how are we to trust that what humans say about the gods' laws is true? Precisely insofar as we truly long to obey the gods' laws, it would seem that we cannot simply be satisfied with merely human claims about what those laws are. At all events, Cebes seems to believe that the only genuinely trustworthy sign that a law is truly divine is that it is clearly good for those who obey it and hence clearly worthy of divine rulers. It seems, then, that his desire to find a clear reason for the prohibition against suicide reflects his pious conviction that the gods are good rulers and his pious desire to fulfill their demands.

Now, as we have seen, Socrates wants to encourage Cebes in his desire to understand the prohibition against suicide. But he also wants him and indeed all his companions to obey that prohibition. Accordingly, once he has explained why Cebes might reasonably question that prohibition, Socrates proceeds to argue on its behalf. He first gains Cebes' agreement to the pious claim that the gods take care of us and are our masters. He then suggests that, just as Cebes would get angry at one of his slaves for killing himself without his permission and would try to punish him, so might the gods get angry with us and punish us, presumably in an afterlife, for killing ourselves without their permission. Therefore, he concludes, it may not be unreasonable for a man to refrain from committing suicide until the god sends some necessity as he has done, Socrates claims, in his own case (62b6–c8). In this way, Socrates provides Cebes with a clear reason for obeying the divine prohibition against suicide and thereby shows himself to be a defender of piety.

Socrates' argument here does not, however, indicate as clearly as it might have that suicide is unjust. For, according to that argument, the relations between gods and men resemble those between human masters and their slaves. Now, Socrates clearly suggests that, inasmuch as the gods have the power to punish us, their slaves, in an afterlife, they greatly surpass human masters in their power. But he does not clearly say or suggest that the gods surpass human masters in their benevolence toward their slaves. He seems to leave open the possibility that the gods rule over us as selfishly or unjustly as human masters rule over their slaves. Nevertheless, Socrates' argument does clearly suggest to Cebes that it would be most imprudent for him to commit suicide. For by doing so, he might suffer from a much greater persecution than he has witnessed in this life.

Socrates qualifies here his earlier claim that the philosopher is willing to die by suggesting that he is willing to die only in such a way as to avoid punishment after death. But he still maintains that it may be reasonable for him to embrace death now since the gods have sent to him a certain necessity and have thereby granted him permission to die. Yet, since Socrates could have avoided his execution by escaping from prison, it is not, strictly speaking, necessary for him to die now. The gods did not compel him to stay and die; he freely chose to stay and die (see 98e1–99a4).[19] How, then, does he know that he has the gods' permission to die? Socrates may mean to suggest here that he knows that the gods must approve of his dying now because he knows that it is good for him to die now and he believes that the gods are benevolent rulers of human beings. He may believe, for example, that it is just and hence good for him to obey the laws of Athens.[20] He may also believe that it is better for him to die now rather than later after having suffered the evils of a prolonged old age.[21] Yet, Socrates' argument on behalf of the divine prohibition against suicide is, as we have seen, noticeably silent about the gods' benevolence. And, insofar as Socrates is not confident that they are benevolent, the question remains, how can he be confident that they approve of his decision to die now and hence that it truly is good for him to die now?

III. The Impiety Charge of Cebes and Simmias

Cebes accepts as plausible Socrates' argument against suicide. But he now argues that, precisely if what Socrates says is true, it is most unreasonable for the philosophers to be willing to die so easily. Cebes argues as follows. If, as Socrates has suggested, the gods do, indeed, take care of and rule human beings and if, as Cebes assumes, they are the best of rulers, then it would seem to be unreasonable for the wisest of human beings not to feel distressed when they leave the gods' care. For a wise man does not think that he will take better care of himself once he has become free of their care. Instead, he will desire "always" to be with the one who is better than he is. But a foolish man would perhaps think that he ought to flee from his master and would not understand that he ought not to flee from his good master but ought rather to stay with him as long as possible. Therefore, Cebes concludes, insofar as death means leaving one's divine masters, it is the wise who will be distressed at dying and it is the fools who will rejoice (62c8–e7).

Cebes argues here that, insofar as the philosophers are easily willing to die, they must not be truly wise. For the truly wise man will recognize that no man can attain happiness without the assistance or guidance of the gods. He will recognize that the gods' care is the greatest good for a human being. And, consequently, he will desire "always" to be with his divine masters. The truly wise man will, then, be a pious man. And therefore, insofar as death separates him from his divine masters, it is unwise and also impious for the philosopher to be easily willing to die. Cebes argues, then, that, insofar as they are easily willing to die, the philosophers reveal that they do not understand their need for the gods' care or guidance and thereby reveal that they are both unwise and impious.

Now, since Cebes himself has been tempted by thoughts of suicide, it would seem that, insofar as his argument is directed at the philosophers' readiness to die, it is a merely hypothetical argument. Although Cebes would regard their wish to die as unwise and impious if he were convinced that the gods take care of us in this life, his own interest in suicide suggests that he doubts that human beings actually enjoy such care. Nevertheless, while he doubts the truth of the pious claim that the gods take care of human beings in this life, he seems to be wholly convinced by the pious claim that without the gods' care man is a miserable creature. And insofar as the philosophers' readiness to die reflects their belief that human beings can take care of themselves throughout their lives without divine guidance, Cebes does argue that they are, in fact, unwise and impious. Cebes' argument here, then, is not so much a challenge to the wisdom and piety of the philosophers' readiness to die as it is a challenge to the wisdom and piety of their whole way of life.

Socrates is, in Phaedo's opinion, pleased with Cebes here. And Socrates confirms this impression by praising Cebes to his other companions for always investigating certain arguments he hears rather than allowing himself to be quickly persuaded by them (62e8-63a3). Socrates indicates here that he wants his companions to overcome whatever reticence they may feel on this day, to challenge his claims, and specifically to express their doubts, as Cebes has, about the wisdom of the philosophic life.

Simmias now speaks up to support Cebes' suggestion that the philosophers are both unwise and impious. But he restates that suggestion as a personal accusation against Socrates. He says that, in his opinion, Cebes is directing his argument at Socrates in particular, since he is bearing it so easily to desert both his friends and his divine rulers. As Socrates surmises, and Simmias emphatically agrees, Simmias here accuses Socrates of injustice as though he were in a court of law (63a4–b3).

Even though Simmias claims here that he is simply restating Cebes' suggestion that the philosophers are impious, he actually changes that suggestion in a most significant way. For while Cebes emphasizes that the philosophers' impiety is unwise, Simmias emphasizes that it is unjust and adds that the philosophers are unjust to human beings as well. And consequently, while Cebes tries to explain to Socrates the folly of the philosophers' willingness to leave their divine masters, Simmias makes a formal and general accusation of injustice against Socrates and thereby implies that he must either prove his innocence or somehow pay a penalty for his crime.

It is true that Cebes also suggests that human beings "ought," or have a duty, to remain with the gods and thereby implies that, insofar as Socrates is fleeing the gods, he is acting unjustly toward them (see 62d8–e3). But, in contrast with Simmias, Cebes emphasizes that the gods' care is good for human beings and hence that it is clearly in Socrates' best and highest interest to fulfill his duty to remain with them (see also 62a1–9). And in further contrast with Simmias, Cebes does not accuse Socrates of unjustly deserting his friends, perhaps because he is not sure that it is in Socrates' best interest to remain with them. After all, insofar as Cebes has thought about committing suicide, he himself has thought about deserting his friends. He restricts himself, then, to accusing Socrates of unjustly deserting those beings—the gods who take good care of human beings—with whom it is clearly in his best interest to remain. Accordingly, even though he does suggest that Socrates is acting unjustly toward the gods, Cebes does not accuse him as though he were in a court of law and thereby imply that he should be punished for his injustice. For, by unjustly abandoning the gods, Socrates is foolishly depriving himself of their beneficent care and is consequently already suffering for his injustice. Moreover, insofar as no human being deliberately deprives himself of what is good for him, Socrates' injustice must be, according to Cebes, involuntary. By emphasizing, then, that it is in one's best interest to be pious and foolish to be impious, Cebes suggests that, insofar as Socrates is guilty of impiety, he does not deserve to be punished but should rather be enlightened.[22] And consequently, Cebes attempts to correct Socrates' injustice by explaining to him, at some length, that it is good for him to act justly toward the gods and hence good for him to be pious.

Simmias also says that the gods are good rulers of human beings and thereby seems to agree with Cebes that it is in Socrates' best interest to fulfill his duty to remain with the gods. But Simmias emphasizes that Socrates is acting against his gods, that he is betraying them, and that such disloyalty is simply wrong. Furthermore, he also accuses Socrates of unjustly deserting his friends. And even though he does not argue that it is in Socrates' best interest to remain with them, he nevertheless implies that because they are his friends they deserve his loyalty. By accusing Socrates of deserting both his friends and his divine rulers, Simmias suggests that together they constitute a kind of political community to which Socrates belongs and to which he is bound by ties of friendship and duty. And as it is unjust for a man to desert his fellow citizens and his rulers, even and especially if he thinks it is in his self-interest to do so, so is it unjust for Socrates to desert his friends and his gods. Simmias, then, adopts the position that the truly just man will be loyal to his rulers and his friends and will fulfill his duties to them not because he has calculated that it is in his best interest to do so but simply because he recognizes that, being his rulers and his friends, they deserve his loyalty. And he suggests that, insofar as Socrates is led by considerations of self-interest to embrace death and hence to abandon his divine rulers and friends, he is guilty of deliberately and selfishly betraying them and consequently deserves to be punished.

Socrates responds to Simmias by suggesting that both he and Cebes are accusing him of injustice just as the Athenians had accused him at his trial (63b1-2). By identifying both Cebes and Simmias with his Athenian accusers, Socrates invites us to consider in what ways their two distinct charges may reflect two distinct aspects of the Athenians' impiety charge. On the one hand, the Athenians accused Socrates of being unjust to the gods of his city, the true rulers of Athens (see 58a10–b7), by withholding from them the honor and loyalty they deserve. Similarly, they accused him of being unjust to his fellow citizens by refusing to care for them and to respect them as he ought to have done. This "Simmian" accusation implies that Socrates is guilty of deliberately and selfishly disregarding his duties to gods and men and hence that he deserves to be punished. On the other hand, the Athenians accused Socrates of failing to understand that the gods' care is good for him and hence that it is good for him to honor them and to obey them. This "Cebian" accusation implies that Socrates is guilty not only of injustice but also and above all of ignoring his own best interests and hence that he deserves to be pitied and enlightened rather than punished. For, by foolishly depriving himself of the gods' care, Socrates is unwittingly punishing himself. Now, the fact that the Athenians decided to punish Socrates rather than attempt to show him the folly of his ways would seem to indicate that they thought him guilty of wilful injustice rather than of ignorance. Yet, insofar as the Athenians believe that the gods are good rulers of human beings and that the pious man is not only just but happy, they must believe, if only half-consciously, that, Socrates is not only unjust but also ignorant and hence that his injustice is involuntary. In this way, the two charges of Cebes and Simmias both reflect and clarify the ambiguous character of the Athenians' impiety charge against him.[23]

We see, then, that, on the last day of his life, Socrates attempts to reassure his friends that his imminent execution does not call into question the wisdom of his philosophic life by showing them, through both his words and his bearing, that he is ready and even eager to die now. But Socrates' posture in the face of death provokes his friends to accuse him of impiety and hence to challenge not only the wisdom but also the justice of his way of life. And by making this accusation, his friends repeat the very charge for which his enemies have convicted him and condemned him to death and for which they are about to execute him. Yet, as Socrates himself observes, by accusing him as they do, Cebes and Simmias also give him the opportunity to give them a more persuasive defense of his way of life than he was able to give the Athenians at his trial (63b4-5; see also 69e3-5). They give him the opportunity, then, to persuade them and his other companions before he dies that the philosophic life is, despite their doubts, the best way of life for a human being. And they also give him one last opportunity to persuade them and through them men at large that, notwithstanding the verdict of the city of Athens, he is not, in truth, guilty of injustice against gods and men (see 84d8–e3).

Chapter 4

Socrates' Defense of the Philosopher's Readiness to Die

I. Socrates' Hope for an Afterlife

Socrates responds to the charges of Simmias and Cebes by admitting that it would, indeed, be unjust of him not to be distressed at dying if he did not think that, once he was dead, he would come to be with other gods who are wise as well as good and with human beings among the departed who are better than those here. But he assures his friends that he does hope to arrive among good men, although he would not strongly affirm that he will. And he also assures them that, if he would strongly affirm anything else about such matters, he would strongly affirm that he will come to be with gods who are very good masters. Accordingly, he is of good hope that there is something for the departed and that, as is said of old, it is much better for the good than for the bad (63b4–c7).

Socrates here assures his friends that his readiness to die does not reflect any desire on his part to be free of the gods. On the contrary, by seeking to die now he is seeking to be with other gods who are wise as well as good masters. Socrates responds to his friends' impiety charge, then, by declaring that he does wish to enjoy the care of divine rulers and hence that he is pious, even though his piety is not of this world.

Furthermore, Socrates responds to Simmias' charge that the philosopher is an unjust man who selfishly disregards his duties to the political community constituted by his friends and his divine rulers, by declaring that he is not selfish, that he does wish to belong to a political community, but that he wishes to die because he wishes to belong to one which is better than his earthly community. Socrates suggests here, then, that, insofar as he expects to belong to a political community in the afterlife and to enjoy the company of good men and the care of good and wise gods there, his readiness to die is pious, wise, and just.

Yet, as a response to Cebes' specific charge that it is unwise for him to be so willing to die now, Socrates' defense here is remarkably tentative. For, while it might be wise for him to embrace death if he were reasonably confident that he would arrive among good men in the afterlife and enjoy with them the care of the gods, Socrates expressly states that he is not at all confident that he will arrive among such men or enjoy such care once he is dead (63b8–c2). But if he is so uncertain about what his fate will be once he is dead, how can it be wise or reasonable for him to be willing to die so easily? Furthermore, as a response to Simmias' charge of injustice, what Socrates says here in defense of his readiness to die is even more questionable. For is it just for him to abandon his friends and his divine rulers in this life even in order to be with better men and rulers in the afterlife? Does the prospect of enjoying the company of better men and the care of better rulers relieve the philosopher of his duties to his actual friends and rulers?

Simmias, however, does not challenge Socrates' defense of the justice of his readiness to die. Instead, he urges Socrates to share with his friends the reason for his hopes for the afterlife. For this, he says, seems to him to be a common good. And he also says that it will be a sufficient defense of Socrates' readiness to die if he persuades them that he has good reason to be so hopeful in the face of death (63c8–d2). Despite his having sharply accused Socrates of unjustly deserting his divine rulers and his friends in this world only moments before, Simmias is now quite willing to acquit him of this charge if he will only benefit his friends by showing that it is reasonable to hope for a happiness in Hades far greater than any that is attainable in this life and hence that it is truly good for him—and would be good for them—to abandon this world. In this way, Simmias himself abandons his previous identification of justice with loyalty to one's divine rulers and friends. He redefines justice as that which is a common good for Socrates and his friends. And he suggests that Socrates would promote their "common" good if he were to show them that it is reasonable to abandon one's friends and to seek one's individual happiness in the afterlife.

Socrates responds to Simmias by saying that he wants to give his companions an account of how it appears to him that a man who has really lived the philosophic life has plausible reasons for being confident in the face of death and for being of good hope that he will win the greatest goods for himself in an afterlife (63e8-64a3). And he thereby indicates that, by defending the philosopher's readiness to die, he will also be defending the philosopher's way of life as a whole. For, insofar as he shows that the philosopher has good reason to hope for the greatest happiness after death, he will have shown that the philosophic life is simply the best way of life for a human being. We see, then, that Socrates' primary intention in the *Phaedo* is not to discuss the question of the immortality of the soul but rather to persuade his young friends that, notwithstanding their doubts, the philosophic life remains the best way of life.[1] He is led to discuss the question of immortality by his friends' doubts about the piety and justice of the philosophic life and by his desire to assuage their doubts. Yet even if Socrates should go on to show them that the philosopher may reasonably hope to attain the greatest goods for himself after death, it is still not clear that he will have thereby justified the philosopher's readiness to die. For even if it is good and hence wise for the philosopher to seek happiness in the afterlife, it is still not clear that it is just for him to abandon his friends and rulers in this life in order to attain such happiness for himself.

II. The Philosopher's Longing for Death

Socrates begins his defense of his readiness, as a philosopher, to die, by telling Simmias and Cebes that it may escape the notice of other human beings that those who are devoted to philosophy in the correct way practice nothing else but dying and being dead. And if this is true, he says, then it would be strange if they were eager throughout their lives for nothing but death and then were distressed when death finally comes (64a4-9). Socrates here reveals to his friends that the philosopher is not only ready or even eager to die but that he devotes his whole life to learning how to die and that he longs throughout his life for nothing but death. And he thereby reveals to them that the philosopher spends his whole life learning how to separate himself from his friends and his rulers and longing for his final separation from them (compare 64a4-9 with 62c9-63a9).

Simmias responds to this seemingly strange portrait of the philosophers by laughing, even though, as he claims, he is in no laughing mood on this day. He evidently feels ashamed to be laughing on the day of his friend's execution. But he blames Socrates himself for his laughter. For, as Simmias explains, he supposes that the many who heard this would think it well said against the philosophers and that the many in his native Thebes would agree that the philosophers really do want to die and, moreover, that they deserve to die (64a10-b6). Now, Socrates' claim that the philosophers long throughout their lives for nothing but death is admittedly strange. It is also strange that he should seem to agree with the opinion of the many that the philosophers live such wretched lives that they must want to die. Yet Simmias' laughter shows that he finds the philosophers' apparent disdain for life not only strange but also ridiculous and foolish. It shows that, despite his apparent devotion to the philosophers, he feels a certain sympathy for the many's contempt for them. It is understandable, then, that Simmias should feel ashamed of his laughter here and should try to deny that he feels like laughing on the day that Socrates is to be executed by the Athenian many. For his laughter is a sign of his sympathy for Socrates' enemies, a sign of his disloyalty to his friend, and hence, it would seem, a sign of his own injustice.[2] Moreover, Simmias' remark that, according to the many, the philosophers deserve to die reminds us that, like the Athenian many, he, too, has accused Socrates of injustice and has implied that he deserves to be punished for his crime. We see, then, that, despite his apparent friendship for the philosophers and for Socrates, Simmias feels a considerable sympathy for their enemies and hence is a most uncertain friend of theirs. And perhaps it is because Socrates sees this as well that, while he will address Cebes three times as his friend in the course of this conversation, he will never address Simmias as his friend (compare 72c5, 80a6, e1 with 67b7, 68b3, 76d1, 82c2, 85e1, 110b5; see also 91b1, 103b6).

Socrates acknowledges that what the many say about the philosophers is true and thereby seems to justify Simmias' sympathy for the many's view of the philosophers. But, by saying that the many do not understand in what sense the true philosophers want and deserve to die and what kind of death they deserve, Socrates suggests that Simmias should not simply trust what the many say about them. Accordingly, Socrates proposes that they disregard the many altogether and try instead to understand for themselves the philosopher's eagerness for death (64b7–c1).

In order to clarify his claim that the true philosophers are eager throughout their lives for nothing but death, Socrates now asks Simmias whether "we" believe that death is something. When Simmias replies that we do indeed believe that it is something, Socrates asks him whether it is anything other than the separation of the soul from the body whereby each exists apart from the other. Simmias answers, without any hesitation, that death is nothing other than this (64c1-9). And on the basis of this agreed upon definition of death, Socrates proceeds to argue that the philosophers are eager throughout their lives for nothing but the separation and release of their souls from their bodies.

Simmias' agreement with this definition of death is extremely important for Socrates' defense of the wisdom and the justice of the philosopher's readiness to die and, indeed, of the philosopher's whole way of life in the *Phaedo*. In the first place, by readily agreeing here that the soul survives after death, Simmias allows Socrates to assume throughout what he explicitly calls his defense of the philosopher's readiness to depart from this life that there is an attractive, or at least potentially attractive, alternative to this life, namely, the afterlife. In this way, Simmias grants, at least to begin with, the plausibility of Socrates' claim that it is reasonable and wise for the philosopher to long for death. And even though Socrates' defense prompts Cebes to challenge the assumption that there is an afterlife (69e6-70b4), the question of whether there is an afterlife emerges only after both Simmias and Cebes have come to feel in their hearts the power of the hope for a life beyond this one.

Furthermore, and more importantly, Simmias' agreement to this definition of death marks a crucial and lasting change in the entire context within which the philosopher's readiness to die is discussed. Up until this point in the conversation, the philosopher's readiness to die has been discussed within the context of his relation to his friends and his divine rulers and hence within a political context. The implicit definition of death throughout this early discussion has been a political one, namely, the separation of the philosopher from his political community as it is constituted by his friends and his divine but earthly rulers (see 62b2-63c7). And consequently, Cebes and Simmias have together demanded, on behalf of his friends and his divine rulers, that Socrates defend the justice as well as the wisdom of his readiness to die just as the Athenians had demanded, on behalf of his fellow citizens and his gods, that he defend the justice of his way of life. It has seemed, then, that, in order to defend his readiness to die, Socrates would have to defend to his friends the justice of his readiness to abandon them and his rulers for the sake of attaining for himself the greatest goods. And consequently, it has seemed that Socrates would have to explain why it is just for the philosopher to be devoted to his own good rather than to fulfilling his duties to his friends, his rulers, and his political community as a whole.

But now, by agreeing to the wholly apolitical definition of death as nothing other than the separation and release of the individual soul from the individual body, Simmias allows Socrates to portray the philosopher's eagerness for death as nothing more than his eagerness to release his own soul from his own body. He allows Socrates to portray the philosopher's eagerness to die as a reflection of his noble superiority to the body rather than as a reflection of his disloyalty to his friends and rulers. And he thereby allows Socrates to set aside the question of whether it is just for the philosopher to disregard his duties to others in order to attain the greatest goods for himself.

Accordingly, once Simmias agrees that death is nothing but the separation of the soul from the body, Socrates is able to consider with him what the philosopher's posture is toward the body rather than toward his friends and rulers. He quickly gains Simmias' agreement to the following propositions: that the true philosopher despises the pleasures and the adornments of the body, that he consequently distances himself from his body as much as is possible, and that he devotes himself above all to his soul. And Simmias also goes along with Socrates' suggestion that the philosopher distinguishes himself from other human beings by his desire to release himself from "the community of the body" (64c10-65a3). Now, all of these statements would seem to call into question the justice of the philosopher, for they would seem to suggest that he despises his fellow human beings and his rulers, that he distances himself from them as much as possible, and that he devotes himself above all to his own happiness. Simmias, however, seems to forget altogether the question of the philosopher's justice in his relations with men and gods in this life, even though he himself had raised that question in his accusation against Socrates. For when Socrates suggests that it is because of the philosophers' contempt for the body and its pleasures, rather than because of their seeming injustice to their fellow citizens and gods, that the many believe the philosophers deserve to be executed, Simmias agrees, without any hesitation, that what Socrates says is very true (65a4-8).

We see, then, that Socrates' defense of the philosopher's readiness to die and, indeed, of the philosophic life as a whole in the *Phaedo* abstracts from the question of the philosopher's relation to his political community and thereby abstracts from the question of the philosopher's justice to men and gods in this life. One sign of this is that, while Socrates will go on to give Simmias a somewhat detailed account of the philosopher's courage and moderation, he will pointedly omit a similarly detailed account of the philosopher's justice (compare 68c5-69a4 with 69b1–c3). What makes this abstraction possible and also perhaps defensible is that Simmias and Cebes evidently feel little attachment to any political community. They have been willing to leave their native city of Thebes, and they have been willing to violate the laws of Athens. Furthermore, while they have accused Socrates of injustice to his divine rulers, on the day of his execution, at least, they evidently doubt that the gods really do take care of and rule over human beings in this life. It seems, then, that their doubts about the philosopher's readiness to die and about his life as a whole focus more on his wisdom than on his justice to gods and men in this life. Accordingly, by setting aside the question of whether it is just for the philosopher to seek to leave his friends and rulers and by focusing instead on the question of whether it is wise or good for the philosopher to long for the release of his soul from his body, Socrates focuses on the question which is at the heart of his friends' doubts about the philosophic life.[3]

Socrates now proceeds to argue that it is the philosopher's defining passion, his desire for wisdom, which leads him to be eager throughout his life for the release of his soul from his body (65a9ff.). At this point, we may notice a certain asymmetry in Socrates' explanation of his thesis that the true or genuine philosopher is eager for death. In order to clarify that thesis, he has proposed and Simmias has accepted a clear and explicit definition of what death is. We would expect, then, that he would propose a similarly clear and explicit definition of what a genuine philosopher is. But Socrates does not do this. Instead, he goes on to argue that the man who is a genuine philosopher will necessarily long for death. There is, however, a fairly specific definition of what a philosopher is which underlies this entire discussion and which both Simmias and Cebes appear to take for granted (see 69e6-7). Since this implicit definition makes itself felt throughout the discussion of the philosopher's eagerness for death, it is helpful to consider what it is.

Socrates indicates what this definition is by asking Simmias, what about the acquisition itself of wisdom (65a9)? By asking this question, Socrates emphasizes that the philosopher not only loves wisdom but seeks to acquire it for himself. And he both loves it and seeks to acquire it presumably because he believes that it is the greatest of goods (64a1). Accordingly, the philosopher not only seeks to acquire a part of wisdom or to make progress in wisdom but rather seeks to possess the whole of wisdom. And, conversely, since he regards ignorance as the greatest of evils, he seeks to escape from it altogether. Throughout this discussion, then, the philosopher is understood or assumed to be a man who seeks to possess the whole truth and nothing but the truth in order to become perfectly or purely wise (see 66b1-7, 66d7-67b4, 68a7-b7, 69b5-d1, 69e6-7).

In order to see what is distinctive about this understanding of the philosopher, it is helpful to contrast it with the portrait of the philosopher set forth by Socrates in the *Apology*. There Socrates identifies what he calls human wisdom with the knowledge of one's ignorance about the greatest matters and suggests to the Athenians that this is the greatest wisdom attainable for human beings. He thereby suggests that the philosopher devotes his life to the goal of attaining wisdom thus understood, even though he also suggests that such wisdom may be worth little or nothing.[4] Socrates' young companions in the *Phaedo*, however, deny that such human wisdom can truly satisfy the genuine philosopher's desire for wisdom or truly justify his life-long quest for wisdom. They believe that, since the philosopher regards ignorance as the greatest of evils, he must seek not only to become aware of his ignorance but also to become wholly free of it. And since he regards wisdom as the greatest of goods, he must seek to possess a wisdom which is untainted by the evil of ignorance and hence which is pure (see 66d7-67b6, 68a7-b7, 69b5-d2, e6-7). Simmias and Cebes believe that only such a perfect or divine wisdom can truly satisfy the philosopher's desire for wisdom and that only the actual attainment of such a wisdom can justify his willingness to endure the hardships he endures and to run the risks he runs in his pursuit of wisdom.

Now, Socrates does not challenge his companions' opinion that the philosopher dedicates his life to the goal of attaining a perfect or pure wisdom. Instead, he tries to show them that, precisely if that opinion is true, the philosopher will long throughout his life for death. The precise thesis, then, which Socrates is attempting to argue for in his defense of the philosopher's readiness to die is that the philosopher, that is, the man who seeks to acquire nothing less than a wisdom which is free of any taint of ignorance, will be eager throughout his life for nothing less than the final release of his soul from his body.

Socrates begins his argument by asking Simmias whether or not the body is an impediment if someone should take it along as a partner in his search for wisdom. In order to clarify this question, he asks whether the senses of sight and hearing possess some truth for human beings or whether, as "even the poets are always babbling to us," we do not hear, see, or, in sum, perceive anything in a precise or clear way (65a9–b6). Now, by associating the claim that our senses never provide us with precise and clear knowledge of anything with the seemingly dubious authority of babbling poets, Socrates seems to invite Simmias to question that claim and to favor the more cautious claim that the senses afford us at least some access to the truth. But furthermore, it would seem that common sense alone would compel Simmias to agree that our perceptions of things offer us at least some knowledge of the truth. After all, Socrates himself, at the beginning of this conversation, suggested that his perception of the pleasure in his leg offered him at least some insight into the truth about the nature of pleasure and pain (60b1–c7).

Yet, when Socrates goes on simply to assert that it is clear that the soul is deceived by the senses whenever it attempts to examine something with their assistance, Simmias agrees that what he says is very true. And on the basis of this agreement, Simmias goes on to agree that it is only by reasoning, if at all, that the soul may grasp the truth; that the soul reasons "most nobly" when it is not troubled by the senses or the pleasures and pains of the body; and, consequently, that the soul of the philosopher is led by its desire for wisdom not only to despise the body but also to flee from it and to seek to become wholly free of it (65b9–d3). Simmias' agreement, then, that the senses do not possess any truth for human beings but rather deceive the soul leads him to agree that the philosopher must shun his senses, must seek to release his soul from the body, and hence, it seems, must seek to leave this world altogether in order to strive for the wisdom he longs to possess. And it thereby leads him to agree with Socrates' thesis that the philosopher will necessarily long throughout his life for nothing but death.

Now, insofar as the claim that the senses are not at all truthful goes against common sense and insofar as Socrates does not offer any argument in support of that claim, Simmias' agreement to that claim would seem to be wholly unreasonable. Yet Simmias' denial that we can ever know anything by means of our senses may, in fact, be reasonable if he believes that we only truly know something when we know it in a *perfectly* precise and clear way. In other words, if Simmias believes that wisdom is so noble and pure a thing that only a wisdom which is free of any taint of ignorance or uncertainty may qualify as genuine wisdom, then it would be reasonable for him to deny that we can genuinely attain wisdom or knowledge by means of our senses. For, if he identifies knowledge as such with perfect knowledge, then no matter how precise and clear our perceptions of things may be, he would always find that, as long as the things we perceive are always somewhat obscure and opaque and as long as they resist our efforts to understand them perfectly, we never truly understand or know what we perceive.[5] Now Simmias does, in fact, subscribe to this lofty view of wisdom and knowledge. One sign of this is that, when, later in the discussion, Socrates suggests that genuine philosophers identify knowledge itself with pure knowledge and then asks Simmias whether he agrees with them, Simmias answers that he agrees most emphatically (66d7-67b6; see also 68a7–b7). Simmias, then, denies that the philosopher can attain wisdom at all by means of his senses because he denies that anything less than perfect wisdom counts as genuine wisdom.

Simmias may also believe that, insofar as the philosopher seeks perfect knowledge of all the beings, he must seek knowledge of the divine beings as well. Yet, as we are told by the poets, the gods, in particular, are not simply visible beings and hence are not simply knowable by means of our senses.[6] And if what the poets say is true, then it is impossible to know fully the nature of the gods by means of our senses. Simmias' belief that the philosopher cannot attain the wisdom he seeks by means of his senses may reflect, then, not only his lofty view of wisdom but also his belief that the philosopher seeks to possess, above all, a perfect or divine wisdom about the divine beings themselves.

Yet, even if Simmias believes that the senses cannot provide the philosopher with the perfect wisdom that he seeks, it is still not clear why he agrees that the senses "deceive" the philosopher and thereby actively prevent him from attaining such wisdom. For Simmias thereby suggests that the senses are not only useless to the philosopher but harmful or evil as well and hence that the philosopher must not only despise the senses but must flee from them altogether. But if it is clear that the senses do not possess any truth for human beings, how can they deceive the philosopher? By agreeing that the senses are deceptive, Simmias suggests that they are so persuasive that they inevitably lead the man who consults them to believe that they do, indeed, possess the truth. More specifically, insofar as the senses are incapable of providing the philosopher with the perfect wisdom he seeks, they seem to reveal the truth that such wisdom is simply unattainable and hence that the goal of the philosophic life is simply unreachable. It is by persuading the philosopher that the wisdom he seeks is unattainable that the senses deceive him—if, that is, such wisdom is, in truth, attainable for human beings. It seems, then, that Simmias' belief that the senses are deceptive rather than truthful reflects his assumption or faith that the goal of the philosophic life—perfect wisdom—is reachable.[7]

Socrates now proceeds to examine whether, according to Simmias, the wisdom the philosopher seeks is, in fact, attainable. He asks Simmias whether "we" say that there is something "just itself." Simmias agrees emphatically, with an oath to Zeus, that we do, indeed, say that there is such a purely just being. And he goes on to agree that there is something noble and good, as there is bigness, health, and strength; that we cannot know these pure and perfect beings by means of our senses; and that the knowledge of such beings constitutes the wisdom which the philosopher loves and seeks to possess (65d4–e5).

Now, since neither Socrates nor Simmias offer any arguments for the existence of these perfect, invisible beings, it would seem that Simmias merely assumes or accepts on faith that they actually exist.[8] Nevertheless, inasmuch as he identifies genuine knowledge with perfect knowledge and insofar as he believes that such knowledge is attainable, it makes sense that he should believe in the existence of these perfect beings or forms (see 102a10–b2). For, since to know always means to know something, if perfect knowledge is possible, then there must exist beings which are themselves perfectly knowable. And insofar as the things that we perceive are not perfectly knowable, the beings which are perfectly knowable must exist apart from and beyond the world our senses reveal to us. Furthermore, Simmias seems to identify these perfect beings with the divine beings, namely, the gods (see 65d4-6, 85e3-86a3; compare also 78c10-79a14, 79e8-80b5 with 63a7-9).[9] And, indeed, if perfect knowledge of all the beings is attainable, then the divine beings themselves must be perfectly knowable. For if the gods are ultimately mysterious beings and if they rule over all the other beings, then it would seem to be impossible to know in a perfect or perhaps even in a meaningful way any of the beings at all (see 62d3-5). On the assumption, then, that only perfect knowledge counts as genuine knowledge and that such knowledge or wisdom is attainable, it seems to be reasonable and even necessary to believe that the true objects of knowledge exist apart from the sensible world and that those perfect and divine beings are perfectly knowable.

Simmias' belief that the senses are deceptive rather than truthful and his belief in the existence of imperceptible but perfectly knowable beings are based, then, on his assumption or faith that the perfect or pure wisdom the philosopher seeks is attainable, that the goal of the philosophic life is a reachable goal, and hence that that way of life is a reasonable and good way of life. Yet, inasmuch as Simmias actually doubts the goodness and the wisdom of the philosophic life, he must doubt that those beliefs constitute sufficient proof that the goal of the philosophic life is, indeed, attainable. In other words, Simmias must sense that, even if it is true that there are perfectly or purely knowable beings which exist apart from and beyond the sensible world and the knowledge of which constitutes the wisdom the philosopher seeks to possess, it does not necessarily follow that he will, in fact, attain that wisdom and hence that his way of life is, in fact, a reasonable or good way of life. And Socrates now proceeds, it seems, to justify those doubts by showing Simmias that it is impossible for the philosopher to attain the pure wisdom he seeks as long as he is alive.

The discussion up till this point has suggested that, in order to attain pure wisdom, it is necessary for the philosopher to purify himself of the senses. For they constantly tempt him to believe that the sensible world is the only world and hence that it is the true world. And since it is not possible to know the sensible world perfectly, the senses tempt the philosopher to conclude that his search for perfect wisdom is in vain. Accordingly, when Socrates suggests that, if anyone can attain perfect wisdom, it will be the man who shuns his senses as much as possible, who releases himself as much as possible from his body, and who uses his pure mind, itself by itself, to hunt after each of the pure beings, Simmias agrees emphatically that what he says is true (65e6-66a10). And by agreeing that it is impossible for the philosopher to attain perfect wisdom as long as his soul is united with his body, he agrees that it is impossible for him to attain the goal of his philosophic life as long as he is alive. Accordingly, the philosopher can only attain the wisdom that he seeks, if at all, when he is dead. Simmias' agreement here suggests, then, that Socrates has persuaded him that, insofar as the philosopher longs throughout his life for nothing but wisdom, he will long throughout his life for nothing but death.

Yet Socrates' argument here seems to show that, if, as Simmias believes, the philosopher devotes his life to the pursuit of a perfect or pure wisdom, the philosophic life is most unreasonable. And it thereby reveals most clearly why it is that Simmias doubts the wisdom and the goodness of that way of life.[10] For, according to Simmias, the philosopher dedicates his life to a goal which, although lofty and splendid, is unreachable while he is alive. Moreover, precisely inasmuch as that goal is so lofty, the philosopher cannot even approach it while he is alive. For, insofar as Simmias believes that anything less than perfect wisdom does not count as genuine wisdom, he must also believe that progress in wisdom, through which the philosopher might gradually increase but never complete his wisdom, is impossible in this life. In Simmias' eyes, then, the philosopher is a man who is possessed by a passionate love which is never even partially satisfied in his lifetime. He is led by this love to deny himself the pleasures of the body, to shun the world that his senses present to him, and to suffer the evils of persecution. And he makes these sacrifices and undergoes these hardships for the sake of a beloved which can never, it seems, be his. But how can it be sensible for a human being to suffer so for the sake of an unreachable goal? How can a way of life which is so rich with the pain of longing and so destitute of the pleasure of satisfaction be good or reasonable for a human being? It seems that it cannot be. It is therefore no wonder that Simmias is tempted to despair of the philosophic life. For, as Socrates shows through this discussion, Simmias' lofty vision of the philosophic life contains within it the seeds of such despair.

It is true that, insofar as Socrates and Simmias have already agreed that there is a life after death for human beings, they have left open the possibility that the philosopher may attain the wisdom he seeks once he has died. Indeed, Socrates has shown Simmias through this discussion that, in order to believe that the goal of the philosophic life is reachable, he must not only believe that the sensible world is not the true world and that there are perfectly knowable beings who exist apart from the sensible world but also that there is an afterlife in which the philosopher will at last attain perfect wisdom. But Socrates has not shown that the philosopher has good reasons for hoping that he will attain such wisdom once he is dead. His hopes of reaching the goal of his philosophic life would seem, then, to be mere hopes. And how can the philosopher, who claims to live his life according to reason, base his life on the mere hope that he will attain the wisdom he seeks once he is dead?

Moreover, even if we grant, as Simmias does, that there is an afterlife, it is still not clear how the philosopher can be confident that he will acquire wisdom once he arrives there. For how does he know that the divine rulers of Hades will look favorably on his life-long devotion to philosophy? Socrates himself has admitted that he is not at all confident that he will arrive among good men in Hades (63b9–c2; see also c5-7). And he has even expressed concern that he may be punished in Hades for impiety (60d8-61b1). How, then, does he know that he will not be condemned for impiety there as he has been condemned for impiety here? Precisely if there is an afterlife in which the gods reward and punish men, we may wonder if the philosophic life is not a most unreasonable way of life for a human being.

III. The Argument that the Philosopher Deserves the Reward of Everlasting Happiness

Socrates now proceeds to argue that the philosopher does have good reason to hope that he will attain perfect wisdom, and thereby reach the goal of his life, once he is dead. He presents this argument in the form of an opinion which, he claims, genuine philosophers will necessarily hold (see 66b1-2, 67b3-4).[11] The philosophers' opinion, which Socrates presents in their voice, consists of three distinct parts. First they argue that it is impossible for them to acquire the wisdom they desire as long as they are alive (66b3–e2). Then they claim that they cannot become purely wise as long as they are alive but only, if at all, once they have died (66e2-67a2). Finally, they assert that it is not permitted by the gods for them to become purely wise once they are dead unless they purify their souls of any contact with or infection from the body while they are alive (67a2–b2).

The core of the philosophers' opinion would seem to be their claim that they will acquire pure wisdom once they are dead. Yet, their opinion is almost entirely devoted to arguing that they deserve to be rewarded with the pure wisdom that they desire. In the first part of their opinion, they argue that they are not responsible for their failure to acquire pure wisdom in this life (66b3–e4). And in the third and final part they argue that, if they purify themselves of evil in this life, they will be rewarded with pure wisdom in the next life (67a2–b2). The philosophers evidently believe that, if they deserve to be rewarded with pure wisdom and if they cannot possibly acquire it in this life, then justice demands that there be an afterlife in which they will be rewarded according to their desert. The philosophers' hope for attaining wisdom after death, then, is based on their explicit argument that they deserve to be rewarded with pure wisdom and on their implicit assumption or faith that there are just gods who reward and punish human beings according to their desert.

The philosophers begin by telling one another that, as long as they have a body and their soul is kneaded together with such an evil thing, they will never acquire sufficiently the wisdom they desire (66b5-7). It is not "they," then, but their bodies—which they speak of as wholly distinct from themselves—which are responsible for their failure to acquire pure wisdom. Their true selves—their souls—desire pure wisdom and hence desire to become pure, wise, and good. But their bodies prevent their souls from satisfying this desire. The philosophers readily admit, then, that their bodies do not desire pure wisdom and hence are evil. But they sharply distinguish their selves from their bodies and argue that "they," who do desire pure wisdom, are not evil and therefore do not deserve to be blamed—or punished—for their failure to acquire pure wisdom in this life.

But how does the body prevent the soul from acquiring the wisdom that it desires? In the first place, the philosophers claim that the body busies the soul in countless ways by compelling it to nourish the body and to care for it when it is ill (66b7–c2). Yet attending to the body's need for food and health would not seem to take up all or even most of the philosophers' time and hence would not, by itself, prevent them from acquiring the wisdom that they say they desire (see 66b5-8, e2-4). Furthermore, the philosophers do not explain here how the body—which they speak of as being wholly distinct from the soul—is able to compel the soul to attend to its needs. Accordingly, the philosophers make the further claim that the body "fills" their souls with passionate loves, desires, fears, images of all kinds, and much nonsense so that it is impossible for them ever to think of anything because of it. For example, by filling the soul with the desire for wealth, the body compels the soul to make war for the sake of wealth and thereby diverts the soul from the pursuit of wisdom (66c5–d2). Similarly, by filling the soul with the desire to live and the fear of death, the body compels the soul to attend to its need for food and health (66b7–c2). And, worst of all, according to the philosophers, by implanting such powerful passions in the soul, the body prevents the soul from pursuing wisdom even when it has the leisure to do so. For, even then, the soul is so agitated by the desire for things other than wisdom that it is unable to discern the truth. The principal way, then, in which the evil body prevents the soul from acquiring wisdom is not by depriving it of the leisure to pursue wisdom but rather by infecting the soul with evil passions that overwhelm its very desire for wisdom (compare 66b7–c2 with d3-7).

The philosophers blame their failure to acquire the wisdom they claim to be lovers of on their compelling desires and loves for things other than wisdom (66e2-4; see also b3-7). And by claiming that these evil passions are rooted in the body and not the soul, they absolve themselves of all responsibility for their failure to acquire pure wisdom. For in their heart of hearts— in their souls—they love only wisdom. By drawing a sharp distinction between their bodies and their souls, then, the philosophers can at once admit that "they" do not purely—or even strongly—desire to become purely wise and still contend that "they" do indeed desire with all their heart to become purely wise.[12]

Yet, while the philosophers' argument that they are not responsible for their failure to acquire wisdom proves that they do not deserve to be blamed or punished for their failure, it does not prove that they positively deserve to be rewarded with pure wisdom. Indeed, that argument suggests that, given their nature as human beings, it is impossible for them ever to deserve to be so rewarded. For if, as they argue, the body necessarily enslaves the soul by filling the soul with its desires and loves for things other than wisdom, how can the philosophers claim that they, that is, their souls, love only wisdom (compare 66c2-5 with e2-4; see also d1-2)? And, if it is true that the body fills the soul with its passions and hence with its very nature, how can the philosophers sharply distinguish between their souls— that is, their selves—and their bodies (compare 66c2-5 with 67a2-6)? If, finally, it is true that the evil body fills the soul with its evil nature and thereby compels it to be evil, impure, and unwise in this life, how can their souls ever become good, pure, and wise and hence deserving of rewards in an afterlife? It would seem that the philosophers' argument shows that their nature as human beings—as beings who consist of both body and soul (see 79b1-3)—necessarily prevents them both from deserving to be punished for their impurity and ignorance but also from deserving to be rewarded with pure wisdom. And for this reason, it seems, the philosophers conclude this argument by admitting that it is possible that they will never acquire the wisdom they claim to be lovers of (66e2-67a2).

The philosophers respond to this difficulty by exhorting one another to avoid, as much as is possible, all contact with the body, to refuse to fill their souls with its nature, and hence to purify themselves of the evil body while they are alive (67a2-6). And having thus become pure and having released themselves from the folly of the body, they will deserve the reward of pure wisdom and hence attain such wisdom once they are dead. For in the afterlife, they claim, the one who is impure is not permitted by the gods to grasp what is pure (67a6–b2). The philosophers argue here, then, that by purifying themselves of the folly of the body in this life, they will deserve the reward of a wisdom which is itself untainted by folly or ignorance in the afterlife. In this way, the philosophers argue for the reasonableness of their hopes of attaining the wisdom they love after death and thereby argue for the reasonableness of the philosophic life itself.

Is the philosophers' argument, then, a persuasive one? We must first note that their entire argument rests on the implicit assumption that there are just gods who reward and punish human beings according to their desert in an afterlife. We must also note that they do not provide a single argument or piece of evidence to support that assumption. The philosophers' argument for the reasonableness of their hope of attaining wisdom after death and hence for the reasonableness of the philosophic life is itself based, then, on a claim of faith rather than a claim of reason. Nevertheless, in the absence of a compelling refutation of the pious claim that there are righteous gods who reward the good and punish the wicked in an afterlife, it may be reasonable to defer to the pious and to accept their claim as a plausible one.

Yet, precisely if we accept this pious claim, precisely if it is the souls of the good who are rewarded after death, we must question the philosophers' confidence that they will be rewarded once they are dead. For their confidence is based both on their argument that it is not they but their evil body which is responsible for their failure to acquire pure wisdom in this life and on their argument that it is by virtue of having purified themselves of their evil body that they deserve the reward of pure wisdom in an afterlife. These two arguments, however, contradict one another. According to the first argument, the body necessarily prevents them from acquiring pure wisdom in this life by filling their souls with its evil passions. But, according to the second argument, it is, indeed, possible for them to prevent the body from filling their souls with its evil nature and passions and therefore it is possible for them to purify themselves of the body in this life (compare 66c2–d7 with 67a2–b2). Taken together, these two arguments at once affirm and deny that it is possible for the philosophers to purify themselves of evil in this life and thereby affirm and deny that it is possible for them to deserve the reward of pure wisdom in the afterlife. And since the philosophers contradict themselves regarding this crucial question, how can it be reasonable for them to be confident that they will be rewarded once they are dead?

Even if we consider each argument separately, neither seems to offer a sound basis for the philosopher's hope of attaining pure wisdom after they die. If the first argument were true, then the philosophers would never be able to purify their souls of evil passions or of ignorance in this life since both are rooted in the body and the body is the master of the soul. They and, indeed, all human beings would be necessarily evil and ignorant beings. And consequently, no human being could ever deserve to be rewarded in an afterlife. On the other hand, if the second argument were true, it would be possible for the philosophers to purify themselves of the evil passions and to release their souls from the folly of the body in this life. And having thus overcome the obstacles in their pursuit of purity and wisdom, it would be possible for them to become purely good and wise in this life. But consequently, the philosophers would no longer have any reason to long for the reward of pure wisdom in the hereafter. For this reward would already be within their grasp in the here and now. In opposite ways, then, each argument suggests that the philosophers will not be rewarded with pure wisdom after death. For either they are blamelessly evil and ignorant men who cannot deserve to be so rewarded, or they are purely good and wise men who have no need to be so rewarded.

Yet, the simple fact that the philosophers describe themselves as philosophers or lovers of wisdom indicates that they are not yet purely wise.[13] Indeed, the whole reason that they argue that they deserve the reward of pure wisdom after death is their belief that they cannot attain the wisdom they seek in this life (66e4-6). Their very longing, then, for the reward of pure wisdom after death belies their claim that they are already purely wise and hence deserve that reward. Accordingly, precisely if we accept the philosophers' belief that there are gods who are just and who reward and punish human beings according to their desert, we must conclude, it seems, that their hope of being rewarded after death is unreasonable.

But, if it is true that the philosophers can never attain the purity and wisdom which would entitle them to rewards in the afterlife, then it must also be true that they can never deserve to be punished for their failure to become pure and wise in this life. For it would be manifestly unjust for the gods to punish human beings for their evil if they cannot possibly purify themselves of evil. And the philosophers' entire argument is based on the premise that the gods are just (see 67b2). It would seem, then, that, inasmuch as there cannot be an afterlife in which the philosophers will either be rewarded or punished, if the gods are simply just, there cannot be an afterlife at all.

An awareness of the difficulties with the philosophers' argument here may lead us to wonder about the reasonableness of any hope for a perfect and everlasting happiness in an afterlife which is based on the claim that we can deserve such happiness. For insofar as we long for perfect happiness in the hereafter, we must long not only to free ourselves from this world but also to free our presumably immortal souls from our clearly mortal bodies. We must admit, then, that our existence in this world as human beings, that is, as embodied souls, is imperfect and hence that we ourselves are imperfect. But how can imperfect beings deserve the reward of perfect happiness? And how can admittedly imperfect beings believe that they deserve such a reward? It would seem, then, that, insofar as the hope for perfect happiness in an afterlife depends on the belief that human beings can deserve such happiness, it is simply not a reasonable hope.

Yet, despite the difficulties with the philosophers' argument, Simmias does not raise any objections to it. Instead, he expresses his emphatic agreement that it is necessary for all those who love learning, including, presumably, himself, to accept this argument. Socrates replies by saying that, if this argument is true, there is much hope for the one who arrives where he himself is going—that there, in Hades, he will attain sufficiently that wisdom for the sake of which they have busied themselves throughout their lives. Therefore, he concludes, he may now go on his appointed journey with good hope, as may any man who believes that he has provided himself with a mind which has been, as it were, purified. And Simmias agrees emphatically with this conclusion (67b3–c4). It would seem, then, that, through his presentation of the philosophers' argument, Socrates has successfully persuaded Simmias that it is reasonable for him to be of good hope in the face of death and has thereby successfully defended his readiness, as a philosopher, to die.

Socrates, however, does not seem to be entirely satisfied with this conclusion. For he now proceeds to elaborate the philosophers' argument and to examine it further. As he has indicated, the philosopher's good hope in the face of death is based on his belief that his mind has been, as it were, purified and that, consequently, he deserves to be rewarded with pure wisdom by the just gods in Hades. And, in order, it seems, to clarify the basis of this hope further, Socrates suggests to Simmias that purification is the separation of the soul from the body "as much as is possible" in this life (67c5–d2). Now, as his formulation here implies, this definition of purity is somewhat loose, since, strictly speaking, in order to become pure one would have to become free of any taint of the evil body. Yet Socrates may mean to suggest here that strict purity is not demanded by the gods. He may mean to suggest that the gods are not strictly or simply just but that their justice is softened by mercy or generosity. We might expect him to argue, then, that, contrary to what the philosophers' argument has suggested, the philosopher may be of good hope that he will be rewarded with pure wisdom if he has purified his soul of the body not completely but as much as is humanly possible (compare 67b10–d2 with b2).

Socrates, however, goes on, instead, to remind Simmias that death is the release and separation of the soul from the body and hence that death is the true and final purification of the soul of the body. And he proceeds to argue that, since it is only those who love wisdom in the correct way who are "always" eager to release their souls from their bodies, it would be ridiculous for them to be distressed when death finally brings about such a release (67d4–e3). Socrates argues here, then, that, since the philosophers are always eager to purify their souls, it would be unreasonable for them to be distressed when this purification is finally brought about by death.

Yet this argument calls into question the whole basis of the philosopher's confidence in the face of death. For before, Socrates had suggested that the philosopher is of good hope because he believes that he has, as it were, purified his soul of evil in this life. But now he argues that the philosopher is "always" eager for the purification that death brings and thereby suggests that the philosopher does not believe that he has genuinely purified his soul of evil in this life (compare 67d5–e2 with b7–c3). What, then, is the basis of his good hope that he will attain the reward of pure wisdom once he is dead? How can he believe that he deserves that reward if he admits that he has not adequately purified his soul of evil in this life?

Furthermore, by suggesting that death is the true and final purification of the soul, Socrates seems to suggest that all human beings, when they die, automatically become pure. But if this is so, how can the philosopher, in particular, deserve to be rewarded when he dies? Indeed, insofar as all human beings naturally and effortlessly become pure when they die, how can any human being deserve to be rewarded after death by virtue of his purity?

Socrates does suggest here, however, that it is only the philosophers who are always eager to be purified through death. Even though all human beings are impure as long as they are alive and are purified of their bodies when they die, it is only the philosophers who long throughout their lives for the purification that death brings. Accordingly, Socrates goes on to claim that, of all human beings, the philosophers are least afraid of death (67e4-6). Perhaps, then, it is by virtue of their singular longing to die and become pure that the philosophers may deserve the reward of pure wisdom from gods who are generous as well as just.

Socrates now urges Simmias to examine more carefully why it is that the philosophers are least of all human beings afraid of death. He asks whether, if they desire to release their soul altogether from their body, it would not be quite unreasonable if they were afraid and distressed when this release actually took place and if they were not glad to go there where they may hope to attain the wisdom which they have passionately loved throughout their lives. For, "many" men, Socrates points out, whose human beloveds and wives and sons have died have been ready to follow them into Hades, led by the hope of seeing and being with them there. Will, then, someone who is genuinely in love with wisdom and who has eagerly embraced "this same hope," that nowhere but in Hades will he genuinely possess his beloved, be distressed when he dies? Will he not rather be glad to go there? One must suppose so, Socrates declares, if that man really is a philosopher. For such a man will eagerly embrace the opinion that nowhere else but in Hades will he possess wisdom in a pure way. In this way, then, Socrates explains to Simmias the philosopher's singular confidence in the face of death. And Simmias is not only persuaded but moved by this account of the philosopher's passionate hope of possessing his beloved in Hades. For when Socrates asks him whether, if what he has been saying is so, it would not be quite unreasonable for such men to fear death, Simmias agrees emphatically, with an oath to Zeus, that it would be quite unreasonable. He also expresses his strong agreement with Socrates' claim that the mere sight of a man who is distressed when he is about to die is a sufficient proof that he is not a lover of wisdom but rather a lover of the body (67e6-68c4).

Yet, notwithstanding the vehemence of Socrates' account here and notwithstanding Simmias' agreement with it, that account raises grave doubts regarding the reasonableness of the philosophers' hope for the afterlife. For Socrates says that the philosophers cherish the "same hope" that bereaved lovers of human beings cherish regarding the afterlife. But he never even attempts to argue that the hope of such lovers to be reunited with their loved ones in Hades is reasonable. Indeed, the hope of such lovers would seem to be a desperate hope conceived in the wake of a heartbreaking loss. But, if the philosophers cherish the very same hope of possessing their beloveds in Hades, how reasonable can their hope be?

Furthermore, while Socrates had previously said that the philosopher's good hope in the face of death is based on his belief that he has, as it were, purified his intellect in this life, now he suggests that it is based on his opinion that nowhere but in Hades will he possess the wisdom he has passionately loved throughout his life (compare 67b10–c3 with 68a7–b6). In other words, he now suggests that the philosopher's hope reflects, not the strength of his conviction that he deserves wisdom as a reward, but rather the intensity of his desire for wisdom and the depth of his despair of ever satisfying that desire in this life. But how can the mere desire, however intense, for happiness after death provide anyone with reasonable or even plausible grounds for hoping that such happiness will, in truth, be his? Finally, while Socrates had suggested before that the philosophers might deserve the reward of wisdom after death by virtue of their singular eagerness for death, he now reminds us that such eagerness for death is not a distinguishing trait of the philosophers. As he points out, "many" men who love human beings rather than wisdom have been ready to die in the hope of meeting with their beloveds in Hades. It is not at all clear, then, that the philosophers are least of all human beings afraid of death. And consequently, while Socrates goes on to say that a man who is distressed at dying cannot be a philosopher, he carefully refrains from saying that a man who is unafraid of death must be a philosopher. For, as his account here shows, the longing for death does not, in fact, distinguish the philosopher from other men.[14] But how, then, can the philosopher reasonably hope to fare better than other human beings in Hades?

Socrates now attempts to distinguish the philosophers from other human beings by arguing that it is only they who are truly virtuous, that it is only they who are truly willing to sacrifice the pleasures of this life, and, therefore, that it is only they who will be rewarded by the gods in Hades. He first gains Simmias' agreement that, since the philosophers do not fear death and since they despise the body and its pleasures, they possess to an extraordinary degree what the many call courage and moderation. Yet, since other human beings appear to possess these virtues as well, Socrates goes on to argue that the courage and moderation of all human beings who are not philosophers is not genuine but absurd. For example, since they all believe that death is a great evil, when they face death they do so because they fear even greater evils. Their courage, then, is unreasonable, Socrates says, since they overcome their fear of death because they themselves are overcome by another fear. And consequently, they are courageous by means of a certain cowardice. Similarly, those who are not philosophers are moderate by means of a certain lack of discipline. For when they deprive themselves of certain pleasures, they do so because they fear being deprived of other, presumably greater, pleasures. They overcome their desires for certain pleasures, then, because they themselves are overcome by their desire for other pleasures (68c5-69a5).

Socrates suggests here that the courage and moderation of human beings who are not philosophers is spurious because it does not reflect a genuine concern for virtue or a genuine superiority to the fear of pain and the desire for pleasure. Their so-called virtues are simply means by which they seek to minimize their pain and maximize their pleasure and consequently reflect their enslavement to their fears and desires. Accordingly, Socrates goes on to suggest that the truly virtuous man, that is, the man who is not only truly courageous and moderate but also, he now adds, truly just, does not seek to exchange lesser pleasures for greater ones or greater pains for lesser ones but has, rather, already purified himself of all such things. And he further suggests that true virtue is therefore not possible without wisdom. For only when one has attained wisdom is one truly free of the desire for pleasure or the fear of pain. Those men who are not philosophers, then, lack true virtue because they lack the wisdom which is the foundation of true virtue (69a6–c3). And those men who are philosophers, Socrates implies, are the only men who are truly superior to the desire for pleasure and truly concerned with virtue. For, insofar as the philosophers devote their lives to the pursuit of wisdom, they also devote their lives to the pursuit of virtue as a whole. In this way, Socrates portrays the philosopher as a man whose singular love of wisdom is bound up with a singular love of virtue as a whole, including the virtue of justice. And by suggesting that the philosopher alone is truly concerned with justice in particular, Socrates affirms the justice of the philosophic life.

Socrates concludes by suggesting that only those men who have purified themselves and have thereby become truly wise and virtuous in this life will dwell with the gods in Hades. All the others will be punished for their impurity by being condemned to lie in filth forever. And since only those who have philosophized in the correct way become pure in this life, only they will be rewarded by the gods in the afterlife. Therefore, he tells Simmias and Cebes, it is reasonable or at least plausible for him to believe that he will meet with masters and companions in Hades who are good or at least no worse than those here (69c3–e2). And with this statement Socrates ends what he explicitly calls his defense of his readiness, as a philosopher, to die and therewith his defense of his philosophic life as a whole.

Socrates' defense culminates with the argument that, since the philosopher has attained pure wisdom in this life and has thereby purified himself of the fears and desires of the body, he deserves to be rewarded by the gods in the afterlife and therefore has good reason to be hopeful in the face of death. Yet, insofar as the philosopher remains a philosopher, insofar, that is, as he remains a lover of wisdom throughout his life, he must not yet have attained wisdom in this life. Indeed, according to the argument that Socrates has made and that Simmias has agreed to, it is impossible for the philosopher to attain the wisdom he seeks in this life (65d4-67b6). And it is precisely because he believes that he cannot possess his beloved wisdom here that he longs for death in the hope that there at last wisdom will be his (67e3-68b7).[15] Since, then, the philosopher cannot become wise or pure in this life, he cannot deserve rewards in Hades. And therefore, it seems, we are compelled to conclude that, if the gods are simply just and consequently reward and punish human beings strictly according to their desert, the philosopher's hope for rewards after death is an unreasonable hope.

Must we conclude, then, that Socrates' defense of the philosopher's readiness to die and of the philosophic life as a whole is a failure? There is at least one respect in which it may not be. We recall that Socrates undertook this defense in response to the charge of Cebes and Simmias that he and all philosophers are unjust to the gods and hence impious. And by reviving the Athenians' impiety charge against him, they had raised, at least implicitly, the possibility that he will be punished by the gods for his impiety in the afterlife (compare 62c9-63b3 with 62b7–c8). We also recall that, even earlier in the conversation, Socrates himself had expressed the concern that he might be guilty of impiety and that he might consequently have to pay a penalty in Hades (see 60d8-61b1). We see, then, that the dialogue raises the question whether the philosophic life is not a most unwise way of life because it exposes the man who leads it to the threat of divine punishment after death. Now, insofar as Socrates' defense of the philosophic life is directed specifically at this question, that defense may be successful. For, by showing that it is impossible for the philosopher to become truly wise and virtuous in this life, Socrates shows not only that he cannot deserve to be rewarded in the afterlife but also that he cannot deserve to be punished there for his failure to become wise and virtuous here. In other words, by showing that the philosophers and, indeed, all human beings are necessarily unwise and impure, Socrates shows they that they cannot be justly blamed or punished for their ignorance and their impurity. Accordingly, precisely if there are gods who are simply just and who consequently reward and punish human beings in strict accordance with their desert, there cannot be an afterlife in which human beings are either punished or rewarded and hence there cannot be an afterlife at all. In this way, then, Socrates does vindicate the philosophic life here by showing that, while the philosopher may not hope for the greatest of goods after death, he also need not fear the greatest of evils, namely, everlasting punishment.

Yet, despite the importance of this aspect of his defense, it still seems that Socrates fails here to vindicate the reasonableness and the goodness of the philosophic life. For, assuming, as Socrates here does, that only a wisdom which is free of any taint of ignorance may qualify as genuine wisdom and that the philosopher devotes his life to the goal of attaining wisdom thus understood, he shows that it is impossible for him to reach that goal in this life. And assuming, as he here does, that the gods are simply just and hence that they reward and punish human beings strictly according to their desert, he shows that it is impossible for the philosopher to reach his goal in the afterlife. Socrates seems to show here, then, that the goal of the philosophic life is simply unreachable and hence that that way of life is simply unreasonable.

The fact that Socrates fails to defend the reasonableness of the philosophic life on the basis of these two assumptions may lead us to wonder about the reasonableness of those assumptions. After all, Socrates never argues for the assumption that a pure wisdom, untainted by the senses, is the only true wisdom. Indeed, we recall that, at the very beginning of this conversation, Socrates himself had suggested that his senses had enabled him to learn something about the nature of pleasure and pain and had thereby enabled him to make some progress in wisdom (60b1–c7).[16] We also recall that it was Simmias rather than Socrates who had affirmed most strongly that the wisdom which the philosopher seeks is pure and hence unattainable in this life (see 66d7–67b6, 68a7–b7). If, then, Socrates actually believes that wisdom mixed with ignorance or human wisdom may count as genuine wisdom and that the senses do afford us access to such wisdom in this life, he might be able to argue that the philosopher may make progress in wisdom in this life and might thereby be able to vindicate the reasonableness of the philosophic life.

Socrates also never argues for the assumption that the gods are simply just beings who reward human beings strictly according to what they deserve. Indeed, he himself suggests on a number of occasions that the gods may reward the philosopher with the wisdom he seeks even if he does not, strictly speaking, deserve such a reward. For example, at the end of his defense, he suggests that, since he has striven as much as possible and in every way to become wise and pure in this life, the god may be willing to grant him the reward of pure wisdom in the afterlife (69d2-6; see also 67b10–d3). Socrates alludes here to the possibility that the gods may be generous as well as just and hence may not require us to fulfill the strict demands of justice in order to enjoy their care in Hades. Perhaps, then, the philosopher may reasonably hope to attain pure wisdom and thereby reach the goal of his life after he dies, not because he believes that justice demands that he be so rewarded, but because he believes that the gods may graciously reward his efforts to become deserving of their rewards.[17] In this way, perhaps, Socrates could successfully defend the reasonableness of the philosopher's way of living and dying.

Chapter 5

The First Argument for the Immortality of the Soul

I. Cebes' Doubt that the Soul is Immortal

Once Socrates has concluded his "apology," he expresses to Simmias and Cebes the hope that he has been more persuasive in this defense speech than he was in the one he gave to the Athenian jurors at his trial (69e3-5). By saying this, Socrates reminds his friends that, now that he has made his defense speech in compliance with their demands, they, his judges, must give their verdict. And Cebes does speak up to express his agreement with certain parts of Socrates' defense but also his dissatisfaction with other parts. Simmias, however, is silent. And this silence on his part is surprising. For, in addition to the fact that he has been Socrates' interlocutor throughout his argument in defense of the philosophic life, it was he who demanded most emphatically that Socrates give this defense speech in the first place (see 63a4–b5, c8–d2). Moreover, Simmias' demand had seemed to reflect not only his genuine doubts about the goodness of the philosophic life but also his genuine desire to resolve those doubts and to learn whether it truly is a good way of life. We would expect him, then, to reveal here, as Cebes does, whether or to what extent he is persuaded by Socrates' defense. Yet, when the moment comes for him to give his judgment, Simmias demurs. He refuses to take a final or even a provisional stand regarding the truth of that defense. And this refusal forces us to wonder about the seriousness of Simmias' concern to learn the truth about the question of the goodness of the philosophic life. For, however much he may care about that question, he evidently does not care enough about it, at least at this point in the conversation, to press forward in searching for the truth of the matter.

Indeed, if we look back on the entire discussion up until now, we see that there is reason to wonder whether Simmias has been fully involved with it. He has, to be sure, answered Socrates' questions and responded to his claims throughout the argument in defense of the philosophic way of life. But, for example, the fact that, near the beginning of Socrates' defense, Simmias simply accepts the mere suggestion that the soul survives after death calls into question how seriously he takes that defense. For he must

be aware, even at this stage of the discussion, that that proposition is a
questionable one (see 77b3–5, 85b10-86d4). And it is hard to see how he
could simply accept a claim that is so large and so obviously crucial to
Socrates' entire defense if he were genuinely eager to learn whether or not
that defense is true. More generally, even though Simmias evidently has
doubts about the goodness of the philosophic life, he does not appear to be
especially troubled by them. He is not led by them, as Cebes is, to doubt
the goodness of life itself (compare 61b7–c5 with 61d3-62a9). Furthermore,
his suspicion that the philosophers may be foolishly indifferent to the things
of this world leads him to laugh at them rather than to lament their folly
(64a10–b6). Simmias' relative equanimity in the face of his doubts forces
us to wonder whether he is truly pained by those doubts, whether he is
genuinely eager to resolve them, and hence whether he feels, at least at this
stage of the discussion, that so much is at stake for him in the question of
the goodness of the philosophic life.

In contrast with Simmias, Cebes clearly feels that a great deal is at
stake for him in the question at hand. As we have seen, although both men
have doubts about the goodness of the philosophic life, Cebes' doubts have
led him to think about committing suicide. The question of the philosophic
life is, in a very real sense, a life-or-death question for him. And consequently, he follows Socrates' argument in defense of that way of life with
intense interest and does not hesitate to say what he thinks of it once it has
been brought to a conclusion.[1]

Cebes says that, although he believes that the rest of Socrates' defense has been finely or nobly spoken, what he has said about the soul
causes much distrust among human beings. For they fear that, "on that
day" when a man dies, his soul "is destroyed and perishes" and that, once
it escapes from the body, it is scattered "like smoke" and "no longer exists
anywhere at all." Cebes grants that, if the soul were still to exist once it has
escaped from "these evils" which Socrates has described, there would be
much fine hope that his defense of his readiness to die and of his philosophic life as a whole is true. But he points out that perhaps there is a need
for much encouragement and faith (*pistis*) that the soul of a man who has
died continues to exist and also that it possesses some power and wisdom
(69e7–70b4).

Cebes indicates here that he is persuaded by Socrates' noble account
of the philosopher as a man who devotes his life to the attainment not only
of wisdom but also of true justice and true virtue as a whole (see 69a6–e7).
He also suggests that he agrees with Socrates' argument that, since the
"evil" body prevents the philosopher from attaining the wisdom he seeks
while he is alive, he can attain that wisdom only, if at all, when he is dead
(compare 70a6–b1 with 65e6-66e6). Cebes wonders, however, whether the

soul does, in fact, continue to exist once it is released from the body and
hence whether the soul of the philosopher will finally possess wisdom once
he has died. It is true that Cebes seems to attribute to others the fear that
the soul may not survive after death (70a1-6). It might seem, then, that
Cebes himself has been convinced by Socrates' defense and that he is simply asking for help in responding to the fears and doubts of others regarding the fate of the soul after death and the goodness of the philosophic life.
Yet, the vividness of Cebes' account of the fear that the soul may perish and
his final statement that there may be a need for much encouragement that
the soul still exists after death suggest that he, too, stands in need of such
encouragement, that he himself fears that the soul may be mortal, and
hence that he himself is not entirely persuaded that Socrates' defense is
true.

Cebes suggests specifically that Socrates has not yet shown either
that the soul survives after death or that, if it does, it attains wisdom then.
Now, it is true that Socrates has assumed rather than argued that the soul
is immortal (see 64c2-9). But he has argued, on the basis of that assumption and on the basis of the further assumption that there are just gods
who reward and punish human beings according to their desert, that the
philosophers deserve to be rewarded with wisdom and everlasting happiness and therefore that they will be so rewarded by the gods once they are
dead (see 67a2–c3, 68b8-69d2). It seems, then, that Cebes has not been
entirely persuaded by this argument. Perhaps precisely because he takes
the philosophic life so seriously, he senses that Socrates has not yet shown
that it is possible for the philosophers to deserve the reward of wisdom and
everlasting happiness. And since Cebes cannot be satisfied with Socrates'
defense if he even suspects that it is untrue, he urges Socrates to provide
further assurances not only that the soul continues to exist after death but
also that it attains wisdom then.

It is important to note that, despite Cebes' eagerness to know whether
or not there is an afterlife in which the philosopher will attain wisdom, he
does not call on Socrates here to provide an argument or a demonstration
that such an afterlife exists. Instead, he urges Socrates to provide "encouragement" (paramuthia) and "faith" (pistis) that there is such an afterlife
(compare 70b1-4 with 72e3-73a3, 77c1-5, 88a8–b8). Cebes seems to doubt
that it is possible for any human being to know whether or not there is
such an afterlife and hence seems to regard this question as, fundamentally, a question of faith rather than a question of knowledge or of reason.
Accordingly, when Socrates suggests that they tell myths about whether or
not it is "probable" that the soul is immortal, Cebes gladly accepts this
suggestion.[2] It seems, then, that Cebes turns to Socrates here not for a
definitive proof that the soul is immortal but rather for plausible grounds

for hoping, even in the face of doubt, that the soul is immortal. And Socrates appears to agree to give Cebes encouragement in his hope.

Socrates' apparent willingness to support the hope of Cebes for an afterlife in which the gods reward the philosophers may help to explain why he says here, in an allusion to Aristophanes, that not even a comic poet would say of him now that he is idly discussing inappropriate matters (70b10–c2). For the comic poet Aristophanes had specifically accused Socrates of carelessly blasting men's pious hopes by declaring that there are no gods who reward the good and punish the wicked.[3] Now, however, by encouraging his friends to believe in an afterlife in which the gods reward the good (philosophers) and punish the wicked (non-philosophers), Socrates appears to be championing, rather than dashing, those hopes (see 63b5–c7, 63e8–64a2, 67a6–b2, 69c3–d2; see also 115c4–d6). He appears to be a defender rather than an enemy of men's pious and moral longings. The Socrates of the *Phaedo* appears, then, to be innocent of the charges that Aristophanes levelled against the Socrates of the *Clouds*.

Yet, immediately after this allusion to Aristophanes, Socrates proposes to Cebes that they examine not a myth but an argument for the immortality of the soul. And he proposes that they do so in order to determine, with apparent certainty, whether or not the souls of the dead exist in Hades (compare 70c4-8 with b5-7). In this way, he implies that it is, indeed, possible to determine whether or not there is an afterlife through reason alone and hence that the question of the afterlife does not simply belong to the realm of faith but also, and even primarily, to the realm of reason. Yet it makes sense that Socrates should try to argue here for the claim that the soul is immortal. For his specific intention in this discussion is not to defend the pious hope for an afterlife but rather to defend the goodness of the philosophic life. And, since to live that life means to live one's life in accordance with reason, Socrates could hardly base his defense of that way of life on a claim which cannot itself be justified by reason (see 61c9-62c8).[4]

II. The Argument that the Living Come Back Into Being out of the Dead

Socrates proposes to Cebes that they examine whether or not the souls of the dead exist in Hades by considering an ancient story or argument (*logos*—70c5-6) according to which the souls of the dead journey to Hades from this world and return here from there and come into being out of the dead. If the living do come back into being out of the dead, he asks, would it not follow that our souls exist in Hades? For, he continues, they would not come *back* into being if they had not already existed before. And this, he says, would be a sufficient proof that these things are so, if, in fact, it were clear that the living come into being out of the dead. But if this is not clear, Socrates says, and Cebes agrees, there would be a need for another argument (70c4–d6).

It is important to note that the argument that Socrates proposes to consider here does not fully address Cebes' need for assurance that the soul both continues to exist after death and also "possesses some power and wisdom" then (70b1-4). Socrates argues only that, if it could be shown that the living come back into being out of the dead, then it would follow that the souls of the dead exist "somewhere" (see 72a4-8). And although he calls this place "Hades," his argument does not explicitly address the question of what kind of existence the soul has in that place and hence does not explicitly address the question of whether it attains wisdom there (see 70c4–d4, 71e2). Even if it should prove to be clear, then, that the living come back into being out of the dead, Socrates still would not have shown that the soul possesses wisdom after death and hence still would not have vindicated the philosophic life. On the other hand, if Socrates were to show successfully that the souls of the dead continue to exist, he would at least have reassured Cebes that the soul is, indeed, immortal and would thereby, it seems, strengthen his hope that the soul of the philosopher may, finally, attain the wisdom he seeks after death.

Socrates' formulation of this argument does, however, implicitly raise as a question what kind of existence we may have and in what sense we may continue to exist after we die. Socrates raises this question by changing the ancient story about immortality in the following way. According to that story, when we die our souls go to Hades and then come back to this world, presumably by entering new bodies.[5] The ancient story, then, clearly identifies our selves with our souls and not at all with our bodies. Consequently, when the soul of a dead man returns to life, it is clear, according to that story, that, although the soul is in a new body, it continues to be the same individual soul that it was when it was in Hades and when it was in its old body. Socrates, however, says that he will argue, not that the souls of the dead go to Hades and then return to this world, but rather that the living come back into being out of the dead (compare 70c8–d4 with c5-7; see also 71c11–e1, 71e14-72a8). By saying that the living come "back" into being, he does suggest, as the ancient story does, that the living human beings are essentially the same individuals as the human beings who lived before and then died. But by speaking of the living and the dead rather than of the souls here and the souls in Hades, he seems to stress the difference between the living and the dead. And by saying that the living come back into being "out of" the dead rather than that the souls of the dead return to this world, Socrates points to the possibility that the living and the dead are two fundamentally distinct kinds of beings. Socrates' formulation of the argument that the living come back into being out of the dead, then, raises as a question in what sense we the living may continue to exist and in what sense we may become different beings once we are dead.[6]

Socrates' argument that the living come back into being out of the dead may be summarized as follows. First he gains Cebes' agreement that all beings who come into being and who have opposites come into being out of their opposites (70d7-71a11). Cebes then agrees that being dead is the opposite of being alive (71c1-d7). From these two claims Socrates concludes that the living come into being out of the dead (71d10-72a6).

Now, even though Cebes readily agrees to these two claims and consequently feels compelled to agree to the argument as a whole, the truth of those claims is not, in fact, demonstrated in this discussion. While Socrates does cite the examples of certain pairs of opposite beings which may be said to come into being out of each other, he does not prove here that *all* beings who come into being and who have opposites come into being out of their opposites. And he does not even attempt to prove that being dead is the opposite of being alive.[7] Furthermore, Socrates never addresses here what would seem to be the most obvious objection to the argument that the living come into being out of the dead, namely, that living beings appear to come into being out of other living beings as, for example, Xanthippe's baby appears to have come into being out of her.[8] For these reasons, and others as well, we are forced to conclude that this argument fails to prove that the living come into being out of the dead and hence fails to prove that our souls continue to exist after we die. Yet, what is most unsettling about this argument is its conclusion. For, even though Socrates clearly indicates that his purpose in making this argument is to show that the living come *back* into being out of the dead (70c5–d5) and even though he later claims that the argument seems to prove that the souls of the dead exist and come *back* to life (72a6-8), the precise conclusion he draws from the argument is that the living come into being—and not *back* into being—out of the dead (72a4-6; see also 71d14–e1, 72d8-9). Insofar as he draws this conclusion, he seems to suggest that, according to the argument, the living who come into being out of the dead were never alive before, that they are essentially different from those living beings who were previously alive, and hence that those living beings who were previously alive and then died ceased to exist when they died. In this way, he seems to imply not only that the argument fails to show that we who are now alive continue to exist after we die but that it actually points to the conclusion that we who are now alive will no longer exist once we have died.[9] In order to see how the argument here may, in fact, point to this disappointing conclusion, let us examine it more carefully.

Socrates begins the argument by telling Cebes that, if he wishes to understand it more easily, he should consider not only human beings but also animals, plants, and all things that come into being. He then proposes that they examine whether all such beings that have opposites do not come into being out of their opposites. Socrates seems to imply here that, if he can show that all beings who come into being and who have opposites come into being out of their opposites, he will have shown that the living come back into being out of the dead (70d7–e2).

Socrates next gets Cebes to agree, first, that, when something becomes bigger, it necessarily comes into being out of a smaller being and, then, that, when something becomes smaller, it comes into being out of a bigger being (70e6–71a2). At this point, we would expect Socrates to argue that, since the bigger beings come into being out of smaller beings and vice versa, when a bigger being comes into being it is actually coming *back* into being. For, insofar as Socrates is trying to argue that the living come *back* into being out of the dead, we would expect him to argue here that the bigger being was also bigger at some time in the past, that it then became smaller, and that now the original bigger being is coming *back* into being.

Yet Socrates does not say that the bigger being comes *back* into being out of the smaller being. It would seem, then, that, according to his argument, the bigger being is not the same as the smaller being (see 70e6–8). When a smaller being becomes bigger, it seems, a new, bigger being comes into being out of the original, smaller being. In the process of becoming bigger, the original, smaller being is essentially transformed into a new, bigger being. And therefore, the original, smaller being no longer exists. Similarly, when the original, smaller being came into being, the bigger being that it came into being out of ceased to exist. Consequently, when a bigger being comes into being, it does not come *back* into being since "it," that is, this particular bigger being, did not exist before. And accordingly, after going through a few other examples, Socrates concludes that opposites come into being—and not *back* into being—out of their opposites (compare 71a9-10 with 70c8–d5). But, if we apply what he says here of opposites in general to the living and the dead in particular, we must conclude, it seems, that the living only come into being—and not *back* into being—out of the dead and hence that we the living no longer exist once we have died.[10]

Socrates then goes on to assert that there must be a pair of processes (*geneseis*) which lead back and forth between each pair of opposite "beings" and gives three examples of such processes (71a12–b7). The first example that he gives are the processes of growth and decay between the bigger and the smaller being (71b2–4). Yet the process of decay (*phthisis*) would seem to lead finally not to a smaller being but to a dead being. Similarly, the next example that Socrates gives, of separating and combining, is reminiscent of his earlier definition of death as the separation of the soul from the body and of his implicit, corresponding definition of life, namely, the combination of the soul with the body (compare 71b6 with 64c4-8). Finally, the last example, of cooling and warming, reminds us of the executioner's implicit definition of dying and living as the cooling and warming of the body (compare 71b6-7 with 63d7–e1, 117e4-118a5). Each of these three pairs of processes, then, seem to lead back and forth between the living being and the dead being. And, taken together, these three examples suggest that the warm, fully grown being whose body and soul are combined—the living being—is a fundamentally different being from the cold, decayed being whose body and soul have separated—the dead being. In the light of these examples, it would seem that, according to Socrates' argument, when the living being dies and the dead being comes into being out of it, the living being no longer exists. In this way, Socrates' argument here suggests that we who are now alive will no longer exist once we die, but only the dead beings—the cold and withered corpses—that come into being out of us will remain (see 115c4–d2). And it would therefore seem that, according to this argument, we are not immortal souls who alternate between being alive and being dead but are rather living beings who simply cease to exist when we die (see 105c9-106d1).

Yet when Socrates explicitly applies his argument that opposites come into being out of their opposites to the case of the living and the dead, he drops these examples which imply that the living and the dead are fundamentally different and, instead, compares being alive and being dead to being awake and being asleep. And through this comparison he seems to suggest that the being who is alive is essentially the same as the being who is dead. For when a man is asleep, he would seem to be essentially the same being as the man who is awake. If, then, dying truly is similar to falling asleep, it would seem that, when we die, we do continue to exist and hence that we are immortal.

Cebes evidently grasps this implication of Socrates' comparison of death to sleep. When Socrates asks him whether there is something that is opposite to being alive as being asleep is opposite to being awake, he replies that there is, namely, being dead. And when Socrates asks whether all these beings—namely, the being who is awake, the sleeping being, the living being, and the dead being—come into being out of one another, Cebes agrees. Finally, once he has agreed to these things, he is, as he says, compelled to agree with Socrates' suggestion that the living come into being out of the dead. And when Socrates concludes that our souls are in Hades, Cebes says that it seems to be so (71c1–e3).

Yet, despite Cebes' agreement, Socrates himself forces us to wonder whether that conclusion truly follows from this argument. For he suggests here again that, according to the argument, the living come into being—and not *back* into being—out of the dead (compare 71d14-15 with 70c5–d4). In this way, he continues to suggest that death transforms the living being into a fundamentally different being, namely, the dead being, and hence that "our" souls cannot exist after "we" die but only the dead beings who come into being out of "us" remain. It would seem, then, that Socrates does not believe that the comparison of death with sleep actually strengthens the case for immortality.

In order to understand why this is so, let us reconsider the comparison of death with sleep. It does seem plausible to say that when a man falls asleep he is essentially the same being he was when he was awake. Yet, in an important sense the man who is asleep is not the same being as the man who is awake. For once a man has fallen asleep, he is no longer a conscious or thinking being. A sleeping Socrates, for example, would be no different, while he was asleep, from a mindless or imbecilic Socrates. But then he would no longer be Socrates, the wakeful and awakening philosopher. As the Athenian Stranger says in the *Laws*, "For a man who is asleep is worthy of nothing—no more than one who is not alive."[11] Even if death is a form of sleep for the soul, then, it would still seem reasonable for Socrates to suggest that, insofar as we human beings are thinking beings, in the most important sense we will no longer exist once we have died (see also 70d7–e1, 71d14–e1).

We see, then, that, rather than prove that the living come back into being out of the dead and hence that we who are now alive continue to exist once we have died, this argument actually raises serious questions regarding the truth of these claims. It does so, in the first place, by suggesting that, insofar as we are living beings, that is, warm, fully grown beings whose soul and body are combined, and insofar as death transforms us into cold and decayed beings whose soul and body are separate, we no longer exist once our lives have come to an end. And it also casts doubt on these claims by suggesting that, insofar as we are thinking beings and insofar as death is a form of sleep for the soul, we no longer truly exist once we have died. In this way, the argument leaves us wondering in what possible sense "we" might continue to exist once death has brought our lives to a close.[12]

Cebes, however, does not raise any questions about Socrates' argument here. He evidently does not clearly see the ways in which it both fails to prove that we continue to exist once we have died and calls into question the possibility of our survival after death. But Cebes does seem to sense a difficulty with the argument. Although he first says that it is necessary to agree that that which is alive comes into being out of that which is dead, when Socrates asks whether the living, then, come into being out of the dead, Cebes says only that it appears to be so. And when Socrates concludes that our souls are, then, in Hades, Cebes says only that it seems to be so (see 71d12–e3). Cebes' agreement with the argument, then, seems to be half-hearted.

It may be that Cebes senses here, if only vaguely, that the argument fails to prove that our souls exist in Hades (see 71e2–3). But, even if he believes that the argument does prove the immortality of the individual soul, he must sense that it does not prove that the soul possesses the kind of immortality for which he longs. For Cebes longs for immortality because he longs to possess the good—which he believes to be wisdom—always.[13] Yet the argument Socrates gives here clearly rules out the possibility that we will possess wisdom forever after we die. Even if our souls should attain wisdom after death, they are, according to the argument, compelled to return, again and again, to what Cebes believes are the "evils" of this life and hence to what he believes is the condition of ignorance which is our fate in this life (see 70a6–b1, 66b1–e6). In this way, the argument Socrates gives here compels Cebes, who is so dissatisfied with life that he has thought seriously about suicide, to agree that he can never escape from life once and for all.[14] Moreover, this argument is silent about the possibility that our souls will possess wisdom or, indeed, any form of happiness even in Hades. It only purports to show that the soul will have an everlasting existence after death. Indeed, insofar as Socrates compares death to sleep, he implies that being dead, or being in Hades, is even less desirable than being alive, at least for a man like Cebes. For inasmuch as Cebes longs to possess wisdom, even he would have to admit that he has a greater hope of attaining it while alive and awake than while asleep. Cebes seems to be dissatisfied with this argument for immortality, then, because his deepest hope is not merely for an everlasting existence but also, and above all, for a perfect and everlasting happiness.

Socrates responds to Cebes' half-hearted agreement with the argument that the living come into being out of the dead by asking him whether or not it is clear that there is a process whereby the living die. Cebes emphatically agrees that this is clear. Socrates then asks him whether they will not grant that there is a countervailing process whereby the dead come back to life. Or, he continues, will nature, in this sense, be lame? Now, Socrates does not explain here in what sense nature would be lame or defective if they were to refuse to grant that the dead return to life. Nevertheless, Cebes proceeds to agree that it is altogether necessary to grant that the dead return to life and hence that the living come into being out of the dead. Socrates concludes by saying that it is agreed, then, also in this way, that the living have come into being out of the dead no less than the dead out of the living. And, he adds, inasmuch as this is so, it seems to be a sufficient proof that the souls of the dead necessarily exist somewhere and that from there they come back to life (71e4-72a8).

Cebes responds by saying that, on the basis of what has been agreed to, he believes this to be a necessary conclusion (72a9-10). In this way, he continues to imply that, insofar as he accepts this conclusion, he accepts it only as a grim necessity (see also 71c13). Moreover, by suggesting that it is necessary to accept this conclusion only on the basis of what has been previously agreed to, he seems to express some doubt as to whether those previous agreements were sound and hence as to whether it truly is necessary to accept this conclusion. It seems, then, that Cebes continues to accept only reluctantly the conclusion that our souls cannot remain in Hades forever but must eventually return to this world and all its evils.

Socrates now tries to defend the claim that the living necessarily come back into being out of the dead by giving an account of the consequences that would follow from a denial that it is true. He argues that, if the processes of nature, such as falling asleep and coming together, were not balanced by opposite processes, such as waking up and separating, then all things would eventually be asleep and be together. Similarly, if all living things were to die and were not to return to life, then all such things would eventually be dead and nothing would be alive. Socrates argues here, then, that unless they grant that the dead come back to life, they must conclude that life on earth will eventually cease to exist. And, he implies, this is simply an unacceptable conclusion (72a11–d3; see also d6-9).

Cebes responds by saying that, in his opinion, what Socrates has said is "altogether true" (72d4-5). He is, then, thoroughly persuaded that, if they deny that the dead return to life, they must conclude that all life will eventually come to a complete end. But Cebes also seems to regard this conclusion as unacceptable. For he now seems to agree that the dead return to life, that the living come into being out of the dead, and hence that life will never perish from the earth (see 72d6-73a3). It seems, then, that, in order to avoid the conclusion that all life on earth will eventually come to an end, Cebes agrees that the souls of the dead must return to life.

Yet, Cebes' agreement here is most surprising. In the first place, while Socrates does imply that it is unreasonable to believe that life on earth will eventually perish, he does not argue here that this belief is unreasonable. Socrates only argues that, if they deny that the dead return to life, they must conclude that all life on earth will eventually come to a complete end. Cebes' acceptance of this argument, then, does not compel him in any way to conclude that the dead return to life. But furthermore, if all living beings were to die and none were to come back to life, it would seem that, according to Socrates' argument, once we die, our souls would remain in Hades forever (see 71d14–e3). And since Cebes has apparently been so strongly inclined to regard life as an evil that he has thought seriously about killing himself, we would expect him to welcome the possibility that his soul, at least, will escape from the evils of life once and for all and dwell in Hades forever. Why, then, does Cebes respond to Socrates' argument by simply rejecting the possibility that all life on earth will eventually perish, despite the fact that the argument does not compel him to do so and despite his apparent belief that life is an evil?

Cebes' response here reveals that, however unhappy he may be with his own life, he simply cannot believe that it would be good for all life on earth to perish. Indeed, he evidently feels so repelled by the thought that all life will eventually come to an end that he dismisses that thought altogether. And he thereby betrays his instinctive belief that life is good, despite its many unhappinesses and evils. By presenting his friend with the choice of either agreeing that the dead return to life or affirming that all life will eventually cease to exist, then, Socrates puts Cebes' belief that life is an evil to the test. He reminds Cebes of his instinctive or natural belief that life is good, a belief which his own disappointment with life had evidently led him to forget.[15] And by doing so he weakens his friend's inclination to commit suicide.

This entire exchange may help to explain Socrates' earlier suggestion that, if Cebes will not grant that the dead return to life, then nature will, in this sense, be lame. For Socrates may have been referring not to nature as a whole but to Cebes' nature in particular. He may have been suggesting that, if Cebes' attachment to life is so weak and his hatred of life so strong that he is truly saddened by the thought that the dead will return to life, then his nature must be lame or defective. And insofar as Socrates does, in fact, suggest here that it is unsound to regard life simply as an evil, he also suggests that the philosopher's life-long practice of dying and being dead goes along with a strong—though not an unqualified—attachment to life (see 62c6-8, 98d6-99a4).

Socrates concludes his argument by telling Cebes that they were not deceived when they agreed that there really is a process whereby the dead return to life, that the living come into being out of the dead, that the souls of the dead exist, and that it is better for the good and worse for the bad (72d6–e2). In this way, he encourages Cebes to believe that the soul of a dead human being does continue to exist and that it may even possess wisdom (see 70b1-4). Yet, Socrates' conclusion here points quite clearly to the inadequacy of this argument for immortality. For the argument does not even claim to show that the souls of the good are rewarded after death and that the souls of the bad are punished. More importantly, it does not even claim to show that the soul of the philosopher will attain wisdom and thereby reach the goal of his life once he is dead. It only claims to show

that the souls of all living things—including the souls of plants and animals—continue to exist after death (70d7–e1, 71d14–e1). By stating this
conclusion, then, Socrates reminds Cebes that, if they are to see the philosophic life vindicated, they must turn to another account of the fate of the
soul after death.[16]

Chapter 6

The Argument that Learning is Recollection

I. Cebes' Suggestion that Socrates Make Use of Another Argument for Immortality

Once Socrates has concluded his argument that the living come into being out of the dead, Cebes points out that there is another argument Socrates has often made in the past which, if true, would also seem to show that the soul is immortal. He explains that, according to that argument, our learning in this life is nothing other than the recollection of what we learned at some previous time. But this, he says, would be impossible unless our soul existed before it entered "this human form," namely, the human body. So, in this way as well, Cebes concludes, the soul seems to be immortal (72e3-73a3).

Cebes seems to suggest here that Socrates make use of this argument in order to strengthen the case for immortality. But the argument that learning is recollection is not only an argument for the immortality of the soul; it is also an argument which seeks to defend the goodness of the life devoted to learning and to the pursuit of wisdom.[1] By calling Socrates' attention to this argument, then, Cebes may wish to remind him that, in order to give an adequate defense of the philosophic life, he must show not only that the soul of a man who has died continues to exist, as the first argument claims to show, but also that it attains wisdom after death (compare 70b1-4 with 72d6–e2).

By suggesting that Socrates make use of another argument for immortality, Cebes implies that the one he has just concluded does not, by itself, constitute an adequate defense of the philosophic life. Yet, rather than raise questions about Socrates' defense, Cebes attempts, on his own initiative, to assist him in making that defense (compare 72e3-73b2 with 70b1-4, 89b4-c10). He reminds Socrates of an argument which he might use in order to strengthen his case for the philosophic life. Cebes' behavior here shows that, despite his ostensible role as an accuser and judge of Socrates, he is, in fact, an ally of Socrates, he wants him to make a successful defense, and he is even eager to join him in making it (see 63b1-5, 63e8-64a2, 69d7–e5).

73

Cebes seems to be not only a well-meaning ally of Socrates but also an intelligent one. For his suggestion that Socrates use the argument that learning is recollection in his defense of the philosophic life seems, for a number of reasons, to be a good one. (Indeed, this is the only argument set forth by Socrates in the dialogue which is unequivocally accepted by both Cebes and Simmias—compare 76e9-77b1, 77c1-3, 87a1-4, 91e5-92a5 with 69e6-70b4, 77b1-c5, 85e3-88b8, 107a8-b3).[2] In the first place, insofar as that argument shows that our souls existed before we were born, it shows that the soul is at least capable of existing apart from the body and thereby seems to strengthen Socrates' claim that the soul will continue to exist once it is released from the body (see 72e7-73a3, 76c11-13, 72d9-e1). Moreover, if it is true, as the argument claims, that all our learning in this life is nothing other than the recollection of what our souls knew before we were born, then our souls must have possessed the whole of wisdom before we were born (see 73a7-10, 76c11-13). Unlike the first argument for immortality, this one would seem to give us at least some reason for hoping that our souls may attain wisdom, or rather recover the wisdom we once possessed, after we are dead. It would seem, then, that, by showing that this argument is true, Socrates would be able to provide further reassurance to his companions that the soul of a dead man continues to exist and possesses wisdom and would thereby be able to strengthen his defense of his readiness, as a philosopher, to die.

But furthermore, the argument that learning is recollection, if true, would show that the philosopher need not wait until he dies in order to reach the goal of his life. For, according to that argument, the goal of wisdom is always within our reach throughout our lives.[3] Whenever we appear to be learning, the argument claims, we are actually recovering a part of that wisdom which we once possessed before we were born and which has always remained dormant within our souls.[4] The argument reveals, then, that wisdom is not a remote object of our longing but rather something which is always ours, either potentially or actually (compare 66e2-4, 67e6-b4 with 75e2-6, 76d7-e4). And it thereby reveals that wisdom is attainable in this life. For insofar as wisdom lies within us, there would seem to be no clear limit to the progress we may make in recovering "our" wisdom in this life. It seems, then, that the argument that learning is recollection would enable Socrates to defend not only the philosopher's hopes for the afterlife but also his hopes for this life and to show that the philosophic life is good not only because of the rewards it brings to the man who lives it once he is dead but also because it is an intrinsically rewarding way of life.

Finally, the argument that learning is recollection is one that must be especially heartening for Socrates' young companions and, indeed, for any young person who is struggling to live a life devoted to learning. For insofar as someone young has the experience of learning, that experience almost always coincides with the instruction of a teacher. Consequently, the young student may wonder, at least at some point in his life, whether his learning is not entirely dependent on his teacher and hence whether he is truly capable of learning on his own (see 76b8-12, 77e8-78a9, 99c6-d2). But since teachers almost always die before their students do, a student must almost inevitably face the day when he will be "abandoned" and left to search for wisdom on his own and by himself (see 116a2-7). And on the day Socrates is to die, his young companions must be especially in need of reassurance that they are capable of attaining wisdom on their own and hence that their future pursuit of wisdom will not be in vain. Now, the argument that learning is recollection seems to satisfy this particular need. Insofar as it shows that our learning is nothing other than the recovery of that wisdom which we once possessed, it affirms that learning is possible for all of us and that it does not depend on the instruction of a teacher.[5] We see, then, how promising is Cebes' suggestion that Socrates make use of the argument that learning is recollection. For, if true, that argument seems to offer Socrates a way of both defending the philosophic life as a whole and of encouraging his young companions in particular in their efforts to live that life.

II. The Skepticism of Simmias and the Argument that Learning is Recollection

But is the argument true? And even if it is true, does it truly show, as Cebes suggests, not only that our souls existed before we were born but that they will continue to exist once we have died? These are the questions that Simmias seems to raise when he breaks in and asks Cebes, what are the proofs of these things? And Cebes now attempts to supply those proofs. He first offers the "most beautiful" argument that, when someone questions human beings in a "beautiful" way, he can elicit from them the knowledge of all things which lies within them. Cebes then claims that, if someone leads human beings to diagrams and other such things, he will show "most clearly" that the argument is true.[6] But while Cebes can describe the proofs and while he can praise them as "most beautiful" and "most clear," he evidently cannot reproduce them. Cebes cannot, then, resolve his friend's doubts about the argument. And consequently, Socrates now steps in and tries to persuade the skeptical Simmias that our learning is nothing but recollection and hence, it seems, that the soul is immortal (73a4-b5).

At this point, however, Simmias tries to back away from his questioning of the argument. When Socrates asks him point-blank whether he doubts that what is called learning is actually recollection, Simmias denies that he doubts this at all and claims that he only needs to be reminded of the argument. Indeed, he claims that Cebes' attempt to explain the argument has almost reminded him of it and has even almost persuaded him of it. Nevertheless, Simmias says, he would gladly listen to Socrates' attempt to explain the argument as well (73b6-10).

Simmias' behavior here is quite strange. By asking Cebes what the proofs are of the argument that learning is recollection, Simmias has expressed his doubt that that argument is true. And, since Cebes has not supplied those proofs, Simmias must continue to doubt that the argument is true. Furthermore, since Cebes has claimed that this argument shows that the soul is immortal, one would think that Simmias would be especially eager to know whether or not the argument is true. Why, then, does Simmias not admit to his doubts and urge Socrates to address them so that he might learn whether or not the soul truly is immortal?

Simmias' behavior here suggests that he doubts not only that learning is recollection but that learning itself is possible. More precisely, it suggests that he doubts that it is possible to learn the truth about the most important questions, such as the question of immortality, in this life (see 85b10-c4). For, if he were confident that such learning were possible, he would presumably express his doubts in the hope that he might learn the truth about the soul's fate after death. Cebes, for example, is always eager to express his doubts apparently because he believes that he can escape from his ignorance, at least to some extent, in this life. Accordingly, we see him in this discussion asking Socrates why he has been composing poetry since his condemnation to death, challenging the claim that it is forbidden to kill oneself, wondering about the philosophers' readiness to die, and questioning Socrates' claim that the soul is immortal (see 60c8-d7, 61d3-62a9, 62c9-e7, 69e6-70b4; see also 62e8-63a3, 77a8-9). Despite his doubts about the philosophic life, Cebes persists in hoping that he may learn the truth about things in this life and consequently strives to learn the truth. But Simmias evidently does not share his friend's hope that he can escape from his ignorance in this life. He evidently believes that the effort to learn the truth about things is likely to be in vain. Consequently, Simmias does not make the efforts Cebes does to pursue the truth. He tends to go along with Socrates' claims rather than challenge them (compare, for example, 64c2-9 with 69d7-70b4, 77b1-5, 85e3-86d4). When he does raise questions, he does so in the name of others rather than in his own name and he does not follow up on his questions (compare 61c2-5, 63a4-b3, 64a10-b6 with 61d3-62e7). And now that Simmias has expressed what would seem to be his own genuine doubt about the claim that learning is recollection, he tries to deny that he doubts that claim at all.

Simmias, then, doubts that we human beings can learn the truth about such questions as the fate of the soul after death. And, on the face of it, such skepticism does not seem to be unreasonable. Given the limits of human understanding and given the weakness of our nature as a whole, it may well be impossible for us to know such things as what death holds in store for us (see 107a8–b3). It may well be the case that the question of the immortality of the soul belongs to the realm of faith rather than to the realm of reason (see 85b10–d4; see also 61d10–e4, 69b6-7). Indeed, precisely if we heed Socrates' advice in the *Apology* and strive to become fully aware of our ignorance regarding the greatest matters, we may well have to conclude that we cannot know what will become of us once we are dead (see Plato *Apology of Socrates* 21d2-7, 22c9–e5, 23a5–b6, 29a4–b6, 42a2-5; but see also 41d1-5). And consequently, the skeptical posture Simmias adopts toward Socrates' attempts here to argue for the immortality of the soul may well prove to be a sensible posture.[7]

There is, nonetheless, something dogmatic about Simmias' skepticism here. For, at the very least, given his youth, he cannot know that it is impossible for him to learn the truth about such questions as the immortality of the soul (89a3). And he cannot learn whether or not such learning is impossible unless he himself tries to learn and throws himself into the pursuit of the truth.[8] But this is precisely what Simmias declines to do, at least in this discussion. Unlike Cebes, he does not attempt to penetrate the mist surrounding the question of the immortality of the soul in order to see how far his understanding may go. Instead, he seems to give up on this search for the truth. Simmias behaves here as though he has already decided to abandon the pursuit of wisdom even before he has heard Socrates' complete defense of the life devoted to that pursuit.

Furthermore, if Simmias truly longed to know the truth about the soul's fate after death, if he truly felt the need to learn the truth about this question, he would not be able to discount or minimize, as he seems to, the possibility that he might learn it. For he would be led by his desire for the truth to seek for it and hence, willy-nilly, to hope that he might find it. Simmias' skepticism here suggests that, in his heart of hearts, he does not believe that he needs to know whether or not the soul is immortal. Perhaps he is sufficiently satisfied with his life that he does not long so very much for a life beyond this one (compare 61b7–c5, 63a4-9, 64a4–b6 with 61d3-62a9, 70a6–b1). Perhaps he is sufficiently satisfied with himself to be confident that, if there is an afterlife in which the good fare better than the bad, he will fare well there (compare 63c4–d2 with 70b1-4). In any case, the skeptical posture Simmias adopts here suggests that he does not regard his ignorance about such matters as the immortality of the soul as an evil and hence that he believes that he knows all that he needs to know about such matters. Far from reflecting his genuine awareness of his ignorance or his knowledge that it is impossible to learn in this life, then, Simmias' skepticism seems to reflect his comfortable belief that he does not need to learn and that he is sufficiently wise.

In the discussion that follows, Socrates attempts to persuade his young companion to abandon his skepticism. In the first place, he attempts to persuade him that our souls possessed the whole of wisdom before we were born, that we may recollect that wisdom in this life, and hence that it is reasonable to strive for the attainment of wisdom even in this life. By arguing, then, that learning is recollection, Socrates argues not only for the immortality of the soul but also against Simmias' doubt that learning is possible. But furthermore, Socrates humbles Simmias in this discussion. He first encourages him in his high opinion of himself and of his wisdom and then pulls the rug out from underneath him by making him painfully aware of his ignorance.[9] And while Socrates' treatment of Simmias here may seem strange and even unnecessarily harsh, it is, in fact, necessary if he is to persuade his young friend to abandon his skepticism. For before Simmias can be persuaded to hope for wisdom and to seek for wisdom, he must be freed from his opinion that he is already sufficiently wise. In this discussion, then, Socrates attempts to show Simmias not only that learning is possible but that he, in particular, is in need of learning.

Socrates begins his argument that our learning in this life is nothing other than the recollection of what our souls knew before we were born by giving an account of what recollection is and how it takes place. He first tells Simmias that, if someone recollects something, he must have known that thing at some previous time. Socrates then asks whether recollection does not take place in the following way: someone perceives something and not only comes to know it but also thinks of something else the knowledge of which is distinct from the knowledge of what he is perceiving. Now, if this account is true, recollection would indeed be a kind of learning. For by recovering knowledge which we acquired in the past and then, presumably, forgot, we would be adding to our present store of knowledge and hence would, in this sense, be learning. But, if this account is true, recollection would not be the only way in which we learn. For we evidently do "know" things, according to this account, by perceiving them. In contrast to Socrates' earlier suggestion that the senses are deceptive and therefore an impediment to learning, he now suggests that we do acquire knowledge by means of our senses and hence by means of our body (compare 73c1–d1 with 65a9–d3).[10] But if this is so, how can our learning be nothing other than the recollection of what our (disembodied) souls learned before we were born?

When Socrates asks Simmias whether they may not justly call what he has described recollection, Simmias asks, "How do you mean?" He is simply puzzled by the rather abstract account of recollection he has just heard, and so Socrates proceeds to explain what he means. He tells Simmias that he surely "knows" what lovers experience when they see a lyre or a cloak or anything else their beloved is wont to use: they come to know the lyre and think of the "form" of the boy whose lyre it is. This, Socrates says, is recollection, just as when someone, upon seeing Simmias, is reminded of Cebes. Simmias now agrees emphatically—with an oath—that this, indeed, is recollection (73d5-11). And this exchange itself would seem to provide an example of how recollection takes place. For Socrates' description of the lovers prompts Simmias to recover the knowledge of recollection which he acquired at some time in the past and then somehow forgot.

Yet this dramatic example of recollection would also seem to call into question the claim that our learning is nothing but the recollection of the wisdom our souls possessed before we were born. For Simmias evidently knows what recollection is because he has had the experience of recollecting. But precisely insofar as our souls possessed wisdom before we were born, how could they have had the experience of forgetting what they knew and subsequently recollecting it? And without such an experience, how could they have known what recollection or, for that matter, what forgetting is (see 75d8–e1)? The knowledge of recollection would seem to be available only to imperfect beings, that is, to beings whose ability to retain knowledge is imperfect and who consequently may forget but also recollect what they once knew. And, insofar as our souls were perfect beings before they entered the "human form," it would seem that we could have acquired our knowledge of recollection only after we became imperfect beings and hence only after we became human beings. This dramatic example of recollection, then, points to a kind of knowledge which is available only to imperfect beings such as ourselves. It points to a kind of wisdom which is the fruit of the experience of being human. And, since human wisdom must form at least a part of wisdom as a whole, it would seem that our souls could not have been wholly or perfectly wise before they entered the "human form" and hence that all our learning, at least, could not be recollection.[11]

Socrates goes on to raise still further questions about the claim that learning is recollection. The first five examples of recollection which he mentions here suggest that, when we recollect, we recover knowledge which we originally acquired through perception (73d3-74a8). The lovers, for example, recollect the "form"—that is, the body—of their beloved and therefore recollect what they could only have known by means of their bodily senses. Similarly, Socrates goes on to say that, when someone sees a portrait of Simmias, he may be reminded of "Simmias himself," that is, of what

Simmias actually looks like. Socrates' discussion of recollection suggests, then, that, when we learn, we acquire knowledge through perception and through our experiences and that, when we recollect, we simply recover the knowledge which we acquired in this way. It suggests, in other words, that our learning is entirely the fruit of our experience of being embodied souls, of being imperfect beings, and, in sum, of being human. And it therefore leaves us wondering what evidence there is for the claim that our learning is nothing but the recollection of what we learned before we became human.

At this point, we may also wonder how Socrates intends to persuade the skeptical Simmias that learning is recollection and hence that learning is possible in this life. For, while Simmias might concede that it is possible to learn some things through our senses in this life, he might still believe that it is impossible to learn about the most important things through them. Now, however, Socrates gets the skeptical Simmias to admit that he does know—or at least thinks he knows—one very important thing: namely, that there are "things themselves," or forms that exist apart from the sensible world, that are perfectly knowable and the knowledge of which constitutes true knowledge and wisdom (74a9–b3; see also 65d4-66a10, 75c7–d6, 76e8-77a5, 102a10–b2). He reminds Simmias that he himself must have had the experience of learning about these beings at some point in his life. Socrates goes on to persuade him that he must have acquired his knowledge of these beings and, indeed, the whole of wisdom before he was born, that, insofar as he has learned in this life he has recovered a part of that wisdom, and hence that it is possible for him to learn and to make progress in wisdom in this life (see 76c4-77a5). Indeed, once Simmias claims to know about the separate forms or ideas, he seems to be compelled to agree that he must have acquired this knowledge before he was born. For if the forms truly are beings which exist apart from this world, how could he have acquired knowledge of them unless he existed before he became a part of this world? In other words, if the true objects of our knowledge exist apart from the physical objects—the bodies—we see around us, how could we have come to know them unless "we"—that is, our souls—once existed apart from our bodies and hence before we were born?

Socrates asks Simmias whether or not "we" may say that there is something "equal itself" that exists "beyond" particular things that are equal to one another, such as sticks and stones. Simmias declares emphatically—with an oath to Zeus—that they may, indeed, say this. Socrates then asks him whether they know what "the equal itself" is, and Simmias responds by saying that they know this very well. On the basis of these responses, Socrates goes on to persuade him that they must have acquired their knowledge of what "the equal itself" is before they were born (74a5-

76c15). Now, it is important to note that, by claiming to know what "the equal itself" is, Simmias is not only claiming to know what equality is, that is, what that characteristic is which equal sticks and stones share, but is also claiming to know that equality is a separate, invisible being which exists apart from all perceptible things.[12] For, if he had simply claimed to know what equality is, it would have been possible for him to argue that he has acquired this knowledge in this life by means of his senses and hence to argue against Socrates' contention that he must have acquired it before he was born.

In order to see this point more clearly, it is helpful to consider an alternative response to Socrates' initial question about "the equal itself." We could respond by suggesting that the equal is not a separate being that exists "beyond" particular things but is simply a characteristic which equal things share. And on the basis of this suggestion, we could argue that it is possible to learn what equality is by means of our senses. For example, by observing a pair of sticks that appear to be equal in length and then a pair of stones that appear to be equal in height, we can identify that characteristic which these two pairs share, namely, that of being equal. We could even go on to argue that it is possible to learn what exact equality is through our senses. For example, when observing a pair of sticks and a pair of stones, we might notice that, insofar as each pair consists of two units, they are, in this respect, exactly equal to one another. If, then, Simmias were simply claiming to know what equality is, it would be possible for him to argue that he has acquired this knowledge by means of his senses in this life.[13]

But Simmias is claiming here to know much more. He is claiming to know that the equal is a being that exists apart from the sensible world and that, more generally, there is an entire realm of beings—the separate forms or ideas—that exists apart from this world.[14] And since this is a rather large claim, we might expect Socrates to examine whether Simmias truly knows these things. We might expect him, for example, to ask Simmias what the proofs of these things are or whether he can give a reasoned account of these things (see 73a4-5, 77b5-6). Socrates, however, does not ask these questions or challenge in any way Simmias' claim to know, for example, "the equal itself." Instead, he speaks of that claim as though it were simply true and only asks, "where did we get our knowledge of it?" Furthermore, here and, indeed, throughout almost the entirety of this discussion, Socrates refers repeatedly to "our" knowledge of "the equal itself" and of the separate forms as a whole. He speaks of Simmias and himself as if, together, they formed an inseparable group of knowers. In these ways, Socrates encourages Simmias to think of himself as one who knows, as a wise man, and even as the equal of his older and wiser companion.[15]

Socrates now proceeds to argue that he and Simmias must have acquired their knowledge of the "equal itself" before they were born. He first suggests to Simmias that, since he has never seen things that are purely or perfectly equal, he could not have acquired his knowledge of "the equal itself" through his senses (74b4–d8). He then suggests that, when they see things that are equal, they inevitably think to themselves that those things are only imperfectly equal and thereby implicitly compare them to "the equal itself." But since they could not make such a comparison unless they already knew "the equal itself," they must have already possessed this knowledge before they ever perceived equal things and thought that those things were only imperfectly equal. Accordingly, since they began to perceive things as soon as they were born, it seems, Socrates concludes, that they must have acquired their knowledge of "the equal itself" before they were born. And Simmias agrees that it seems to be so (74d9–75c6).

Now, this entire argument rests on the premise that the form of equality is a separate being which cannot be known by means of our senses. As Socrates says later, the entire argument that learning is recollection is based on the assumption that the forms are separate beings which exist apart from the sensible world. And insofar as Socrates does not demonstrate the truth of that assumption here, he does not actually prove that he and Simmias must have acquired their knowledge of equality before they were born (see 76d7–e7).[16] But what is most striking about Socrates' argument here is its silence about the need for recollection. Socrates does not say here that he and Simmias ever lost or forgot the knowledge of "the equal itself" which they acquired before they were born and hence does not say that they have ever recollected this knowledge. He speaks here as though they were born in possession of this knowledge. And he thereby seems to encourage Simmias to forget that he has ever been ignorant of "the equal itself" and to believe, or rather to imagine, that he has always possessed that knowledge.

Socrates now proceeds to encourage Simmias to think even more highly of himself. For he now points out, as though in passing, that the present argument is not only about the equal itself but also about the beautiful, the good, the just, the pious, and all the forms. And so, he concludes, it is necessary that "we" possessed the knowledge of "all" these beings before we were born (75c7–d5). Yet it simply isn't true that Socrates' previous argument shows that he and Simmias must have acquired knowledge of all the forms and therefore, it seems, must have possessed perfect wisdom before they were born (see 75c7–d5, 76c11-13). At most, it shows that, since they currently possess knowledge of "the equal itself," they must have acquired this knowledge before they were born. But Simmias has not claimed that they currently possess knowledge of the beautiful, the good, and all the other forms. He has not claimed that they are, at present, perfectly wise. Nevertheless, Simmias goes along with what Socrates says here. He may think that Socrates, at least, is wise and hence may have acquired his wisdom before he was born (see 76b8-12). He may also think that, insofar as he knows that the forms exist, he, too, possesses knowledge of those beings and hence that he, too, must in some sense be wise (see 77a2-5). But, more simply, Socrates flatters Simmias here. He invites him to imagine, or rather to dream, that he is now and has always been a perfectly wise man. And Simmias is simply not strong enough to deny himself the pleasures of such a dream.

Socrates now explicitly raises the possibility that he and Simmias not only possessed wisdom before they were born but have possessed it "always" throughout their lives. He points out that, if they acquired knowledge of the forms and have never forgotten it, then they are always born knowing those beings and always know them throughout their lives. And while it is true that Socrates immediately raises the possibility that they lost their wisdom when they were born and hence that those who are said to learn actually recover "their" wisdom, he speaks of this as a mere possibility which is at least no more plausible than the possibility that they actually possess wisdom now (75d7-76a8).

We see, then, that, throughout this discussion, Socrates encourages Simmias in his vain belief that he is sufficiently wise. He encourages Simmias to imagine that he is a knower of the forms, a wise man, and indeed a man as wise as Socrates himself. And having induced this dreamlike state in Simmias, Socrates now rudely awakens him. He suddenly asks, "Which, then, do you choose, Simmias? Are we born possessing this knowledge [of the forms] or do we recollect later the knowledge we acquired before?" He asks, in other words, whether they are, at present, wise men. And while this is a rather simple question, Simmias is simply confused by it.[17] Perhaps he has been hoping that Socrates would somehow show that they did not lose "their" wisdom when they were born and hence that they are wise throughout their lives. Perhaps he has been simply distracted by his dream of wisdom. At any rate, Simmias is suddenly aware that he cannot answer the question. He is suddenly aware that he is ignorant. He can only say that he cannot, at present, choose between the two possibilities Socrates has presented to him (76a9–b3).

Now Socrates rebukes Simmias for his inability to answer and implies not only that he is ignorant but that he is not trying hard enough to escape from his ignorance. He first asks, somewhat sarcastically, "Are you able to choose this and do you have an opinion about it? Could a man who possessed knowledge give a reasoned account of what he knows?" When Simmias agrees, of course, that such a man could do this, Socrates asks, somewhat pointedly, "Can *all* men, in your opinion, give a reasoned account" of the forms? And Simmias now says that, while he would wish that all men could do this, he fears much more that, on the day after Socrates' execution, no human being will be able to do this in a worthy way (76b4-12). In this way, it seems, Simmias renounces his pretensions to wisdom and acknowledges that he is, after all, an ignorant man.

Socrates here not only reminds Simmias of his ignorance but makes him painfully aware of his ignorance.[18] For Simmias must feel embarrassed by his inability to answer Socrates' question and stung by the reproachful tone that Socrates suddenly adopts toward him here. But furthermore, in the light of his pleasant dream of himself as a wise man, Simmias must feel pained by the recognition that he is not, in fact, wise. By reminding him of his ignorance only after having encouraged him to believe himself wise and by rebuking him, then, Socrates attempts to undermine Simmias' good opinion of himself. He attempts to show him that his ignorance is an evil and to make him feel ashamed of his ignorance. He attempts to make Simmias feel stupid and thereby attempts to awaken in him the desire to become wise. And this attempt seems to be successful. For, by expressing the wish that all men were wise, Simmias seems to express the wish that he were wise. And by expressing the fear that all men, other than Socrates, are unable to become wise, Simmias seems to express the fear that he may never be able to escape from his ignorance and thereby seems to acknowledge that his ignorance is an evil.

When we look more closely at what Simmias says here, however, we notice that, while he does acknowledge that he is not wise, he also seems to defend his unwillingness to exert himself in the pursuit of wisdom. For, by expressing the fear that no human being but Socrates is *able* to acquire knowledge of the forms, he suggests that it may be impossible for him or, indeed, for any human being (other than Socrates) to become wise (see 76b10-12). He thereby suggests that he cannot be blamed for giving up in his efforts to pursue wisdom. For, if it is truly impossible for him to attain wisdom, how can he be blamed for abandoning what must be a vain endeavor (see 66b1–e6, 67b3-6)? We see, then, how powerful is Simmias' inclination to abandon the philosophic life. For he would rather believe that (almost) all human beings are incapable of attaining wisdom in this life than attempt to attain wisdom himself.

Yet Simmias' attempt to justify his abandonment of the pursuit of wisdom by suggesting that it is impossible for human beings to attain wisdom would seem to be undermined by the exception he makes here of Socrates. For if he grants that Socrates is wise, how does Simmias know that he, too, may not become wise? Why, then, isn't Simmias encouraged by the example of Socrates to devote himself to the pursuit of wisdom? Simmias' response to Socrates here points to an answer to this question. For his allusion to the fact that Socrates is to be executed on this day suggests that he does not want to follow in Socrates' footsteps because he is afraid of suffering Socrates' fate. It suggests that Simmias is inclined to abandon the philosophic life above all because he is afraid of persecution. It suggests that his most powerful fear, at least on the day of Socrates' death, is not that he may never become wise but that he may be killed in the course of pursuing wisdom. Yet Simmias evidently does not want to admit to himself that he is so afraid. He does not want to think of himself as a soft or cowardly man (see 85b10–d7). Consequently, he attempts to justify his inclination to abandon the philosophic life by embracing the skeptical opinion that it is impossible to attain wisdom. For, if that opinion is true, if the quest for wisdom is truly a hopeless quest, then Simmias may abandon that quest—and protect himself from the threat of persecution—with a good conscience.

Socrates, however, responds to Simmias' suggestion that it may be impossible for him to attain wisdom by returning to the argument that learning is recollection. He presses Simmias to agree that those who learn recollect what they knew before they were born and hence that their souls existed before they entered the human form, apart from bodies, and possessed wisdom. When Simmias balks at this conclusion, Socrates argues that, if they agree that the separate forms exist, they must agree that their souls existed before they were born. And Simmias now accepts this conclusion (76c1–d6). In this way, he is compelled to agree that all human beings are capable, at least, of acquiring wisdom in this life. And he is therefore, it seems, compelled to agree that he cannot abandon the pursuit of wisdom on the grounds that such a pursuit is bound to be in vain.

By persuading Simmias that learning is recollection, then, Socrates deprives him of the cover skepticism would provide for his abandonment of the pursuit of wisdom. He puts Simmias in the position of seeing that, if he is to abandon the philosophic life, he must do so because he is afraid of death. And since Simmias evidently cherishes his good opinion of himself, since he wants to think of himself as a courageous or virtuous man rather than as a coward, the effect of this discussion must be to encourage him to devote himself to the pursuit of wisdom come what may. Yet, insofar as Simmias is afraid of persecution, he cannot simply regard the philosophic life as an intrinsically rewarding life. For even if he accepts that it is possible to attain wisdom in this life, he must still fear the possibility that he, too, will someday have to drink the hemlock. Given his fear of persecution, then, Simmias must regard the pursuit of wisdom as an act of courage, as an attempt to fulfill his duty to virtue and not simply as the pursuit of the self-interested goal of acquiring wisdom for himself. And precisely insofar as he is now willing to devote himself to the philosophic life, he must wonder whether that way of life is truly reasonable, given the threat of persecution. He must see how important it is for him to know whether or not there is an afterlife in which the philosopher is rewarded for his virtue, that is, for the sacrifices he has made in this life. And consequently, he must now feel that he truly does need to know whether or not the soul is immortal. Accordingly, Simmias now expresses, for the first time in the dialogue, his doubt that the soul is immortal (77b1-9). He seems to abandon, at least for the moment, his reluctance to get involved in the discussion and seems to try, at least, to pursue the truth about this question (see also 84d4-7, 85d4-86d4; but see 85b10–d4, 107a9–b3). It does seem, then, that, through his exchange with Simmias, Socrates succeeds in persuading him not only that learning is possible but also that he, in particular, needs to learn the truth about the immortality of the soul.

III. The Objections of Simmias and Cebes

Yet, insofar as Socrates is trying to persuade his friends not only that it is possible to attain wisdom in this life but also that there is an afterlife in which the philosopher will be rewarded, his argument here is a failure. As Simmias suggests, even if the argument shows that our souls existed before we were born, it does not show that they will continue to exist once we are dead (77b1-9). The argument does not show that, when the soul first entered the body, it did not lose its capacity to exist apart from the body just as, according to the argument, it lost its wisdom. The argument does not show, then, that the embodied soul—the human soul—is immortal.

Cebes now speaks up to second Simmias' objection to the argument. He agrees, as Simmias has, that the argument has shown that our souls existed before we were born. But he urges Socrates to complete his demonstration of the goodness of the philosophic life by demonstrating that our souls continue to exist once we are dead (77c1-5). While the two friends, then, accept the argument that learning is recollection, they both urge Socrates to complete his defense of the philosophic life by making a third and final argument for immortality.

When we recall, however, Socrates' reasons for arguing for the immortality of the soul, we may wonder whether, in the light of the argument that learning is recollection, it still is necessary for him to argue for immortality in order to vindicate the philosophic life. For Socrates had previously argued for the immortality of the soul in order to show that the philosopher will finally attain the wisdom he longs for in the afterlife (see

65a9-68b4). That argument, then, had been based on the claim that the goal of wisdom is unreachable in this life. But the argument that learning is recollection purports to show that it is possible to learn and even to acquire wisdom in this life. And Simmias and Cebes have both accepted that argument. Moreover, Socrates has also suggested, albeit quietly, that it may be possible to learn and hence to make progress in wisdom in this life through our perceptions of things and through our human experiences (see 73c1-74a8). If, then, Simmias and Cebes accept that wisdom is attainable in this life, why do they continue to urge Socrates to show that the soul is immortal? And if the goal of the philosophic life truly is reachable in this life, why is it still necessary for Socrates to show that there is an afterlife in order to vindicate the philosophic life?

Socrates now suggests that Simmias and Cebes are continuing to urge him to prove that the soul is immortal simply because they are afraid of death (77d5–e2). He suggests that they long for the afterlife not so much because they love wisdom but rather because they love themselves and consequently are afraid of dying. And he thereby suggests that the primary reason they doubt the wisdom and the goodness of the philosophic life is their fear of persecution. Now, while Socrates presents it in a somewhat playful way, this suggestion actually makes some sense. For, since Simmias and Cebes accept the argument that learning is recollection, they must agree that it is at least possible to attain wisdom in this life. Furthermore, they do not urge Socrates here to show that the soul attains wisdom after death but only that it is immortal (compare 77b1–c5 with 70b1-4). It does seem, then, that Simmias and Cebes want Socrates to prove that the soul is immortal primarily because they want to be reassured that they need not fear death. More generally, it seems that they want him to defend the philosophic life by showing that it is the best way of life, despite the threat of persecution.

Socrates, however, suggests that his friends' fear of death is simply unreasonable. In the first place, he states quite emphatically—indeed, more emphatically than he does anywhere else in the dialogue—that the immortality of the soul has been demonstrated (compare 77c6–d5 with 72d6–e2, 76d7–e7, 80a10–e2, 84a2–b8, 106c9–d1, 106d5-7). They only have to be willing to combine the two previous arguments. For if, Socrates asks, the soul exists before it enters the body and if it is necessary for it to have come into being out of the dead, then how is it not also necessary that it exist once it dies?

Yet even if we grant that the soul somehow comes into being out of the dead, Socrates still has not shown that the soul comes *back* into being out of the dead (compare 70c5–d5 with 71d14–e1). He has not shown that the soul which comes into being out of the dead is the same, individual soul which lived before and then died. Indeed, Socrates himself indicates that he has not demonstrated the immortality of the individual soul by speaking here of *the* soul and not of *our* soul (contrast 77c9–d4 with 77c1–5, 78b7-9). It seems, then, that he has not, in fact, shown that his friends' fear of death is unreasonable.

Nevertheless, Socrates proceeds to mock Simmias and Cebes for fearing death. He characterizes their fear as the childish fear that their soul will be blown apart by the wind once it departs from the body (77d5–e2). In this way, he seems to urge them simply to dismiss their fear as one that is unreasonable and unmanly. Cebes responds by laughing gently and urging Socrates to persuade them that the soul is immortal as though they were frightened children. Cebes seems to admit here that he is afraid of death and that this fear does lie behind his demand for a proof of immortality. Yet he immediately draws back from this admission by urging Socrates to persuade them not as though *they* were afraid but rather as though a child within them were afraid. Cebes attempts to distance himself from his fear of death by claiming that only a child within him, an irrational and unmanly part of himself, is afraid of death and by implying that his more rational and virtuous self, perhaps his soul, is somehow above that fear (compare 77e3-7 with 66b3–c5). Accordingly, he now says, let us, namely, Socrates and the virtuous selves of Cebes and Simmias, attempt to persuade this child not to fear death as though it were a bogeyman (73e6-7).[19]

Cebes' laughter here suggests that he is confident both that his fear of death is unreasonable and that Socrates will remove this fear by presenting a convincing demonstration of the immortality of the soul. Indeed, by making light of his fear of death, Cebes seems to take his cue from Socrates, who had ridiculed his friends' fear as childish. But Socrates now challenges Cebes' confidence that his fear of death can be so easily removed. He urges Cebes and Simmias not to attempt to persuade the frightened child within them by making an argument for immortality but rather to sing to that child every day until they have charmed away its fears (77e8-9). By urging them to use not arguments but songs—and perhaps myths about the immortality of the soul (see 114d6-7)—in order to rid themselves of the fear of death, Socrates seems to suggest that, while the fear of death may be childish and unreasonable, it is so powerful that it is not susceptible to reason but only to charms or music. Indeed, Socrates may be suggesting that the fear of death can only be calmed through charms and spells precisely because it is an all-too-reasonable fear of an all-too-genuine evil. But the clearest and simplest meaning of Socrates' words here is that Cebes and Simmias will not cease to fear death on this day. No matter what arguments Socrates makes to them and no matter what soothing songs he sings to them, they must, he says, sing to their fear "every day" and hence for many, many days after this day. The fear of death is quite simply a fear which Cebes and Simmias must learn to live with for the indefinite future and perhaps for the rest of their lives. Indeed, perhaps even Socrates, who *appears* to Phaedo to be without fear in the face of death (58a3-4), has been composing music since he was condemned to death and on this, the day of his death, has been telling stories about rewards in an afterlife and taking other measures as well in order to calm his own fear of death (see 91a6–b7, 115d2-6; see also 60a3-8, 60c9-61b1, 61d10–e4, 70b6-7, 114d1-7, 117d7–e2). Perhaps learning how to calm one's enduring and powerful fear of death, even at times through music and myth, is a part, at least, of the philosopher's practice of dying and being dead (64a4-6).

Socrates' words here do appear to convey to Cebes some sense of the power of his own fear of death, a fear that must be especially powerful on the day of Socrates' execution. For now Cebes does not laugh. Nor does he suggest that "we" persuade the child within us to stop being afraid (compare 78a1-2 with 77e3-7, following B, T). Instead, he asks Socrates where he and Simmias will find a good song to calm their fear now that he is abandoning them. Cebes no longer speaks as if he were somehow above his fear or as if he expects it to be charmed away on this day. But now he really does speak as if he were a child who is afraid of death. For not only does he admit that he is afraid but, like a child, he seeks reassurance and comfort from someone he regards as a father (see 116a5-7) and believes to be beyond any such fears (see 58a3-4). And, perhaps also like a child, he despairs of ever becoming capable of reassuring himself. Having seen his childish hope that he can simply purge himself of the fear of death shaken, Cebes now appears to be in danger of succumbing to the truly childish fear that, by losing his friend, he is losing the sole human being who can possibly soothe his fear of death. Indeed, perhaps by ridiculing his young friends' childish fear of death, Socrates means to contrast it, not with a superhuman, or inhuman, fearlessness in the face of death, but rather with a mature or manly fear which combines an honest recognition of our fear with a belief that we can calm it by and for ourselves.

Socrates responds to Cebes by urging him and Simmias to seek among the many good men in Greece and among the many races of the barbarians for a song to calm their fear of death. In this way, he tries to reassure them that there are other philosophers and teachers like himself who may help them to ease their fear. But Socrates then adds that they should also seek for such a song among themselves. For perhaps they will not find anyone who is more capable than themselves of calming their own fear of death (78a3-9). And this advice seems sensible. For even if Cebes and Simmias were to find someone else to calm their fear, there would always be a danger that that person would die and hence "abandon" them, as Socrates is about to do. Whether or not our souls are immortal, the fact that all human beings are always in danger of dying and eventually do die points to our ultimate solitude, at least in this life. For to depend on another human being in any way is always to depend on someone who may "abandon" us.

There is, however, a certain difficulty with Socrates' advice to his friends here. By urging them to calm their fear of death, Socrates seems to presuppose that their fear is unreasonable. But, inasmuch as he has not yet shown that their souls are immortal, he has not yet shown that their fear is unreasonable. The question arises, then, why should Cebes and Simmias not act on their fear of death rather than attempt to soothe that fear? More specifically, since they know well, especially on this day, that those who lead the philosophic life live under the threat of persecution, why should they not be guided by their fear of death and abandon that way of life altogether in favor of a life less fraught with danger (compare 64a10–b6 with 77d5–e2)?

Cebes, at any rate, is not simply satisfied with Socrates' advice here. He does promise to follow it, but he also asks Socrates, if it would please him, to respond to his objection that the immortality of the soul has not yet been demonstrated (78a10–b1). And Socrates responds to Cebes by agreeing to address the question of whether it is reasonable to fear death.

It does, then, seem to be necessary for Socrates to prove the immortality of the soul in order to vindicate the goodness of the philosophic life. For even if it is possible for the philosopher to acquire wisdom in this life, it is still not clear that, given the threat of persecution, the philosophic life is a wise or good way of life. In order, then, to encourage his frightened young friends to persist in their efforts to live that life, Socrates must, it seems, show them that the soul is immortal.

There may also be another reason for Socrates to continue to investigate the question of the afterlife. For even if the philosopher can attain wisdom in this life and even if he can escape persecution here, the possibility remains that he might suffer divine punishment once he is dead (see 60d8–e3, 61a8–b1). It may, then, be necessary for Socrates to continue to investigate the question of the immortality of the soul not only in order to reassure his friends that the philosopher need not fear persecution in this life but also in order to reassure himself that the philosopher need not fear persecution in an afterlife.

Chapter 7

The Third Argument for the Immortality of the Soul

I. Socrates' Argument that the Soul Resembles What is Immortal

Socrates' third attempt to prove the immortality of the soul marks a clear ascent from his two previous attempts. Whereas before Socrates has attempted to prove the immortality of the soul by examining previously formulated arguments—namely, the ancient argument that the living come into being out of the dead and the Socratic argument that learning is recollection—now he examines directly what sort of thing the soul is (compare 70c4-8, 72e3-73b5 with 78b4-9). Instead of examining what is said about the fate of the soul after death, he now examines with Cebes the soul itself, so that they may determine for themselves whether or not it truly is immortal (but see 99d4-100a7). We might expect, then, that, if Socrates is to prove to his companions that the soul is immortal, he will do so through this argument.

Socrates proposes to Cebes that they ask themselves a series of questions. What sort of thing is liable to be dispersed? On behalf of what sort of thing ought we to fear that it will be dispersed and that it is liable to be dispersed? Which is the soul? And, finally, ought we to be confident or afraid on behalf of our soul (78b4-9)? Socrates indicates here that, rather than confining himself to examining whether the soul, in particular, is immortal, he will first examine more broadly the nature of mortal and immortal beings and then determine whether the soul is an immortal being. And since the gods are the most obvious examples of immortal beings, he seems to promise here that he will give an account of the nature of the gods in order to determine whether the soul partakes of their immortal nature. Socrates seems to promise, then, that he will show that our souls possess the attributes of divine beings, that they are therefore immortal, and, consequently, that we need not fear for them.

Socrates' third argument for immortality consists of three parts. First, he explains the nature of mortal and immortal beings (78c1-79a11). Then, he argues that the soul is similar to what is divine and immortal (79b1-80b7). Finally, he concludes that the soul "is altogether indissoluble or nearly so" (80b7-10). Now, Cebes seems to be persuaded by this argument that the soul is "altogether" indissoluble and hence immortal (see 79e2-5, 80a8-9, b5–c1). His fear that the soul of a human being perishes on the day of his death seems, then, to be vanquished by this argument (compare 69e6-70b4, 77b1–e7 with 80e1-81a11). And consequently, it seems that Socrates finally succeeds here in vindicating his friend's hopes, and our hopes as well, for immortality.

Yet, if we look closely at the conclusion of this argument, we cannot help but notice that it is, in fact, inconclusive. For it explicitly leaves open the possibility that the soul is only "nearly" indissoluble or immortal and hence the possibility that the soul is not, after all, immortal.[1] In order to see why this argument falls short of proving the immortality of the soul, let us examine it more carefully.

Socrates begins by asserting that it is fitting for things that are put together and also things that are composite "by nature" to be split apart into their component parts. He then asks Cebes whether, "if there is something which is noncomposite," it is fitting for this alone, "if it is fitting for anything," not to be split apart (78c1-4). Socrates' question here raises the shocking possibility that there is no being which does not, sooner or later, split apart or perish and hence that there is no being which is immortal.[2] Cebes, however, does not stop Socrates here and ask him to investigate this possibility at greater length. His evident belief that some beings, at least, are immortal—namely, the gods (see 106d5-9, 62b6–e7, 79b7-13)—leads him to ignore, or perhaps simply not to hear, Socrates' suggestion that perhaps no being is immortal. In what follows, then, Socrates simply accepts the premise that there are immortal beings and investigates whether the soul is such a being.

Socrates and Cebes together proceed to identify the characteristics of immortal and mortal beings and to draw a sharp and elaborate distinction between beings which are noncomposite, indivisible, and hence immortal and beings which are composite, divisible, and hence mortal. Through a series of questions, Socrates gets Cebes to agree, on the one hand, that what is always the same is "most probably" noncomposite (78c6-7)—as, for example, the unchanging forms or ideas are (d1-9)—invisible, and may be grasped only by reason (79a2-5) and, on the other hand, that what is "never" the same is "most probably" composite (78c6-9)—as, for example, the many perceptible things are—and is also perceptible (78d10-79a5). Finally, Socrates elicits Cebes' agreement to the hypothesis that there are only two forms or classes of the beings: visible beings which are "never" the same, and invisible beings which are always the same.

In the course of this exchange with Cebes, Socrates gives one clear indication that the sharp division of the beings into beings which are indivisible, noncomposite, always the same, and invisible and beings which are divisible, composite, never the same, and visible is an inaccurate division. For he says that the many perceptible, composite, and divisible beings, such as human beings, are only "so to speak" never the same (78d10–e5).[3] By inserting this qualification, Socrates suggests that human beings, for example, are not purely changing beings but rather have a certain enduring, albeit not immortal, character or nature (see 79b9-10). But it is precisely this qualification that Cebes fails or refuses to notice (compare 78e2-4 with e5).

Cebes' eagerness to embrace Socrates' sharp distinction between indissoluble, noncomposite, ever constant, and invisible beings and dissoluble, composite, ever changing, and visible beings is surprising since that distinction would seem to undermine the case for our immortality. For, as Socrates proceeds to suggest in a question to Cebes, we human beings are nothing but body and soul (79b1-3). We are therefore composite beings who are, moreover, visible and who constitute Socrates' first example of beings who are, so to speak, never the same (78d10–e5). It would seem, then, that, if Socrates' sharp distinction between immortal and mortal beings is an accurate one, insofar as we ourselves are human beings, we must be mortal beings as well.

Yet, by drawing such a sharp distinction between immortal, noncomposite, ever constant, and invisible beings and mortal, composite, always changing, and visible beings, Socrates actually encourages us to feel, at least, that we are not simply human beings and therefore that we are not simply mortal. For we sense that we are not beings who are "never the same." We sense that we are beings who somehow or other constitute a continuous whole (see, for example, 57a1-4). And, for this reason, we also sense that we are not merely or simply composite beings (see 98c2–99b4). If, then, there are two and only two forms of the beings and if one is never changing, noncomposite, and immortal while the other is always changing, composite, and mortal, it would seem plausible to believe that we somehow belong to the class of immortal beings. And if human beings are composite and always changing but we sense that we are somehow whole and continuous beings, then it would seem plausible for us to believe that we are not, in the truest sense, human. By describing human beings as beings who are "never the same," who are composite, and who are therefore mortal, then, Socrates encourages Cebes in his belief that his truest self may be something different from and higher than his merely human and mortal self: namely, a divine and immortal soul (see also 72e9-73a2).[4]

Socrates' sharp division of the beings into invisible, unchanging, noncomposite, and immortal beings and visible, ever-changing, composite, and mortal beings naturally raises our hopes that he will proceed to argue that our souls are invisible, unchanging, and noncomposite and hence that we are immortal. And Socrates seems to support that hope by eliciting from Cebes his agreement that the soul is invisible (79b7-15). Yet Socrates proceeds to assert only that the soul is "more similar" to what is invisible than the body is (79b16-17). And in the ensuing exchanges, he goes on to suggest, over and over again, that the soul is only similar to, and therefore also distinct from, what is immortal (see 79d9–e1, 80a7, a10–b5).[5] Having raised our hopes that he will prove that the soul is immortal, Socrates proceeds to disappoint those hopes and to render our disappointment complete by concluding that the soul is "altogether indissoluble or nearly so" (80b8-10). The crucial feature of this discussion is Socrates' insistence that the soul is only similar to what is immortal. In order to understand why Socrates insists on this point, we must examine this discussion more closely.

Once he has sharply divided the beings into beings who are invisible and always the same and beings who are visible and never the same, Socrates goes on to reveal that this account is incomplete, since neither our bodies nor our souls belong to either class of beings. Socrates first asks Cebes to which class we say the body is more similar and akin. Cebes replies that it is clear to anyone that the body is more similar and akin to what is visible. According to both Socrates and Cebes, then, since the body is only similar to what is visible, it is not itself purely visible and therefore it is a being which is neither purely visible nor purely invisible (compare 79a6-8 with b4-6).[6]

Socrates next asks Cebes whether the soul is visible or invisible. Cebes answers that it is at least not visible to human beings. Cebes seems to imply here that the soul may be visible to the gods. For even though no explicit mention has been made of the gods in the two previous arguments for the immortality of the soul (not, in fact, since 69c6–d6), since Socrates has been speaking of invisible, unchanging, and indissoluble beings, it is only natural that Cebes should be thinking of the gods (see 80a10–b3). Socrates, however, asserts that they, at least, have been discussing what is visible and invisible with respect to "the nature of human beings" and Cebes agrees with this assertion. Accordingly, when Socrates repeats his question about the soul, Cebes answers that it is invisible. Now, however, Socrates corrects him by stating that the soul is more similar to what is invisible than the body is and that the body is more similar to what is visible than the soul is. And Cebes agrees that this statement is altogether necessary (79b7–c1).

Socrates' statement that the soul is more similar to what is invisible than the body is crucial to the question of whether the soul is immortal. For if what is invisible is identical to what is immortal and if the soul is only similar to, and therefore also distinct from, what is immortal, then the soul must not be immortal. It is true that Socrates does not explain here why the soul falls short of being purely invisible. He does, however, suggest that the soul is both attached to and akin to the body, which is itself more similar to what is visible than the soul. Indeed, by speaking of "the nature of human beings," Socrates indicates rather emphatically not only that the soul and the body are connected to one another but also that together they constitute a certain natural whole and therefore that the connection between them is strong (see 79b1-17). Furthermore, Socrates' words here suggest that the soul and the body are not only connected to one another but also are somehow akin to one another. For, by saying that the soul is more similar to what is invisible than the body is and that the body is more similar to what is visible than the soul is, he identifies both as beings which are neither purely visible nor purely invisible and therefore as beings which are similar to one another by virtue of their impure or mixed character. This exchange between Cebes and Socrates, then, raises the question of whether its natural connection to and kinship with the body are not what prevent the soul from being purely invisible and hence "altogether" immortal.[7]

Socrates turns next to examine whether the soul is "always the same" as the immortal beings "most probably" are (see 78c1-8). He asks Cebes whether, as they were saying before, when the soul makes use of the senses and hence of the body in its investigation of anything, it is not dragged by the body into that which is never the same and it does not wander, become upset, and become dizzy as though it were drunk. Once Cebes agrees, Socrates asserts that, when the soul is by itself and departs to what is pure, everlasting, and immortal, it ceases from wandering and is itself always the same. And is this the experience of the soul which is called wisdom? Cebes agrees emphatically that it is. Then, when Socrates goes on to ask him, based on what has been said both before and now, which form the soul is more similar and more akin to, Cebes replies most emphatically that everyone, even the most unlearned person, would agree, based on this mode of inquiry, that the soul is wholly and in every way more similar to that which is always the same than to that which is never the same (79c2-e5).

Yet, despite Cebes' emphatic agreement that the soul is most similar to that which is unchanging, Socrates' account of the soul actually underscores its changeableness. According to that account, the soul can either make use of the body and be dragged into that which is ever changing or purify itself of the body, depart into that which is pure, everlasting, and immortal, and "become" a being which is always the same (79d3-6). But the very fact that the soul can be dragged by the body into that which is never the same distinguishes the soul from an ever unchanging being and hence distinguishes it from an immortal being.[8]

Furthermore, and more simply, the mere fact that the soul can be affected by the body raises the question of how fundamentally different from the body the soul can be. For how could the body affect the soul at all unless the soul were somehow bodily in its nature? Socrates highlights the similarity between the soul and the body by altering his earlier description of how the body affects the soul (compare 79c1–e1 with 65a9–d3). While he had said before that the body deceives the soul, he now says that the body "drags" the soul down into that which is never the same. Socrates now speaks of the soul as if it were a corporeal being. Moreover, by mentioning the phenomenon of drunkenness, Socrates cites an especially powerful example of how a physical act can affect the soul.[9] But how can the body affect the soul unless the soul is similar to the body in its nature? And if the soul is somehow corporeal in its very nature, how can it ever be free of the corruption and hence of the mortality of the body? By juxtaposing the unchanging and incorporeal nature of immortal beings with the changing and somehow corporeal nature of the soul, then, Socrates forces us to wonder whether his investigation of the nature of the soul will not culminate with the conclusion that it is, by nature, mortal.

Once he has persuaded Cebes that the soul is similar to the immortal beings by virtue of being similar to what is invisible and unchanging, Socrates suggests to him that the soul is similar to "the divine" by virtue of its capacity to rule the mortal body. He asserts that, when the soul and the body are in the self, Nature commands the body to be a slave and to be ruled and commands the soul to be master and to rule. He then asks Cebes, which is similar to the divine and which to the mortal? Or isn't it your opinion that the divine is by nature able to rule and to lead and the mortal to be ruled? Cebes, who had stated earlier that the gods are good masters of human beings, agrees that this is his opinion and also that the soul clearly resembles the divine while the body clearly resembles the mortal (79e8-80a9; see 62c9-e7).

By arguing that the soul is not only similar to the invisible and the unchanging but also similar to the divine by virtue of its capacity to rule over mortal beings, Socrates simply seems to advance his previous argument that the soul is similar to the immortal beings. Yet his mention of the divine rule over mortal beings marks an important shift in his discussion of the nature of immortal beings. Although he had earlier identified the invisible and the unchanging as attributes of immortal beings (see 78c1-9, 79a1-10), only now does he identify the divine capacity to rule over mortal beings as an attribute of immortal beings. Whereas up until now he has described immortal beings as perfect but passive beings, namely, as the things themselves or forms (78d2-7), now he ascribes to them the active power to rule over mortal beings. For the first time in this discussion Socrates seems to identify the immortal beings he has been speaking of with the gods, that is, with beings whom the pious believe to be not only immortal but also our rulers.

Socrates' reference to the gods here seems surprising, since he has not explicitly referred to the gods ever since Cebes urged him to show that the soul is immortal (see 69c3–e2). Yet it makes sense for Socrates to turn to the gods at this point in the discussion. For his attempt to prove that the soul is by nature immortal seems to be leading to the conclusion that the soul is by nature only similar to, and therefore also distinct from, what is "altogether" immortal (see 80b8-10). But, insofar as he is trying to defend the philosophic life by showing that there is an afterlife in which the philosopher will win the greatest goods for himself, this conclusion would be fatal to his defense (see 63e8-64a2, 69d7-70b4). It may be reasonable, then, for Socrates to turn, at this point, to the gods—whom Cebes has described as the best commanders of the beings (62d9–e7)—in the hope that they are supernatural beings who may redeem our mortal nature by granting us the immortality that nature seems to deny us.

Yet, although Socrates does seem to refer here to Cebes' belief in gods who rule over mortals, he also seems to introduce a new goddess, Nature, who "commands" the divine to rule over the mortal and who therefore appears to be more powerful than the other gods.[10] Furthermore, Nature appears to be quite different from the gods Cebes has described. For while Cebes' gods were divine masters over human beings, Nature commands our souls to be our own masters. And while Cebes' gods disapproved of our desire to be free, Nature, as it were, forces us to be free (compare 79e8-80a6 with 62c9–e7). Socrates appears to call on Cebes here to take care of himself and be his own master rather than long for gods who will take care of him. For, he implies, by being his own master, Cebes will be piously following the commandments of a god and imitating that which is by nature divine.

Furthermore, Socrates' own account of the nature of immortal beings as beings who are invisible or incorporeal and unchanging seems to call into question Cebes' pious belief that it is possible for immortal beings to rule over mortal beings. For, inasmuch as immortal beings are incorporeal, how could they affect, and hence rule over, mortal beings? And inasmuch as immortal beings are always the same, how could they adapt their rule to the changing needs and circumstances of their mortal subjects?[11] Finally, and most importantly, what need would immortal beings have to rule over and to understand what is good for mortal beings who cannot, it seems, affect them in any way? Socrates' account here of the nature of immortal beings quietly points to a fundamental contradiction among the qualities the pious attribute to the gods. For, while the pious claim that the gods both are immortal and rule over mortal beings, Socrates here suggests that, precisely by virtue of their immortality and of those qualities which are essential to their immortality, namely, their incorporeality and ever unchanging character, it would seem to be impossible for them to rule over mortal beings.[12]

But, while Socrates' account of the nature of the gods suggests that they are incapable of ruling over mortal beings, his account of the nature of the soul suggests that it both can and must rule over mortal beings. For, inasmuch as the soul is naturally akin to the body, it can affect and hence rule the body (see 63d5–e1, 98c2–99a4, 117c3–e4). Furthermore, inasmuch as the soul necessarily dwells with the body in a single self and is therefore necessarily affected by the body, the soul has a reason both to rule and to understand what is good for the body (79e8–80a1; see also 60b1–c7, 117e4–118a10). Finally, if it is true that the gods cannot rule over mortal beings, then the soul cannot look to divine masters to care for the body but can look only to itself. It is precisely, then, because the soul is akin to and connected to the body that it has both the capacity and the need to rule and to understand the body. Yet this natural kinship with and attachment to the body is also what prevents the soul from being an immortal being. For, since the body is mortal, the soul's kinship and attachment to the body must render it mortal as well. If, then, as Socrates says, it is Nature's command that our souls rule our bodies, it would also seem to be her command that our souls die with our bodies.[13]

Socrates' juxtaposition of the nature of immortal beings with the nature of the soul here seems to suggest not only that mortality is a necessity of our nature but also that our mortality may not simply be an evil for us. By saying that the soul's capacity to rule the body is "divine," he implies that this capacity is somehow good. But Socrates also suggests that the soul's capacity to rule the body is dependent on those aspects of its nature—its kinship with and connection to the body—that render it mortal. If, then, the soul's capacity to rule is a good and if that capacity is necessarily dependent on the soul's mortal nature, it might seem that our mortality is not simply an evil for us and hence that our mortality is not simply to be lamented or feared. In this way, Socrates might appear to fulfill his earlier promise to discuss, not only whether or not the soul is mortal, but also whether or not we ought to fear that the soul is mortal (see 78b4–9). And he also may raise our hopes that, by showing that death is not simply an evil, he will remove or charm away our fear of death.

Nevertheless, even if Socrates has suggested that our mortality is not simply an evil, he has not shown that it is not primarily an evil. For he has not explained whether the good of being able to rule over mortal beings and even the good of being able to understand mortal beings outweighs the evil of never attaining a wisdom untainted by uncertainty in an afterlife. Furthermore, even if he could show that the blessings we enjoy as mortal beings are somehow greater than the blessings we would enjoy as immortal beings, he still would not have shown that death is not primarily an evil for us. For we human beings seek not only to possess what is good for ourselves but to possess it always.[14] And therefore, precisely insofar as our mortal condition is something good, the death that sets a term to that condition must be a very great evil. Socrates' suggestion, then, that mortality is a necessity of our nature and that it is not an unalloyed evil does not constitute an argument that it is unfitting for us to fear death. For we can accept death as inevitable and even recognize that it is connected with a certain good without denying that it is ultimately an evil to be feared.[15]

Socrates now sums up the conclusions of this discussion by stating that the soul is most similar to what is divine, immortal, intelligible, single-formed, indissoluble, and always the same and that the body is most similar to that which is human, mortal, many-formed, unintelligible, dissoluble, and never the same. Do we have, he asks Cebes, anything else to say in addition to these things, or is it not so? Cebes replies that they have nothing to add. Socrates then asks him whether, based on what they have said, it is not fitting for the body to be quickly dissolved but for the soul "to be altogether indissoluble or nearly so" Cebes answers, "of course" (80a10–c1).

Socrates' third argument for the immortality of the soul now appears to be complete. And Cebes, at least, appears to accept that argument as a proof that our souls are "altogether" indissoluble and hence as a proof that we are immortal. Yet, as we have seen, the actual, though implicit, conclusion of that argument seems to be that, while the soul may be very similar to what is immortal and hence may be "nearly" immortal, it is not, in the end, immortal. Specifically, the argument seems to suggest that, given the nature of the soul—and given especially its kinship with and attachment to the body—it cannot be immortal and that, given the unchanging and incorporeal nature of the immortal gods, they cannot rule over us and hence cannot grant us the immortality that nature denies us.[16]

Furthermore, and perhaps more importantly, even if we grant, as Cebes does, that the argument does show that the soul is altogether indissoluble and immortal, we must still wonder whether it shows that *we* are immortal. For, while Cebes appears to believe that our true selves are identical to our souls, Socrates' argument has not established that this is so (see 72e7–73a2). Indeed, he himself has suggested that we are human beings who are constituted by the combination of body and soul (79b1-2). He has suggested, then, that we are essentially composite beings. And if this suggestion is true, then even if our souls continue to exist after we die, just as our bodies do (80c2–d2), we ourselves must nonetheless dissolve or perish once our souls and bodies are separated in death. Despite Cebes' apparent belief, then, that Socrates' argument proves that we are immortal, that argument leaves us wondering what grounds there can possibly be for hoping that we may continue to exist once we have died.

Socrates does not, however, point out to Cebes these grave difficulties with the argument for immortality. Instead, he returns to the pious claim that there is an afterlife in which the gods reward the good and punish the wicked (compare 80d5–81a10, especially 81a9-10, with 69c3–d1, 63c4-6). And he proceeds to argue, on the assumption that there is such an afterlife and hence on the assumption that we are immortal, that, if the philosopher fulfills his duty in this life by purifying himself of the body, his soul will dwell with the gods forever. In this way, Socrates attempts to complete his defense of the philosophic life by attempting to show that the soul of the philosopher will be rewarded by the gods with an everlasting happiness after death and hence that he need not be afraid of death (see 84a2–b8).

Now, it may seem amazing that, given the difficulties that have emerged with the case for immortality in the course of this discussion, Socrates should proceed to ignore those difficulties by simply adopting the pious claim there is an afterlife. We may, however, explain his procedure here in the following way. Even though the preceding discussion has suggested that we are mortal beings, it has not demonstrated that this is so. More precisely, it has not refuted the pious claim that we are, in fact, immortal beings. For example, the pious might point out that, while Socrates has suggested that we are human beings who are constituted by both body and soul, that we are consequently composite beings, and that we are therefore mortal, he has not shown that this suggestion is true. The possibility remains, then, that we are not merely human and mortal beings but rather divine and immortal souls who are only temporarily housed in human and mortal bodies (see 70c4-8, 72e7-73a3).

Furthermore, the pious might continue, even though Socrates has suggested that both the nature of the gods and the nature of the soul must prevent the gods from granting immortality to our souls, that suggestion is based on the assumption that the gods are limited by their own nature and by the nature of the soul. It is based on the assumption that Nature rules the gods (see 79e8-80a5). But this assumption is open to serious question. For what if, as Cebes has claimed, the gods are the commanders "of the beings" and hence the rulers of Nature herself (see 62d5–6)? What if they possess the awesome and mysterious power of uniting, both in their own being and in the being of others, the seemingly contradictory attributes of mortal and immortal beings? What if they possess the power of miraculously transforming the "natures" of the beings in general and the seemingly mortal "nature" of the soul in particular? The possibility that the gods are above nature or supernatural is not, moreover, a merely theoretical possibility. It is, rather, the view of the gods on which popular and traditional religion is based.[17] Insofar, then, as the pious claim that there is an afterlife in which the just gods reward the good and punish the wicked remains unrefuted, it is reasonable for Socrates to treat that claim with the utmost seriousness and to examine whether the philosophic life may be vindicated on the basis of that claim. Accordingly, he now turns to examine the possibility that the gods reward the philosophers with an everlasting happiness after they die.[18]

II. Socrates' Account of the Possibility that the Gods Reward the Philosophers after Death

Socrates now argues that, if there are just gods who reward human beings according to their desert, the philosopher may be reasonably confident that he will receive the greatest rewards in an afterlife. He suggests to Cebes that, if the soul has purified itself in this life by refusing to associate voluntarily with the body, by gathering itself unto itself, and, in short, by practicing philosophy in the correct way, then, when it is finally released from the body, it will be free of "the human evils," attain wisdom and happiness, and dwell with the gods forever (80e1–81a10). Socrates implies here that, if the philosopher can purify his soul of the body in this life, he will have shown that his truest self, his soul, is distinct from and superior to his merely human and mortal self and will thereby have shown that he deserves a fate which is distinct from and superior to the death his body is bound to suffer. And he further implies that, insofar as there are gods who ensure that we receive the fate that we deserve, the philosopher who succeeds in purifying his soul in this life may be reasonably confident that he will enjoy an everlasting happiness once he is dead. In this way, he appears to complete his defense of the philosophic way of life by arguing that the man who lives that life will win for himself the greatest blessings after death. And Cebes, at least, accepts that argument enthusiastically and thereby appears to signal his wholehearted agreement with Socrates' defense (81a11). Nevertheless, even if we grant that there are just gods who reward human beings according to their desert, we must still wonder, is it really possible for the philosopher to purify himself of the body and thereby deserve the divine reward of everlasting happiness?

Socrates proceeds to encourage Cebes in his hope that it is possible for the philosopher to deserve this reward. In the first place, he claims that, if the soul of a man is impure when it is released from the body, having always associated with the body, cared for it, and loved it, then that soul will be punished and punished justly after death for its impurity and wickedness in this life (see 81b1–d9). By emphasizing as he does that the impure and wicked souls deserve to be punished, Socrates emphasizes that it would have been possible for them to have avoided the corruption of the flesh. For those souls would only deserve to be punished if they were truly responsible for their corruption, if their corruption were a consequence of their free choice, and hence if they could have freely chosen to become pure and good. By affirming, then, the justice of the punishments of those souls that have been corrupted by the body, Socrates affirms the possibility that we may purify ourselves of the body in this life and thereby deserve rewards in the afterlife.

Socrates then goes on to suggest to Cebes that it may not even be so very difficult for a human being to avoid the corruption of the flesh. For those men whose souls have been corrupted by the body are, according to Socrates, men who have devoted their lives to hedonism, to crime and tyranny, and to the practice of vulgar and political virtue, that is, to the practice of virtue without philosophy (81e2-82b9). He suggests here that all men who lead nonphilosophic lives have corrupt souls and will consequently be punished by the gods after death. And he thereby suggests to Cebes that, if he simply shuns those other ways of life and devotes himself to philosophy, he will escape the divine punishments that those others suffer and will, instead, enjoy divine rewards in the afterlife.

Finally, Socrates reveals to Cebes that it is not even necessary to be free of all taint of corruption in order to dwell with the gods after death. He tells Cebes that it is not pious for anyone who has not loved wisdom and who is not "perfectly pure" to enjoy the company of the gods "except for the lover of learning" (82b10–c1). Socrates confirms here that no one who has not sought to purify himself through the pursuit of wisdom may be rewarded after death. But he also suggests that it is not necessary to become perfectly pure or wise in order to be rewarded after death. For by distinguishing the lover of learning from the one who is perfectly pure and by saying that it is not impious for the lover of learning to join the race of the gods after death, he suggests that it is possible, at least, for a lover of learning who is less than perfectly pure and wise to be rewarded by the gods with a pure and incorruptible happiness after death. While Socrates had earlier portrayed the gods as strictly just beings who reward only those souls which are simply or perfectly pure, he now suggests that the gods may be gracious beings who reward souls which are not simply or perfectly pure (compare 82b10–c1 with 67b2, 69c3–d1).

Socrates tells Cebes that it is Philosophy, whom he now speaks of as a goddess, who attempts to purify the souls of those who follow her and thereby attempts to help them attain everlasting happiness (82d1-83b2). Those who love wisdom correctly, he explains, hold themselves away from all bodily desires for the sake of joining the gods in the hereafter. But, in addition to this, since they believe that they ought not to oppose the release and the purification from the body that Philosophy offers, they dutifully turn to her, follow her, and are guided by her.

When Cebes asks how the philosopher may fulfill his duty, Socrates agrees to explain this. But before he spells out what the duty of the philosopher is, he first describes the condition the philosopher finds himself in before the approach of Philosophy. Socrates says that, when Philosophy comes to the lovers of learning, their soul is bound and glued to the body. And since their soul is "compelled" to examine the beings through the body as though it were examining them through the bars of a cage, since, that is, their embodied soul necessarily examines the beings by means of the senses, it necessarily wallows in "utter ignorance" of the true beings, namely, the things themselves or forms. Accordingly, when Philosophy comes to the soul in such a condition, she discerns the ingenious character of a prison in which the prisoner is imprisoned by his desire for the prison and is hence an accomplice to his own imprisonment (82e9-83a1).

Socrates emphasizes here that all souls are, to begin with, bound to the body and are consequently in an original state of profound corruption or impurity. For even though the lovers of learning are not hedonists or tyrants or men who practice vulgar virtue, their souls, too, are imprisoned by the body. He stresses here, then, the strength of the connection between the soul and the body and hence the enormous obstacles which must be overcome if the philosopher is to purify himself of the body. But, on the other hand, by comparing the body to a prison and the soul to its prisoner, Socrates also seems to emphasize that it is possible for the philosopher to purify himself of his body. For, according to this comparison, the body is not truly a part of the philosopher's self but is merely the prison in which his truest self, his soul, is forced to dwell. And just as it may be possible for a man to break out of even the most ingenious prison, especially with the help of his friends, so it may be possible for the soul to release itself from the body, especially with the assistance of the friendly goddess, Philosophy.

Socrates now tells Cebes that, when Philosophy comes to the philosopher, she gently encourages his soul and attempts to release it from the body by showing it that the senses are full of deceit, by persuading it to withdraw itself from the senses as much as is possible, and by urging it to trust in nothing other than what it observes apart from the senses and to believe that nothing perceptible is true (83a1–b3). In this way, the goddess urges the philosopher to purify himself of his body by trusting or believing that the visible world is not the true world and, more importantly, by trusting or believing that his visible self, his body, is not his true self or even truly a part of himself. She urges him, in other words, to believe that his only true self is his soul, that his body is not at all a part of his being, and hence that "he" cannot be affected by his body and its corruption. And she suggests that, if the philosopher can embrace this faith, if he can truly believe that his merely human and mortal self is only his apparent self, that it is only a mirage, and that his true self is not at all human or mortal but is rather his divine and immortal soul, then he will have fulfilled his duty and will deserve the divine reward of everlasting happiness.

Now, it is true that this account of the philosopher's duty is relatively gentle. For, according to this account, the goddess recognizes that the philosopher cannot possess complete wisdom in this life. Consequently, she does not demand that the philosopher *know* that nothing perceptible is true and that his body is not a part of his true self but only that he trust or have faith that this is so (compare 82d9-83b4 with 69b5–d2). And yet, despite its relative gentleness, the demand that the philosopher trust that nothing perceptible is true is a demand which no human being can fulfill.[19]

Indeed, the more Socrates explains to Cebes what the duty of the philosopher entails, the more obvious it becomes that that duty is unfulfillable. For he goes on to tell Cebes that the soul of the true philosopher will abstain as much as possible from pleasures, desires, pains, and fears and will reckon that the soul that feels such things will suffer the greatest and most extreme evil, namely, to believe that that through which it feels such things—the body—is most clear and most true, which it is not. And this experience of pleasure and pain binds the soul especially to the body. For, as Socrates explains, each pleasure and pain nails and rivets the soul to the body and compels it to believe that what is perceptible is true. Accordingly, if the philosopher believes that what is perceptible is true, then his soul will necessarily become so similar to the body that it will never be with the gods and be blessed with happiness after death (83b5–e3; see 81a4-9). Socrates indicates here that, in order to avoid believing that what is perceptible is true and hence in order to fulfill his duty, the philosopher must avoid the experience not only of excessive pleasure or pain but of *any* pleasure or pain (compare 83d4-6 with c5-8). But it is clearly impossible for any human being to avoid the experience of pleasure and pain. Indeed, this conversation virtually opened with Socrates' description of a painful experience which he had just had and which he could not possibly have avoided (see 60b1–c7, 59e6-7). And therefore it is clearly impossible for the philosopher to fulfill his duty and hence impossible, it seems, for him or for any human being to deserve the divine reward of everlasting happiness.

At this point, we might wonder whether the gods might not grant us this reward even if we cannot fulfill what Socrates has described as the duty of the philosopher. For even if we cannot, strictly speaking, deserve the reward of everlasting happiness, is it not still possible that the gods will have mercy on us and bestow this reward upon us in the afterlife? Yet, if we consider why it is impossible for any human being to fulfill the duty of the philosopher as Socrates has described it, and, specifically, why it is impossible for any human being to avoid feeling any pleasure or pain, we are led to wonder whether there can be any afterlife at all for such beings as ourselves. For the reason that it is impossible for "us" to avoid feeling bodily pleasure and pain is that our bodies are a part of "us." In other words, "we" cannot avoid the experience of bodily pleasure and pain because "we" are, at least in part, bodily in our very natures. And consequently, we also cannot fulfill the demand to trust that nothing perceptible is true. For, at the very least, we cannot but recognize that our visible selves, our bodies, are truly a part of us and hence are, in some sense, true. The fact, then, that we cannot avoid bodily pleasures and pains indicates that our bodies constitute a part of our very being, of our true selves. It indicates that we truly are composite beings. And therefore it is impossible for us to purify our selves of our bodies or to be separated in any way from our bodies. For, insofar as we are constituted by the union of our souls with our bodies, we cannot undo this union, we cannot divide this whole, without destroying our very selves altogether. It seems, then, that we cannot enjoy the divine reward of everlasting happiness not only because we cannot deserve such a reward but also because, being what we are, we simply cannot continue to exist once our souls and bodies have been separated in death.

One might still object that Socrates has interpreted too strictly what the gods demand of us and that he has also interpreted too narrowly the power of the gods. One might argue that the all-powerful gods may grant the reward of everlasting happiness to the philosophers simply on the grounds that they are more willing than other human beings to sacrifice the pleasures of this life, that they are more willing than others to transcend their concern for their own good, and hence that they are morally superior to other human beings (see 64a10-65a8, 67a2–b1, 68c5–69d2, 80e2-82d7). Yet Socrates himself explicitly says here and elsewhere that the philosophers make these sacrifices *for the sake of* the divine reward of everlasting happiness (see 83e5-7, 82c2-6, 114d8-115a3).[20] The philosopher's "sacrifice," then, is not a genuine sacrifice but is rather the means through which he hopes to win *for himself* the greatest goods (63a8-64a2; see also 91a1–b7). Socrates suggests, then, that the philosophers are no less concerned with their own good than are other human beings and hence that they are not morally superior to other human beings. In this way, he suggests that it may be impossible for any human being to transcend his concern for himself and hence to deserve the divine reward of everlasting happiness.

Socrates goes on to tell Cebes that the soul of the philosopher will not suppose that Philosophy should release it from the body but then, once it is released, succumb to the body's pleasures and pains and thereby bind itself again to it. For by first purifying himself of the body and then surrendering himself to its pleasures and pains, Socrates says, the philosopher would be performing the fruitless task of Penelope, who wove a shroud for Laertes by day and then unwove it by night (84a2-6). Socrates emphasizes here that it would be senseless for the philosopher to fulfill his duty and to purify himself of the body in the hope of enjoying an everlasting happiness after death and then forfeit all hope of such happiness by allowing himself to experience the body's pleasures and pains. He thereby continues to encourage Cebes to believe that it is possible for the philosopher to purify himself of the body and hence to deserve the divine reward of everlasting happiness. Yet, as we have pointed out, it is simply impossible for any human being to purify himself of the body. It is impossible, then, for the philosopher to fulfill his duty to the gods. And it would therefore seem to be senseless for the philosopher even to try to purify himself of the body in the vain hope that he may thereby win for himself the divine reward of everlasting happiness.

Socrates concludes this discussion by asserting to Cebes and Simmias that the philosopher will not succumb to the pleasures and pains of the body. Instead, he will spend his life contemplating and being nourished by the divine and the true, and, when he dies, his soul will go to the divine and the true, and will be freed from "the human evils." And therefore, Socrates asserts, such a soul will not fear that it will be dispersed when it escapes from the body (84a2–b8).

These assertions, however, are greeted not with agreement but with silence. It seems that Cebes and Simmias sense, and sense with disappointment, that it is impossible for any human being to distrust his senses completely and to avoid all pleasure and pain and hence that it is impossible for any human being to deserve to be rewarded after death. And their disappointment must be deepened by the manner in which Socrates has here investigated the question of immortality. For, throughout this discussion, Socrates has championed the hope of Cebes and Simmias for immortality. First, he examined the possibility that the soul is by nature immortal (78b4-80c1). Then, he turned to consider the possibility that the gods reward us with everlasting happiness if we purify our souls of the body (80d5-82b9). And finally, Socrates investigated the possibility that there is a gentle and graceful goddess, Philosophy, who will bestow immortal happiness upon us if we will only have faith that our truest selves are distinct from and higher than our merely human and mortal selves (82b10-84b4). Socrates has striven assiduously and doggedly, it seems, to prove that we can enjoy an everlasting happiness after death. And precisely because his attempt to prove this has been so dogged, his failure must be especially disappointing.[21]

III. Conclusion

Socrates' investigation of the possibility that there is an afterlife in which the just gods reward the philosophers with everlasting happiness seems to culminate, then, with the implicit but unmistakable conclusion that it is impossible for the philosopher or, indeed, for any human being to deserve everlasting happiness and hence that it is unreasonable for any human being to hope for such happiness. And this conclusion would seem to be fatal to Socrates' defense of the reasonableness of the philosophic life in the *Phaedo*. For he has argued that the philosopher longs throughout his life for death because it is only in an afterlife that he can attain perfect wisdom and thereby reach the goal of his life (see 64a4-9, 65a9-68b4, especially 66b5-7, 66d7–e6, 67e6-68a3, 68b3-4). He has argued, then, that the reasonableness of the philosophic life depends entirely on the existence of an afterlife in which the philosopher is rewarded with perfect wisdom and everlasting happiness. But if this is true and if, as Socrates' investigation here shows, it is unreasonable for the philosopher to hope for rewards in an afterlife, then how can he defend the reasonableness of the philosophic life?

Yet the fact that Socrates' own investigation of the possibility that the gods reward the philosopher in an afterlife culminates with the conclusion that the philosopher's hope for such rewards is unreasonable forces us to wonder whether he himself does not agree with this conclusion. It forces us to wonder, in other words, whether Socrates himself does not regard the hope for everlasting happiness as an unreasonable hope. For, as we have seen, all of his arguments on behalf of the hope for immortality and for divine rewards after death fail to vindicate the reasonableness of that hope. And, as we have also seen, all of his arguments point, in a quiet but systematic way, to the conclusion that the hope for divine rewards after death is an unreasonable hope. It would seem reasonable, then, for us to take seriously the possibility that Socrates himself did not actually believe that it is possible for the philosopher or any other human being to enjoy divine rewards in an afterlife.[22]

Now, we might be tempted to reject this possibility out of hand on the grounds that Socrates himself repeatedly claims to believe that there is an afterlife in which he will be rewarded and repeatedly urges his friends to believe this as well. Yet, at least in his initial claim, Socrates only says that, *if* he would strongly affirm anything about such matters, he would strongly affirm that, when he dies, he will arrive among gods who are very good masters (62b9–c7). He thereby explicitly leaves open the possibility that he never made any strong affirmations about these matters and hence that he does not, in fact, believe that he will be rewarded after death (see also 78c3-4).[23]

Furthermore, Socrates' allusion here to the story of Penelope in the *Odyssey* hints at the possibility that he may not be altogether truthful when he claims to believe that there is an afterlife in which philosophers are rewarded. For even though he says that Penelope's act of weaving the shroud for Laertes by day and then unweaving it by night was fruitless and senseless, that act was, as Socrates surely knows, not at all senseless. According to Homer, Penelope's intention was not to complete the shroud she was weaving but rather to deceive her enemies, the violent and outrageous suitors, into believing that she intended to complete the shroud in order to avoid marrying any of them.[24] Might Socrates be suggesting through this example that, by trying to prove that there is an afterlife in which philosophers are rewarded while, at the same time, undoing his efforts by showing that the philosophers cannot deserve rewards in an afterlife, he, like Penelope, is engaged in a deception? Might Socrates be seeking to deceive his enemies—the demos who have condemned him to death for impiety—into believing that he cherishes the pious hope for immortality when he does not, in truth, cherish this hope (see 61a4-8, 84d9–e2)? Might he be seeking to acquire the posthumous reputation of having been pious in order to protect philosophy and the friends of philosophy from the charge of impiety and the persecution of the pious (see chapter 1)?

Indeed, Socrates himself suggests that he has been discussing the question of the immortality of the soul in a somewhat deceptive manner. Once he sees that Cebes and Simmias are dissatisfied with his argument for immortality, he asks them the following question: is the argument not, in your opinion, an *in*adequate one? For, he goes on to say, it still admits of "many" suspicions and objections, if they are to examine it sufficiently. Now, Socrates explicitly acknowledges here that he has not adequately demonstrated that the soul is immortal. Notwithstanding his earlier claims that the immortality of the soul has been demonstrated, he now admits that there are still "many" possible objections to the argument for immortality (compare 84c5-7 with 77c6–d5, 84a2–b8; see also 72d6–e2, 80d5-81a11). And, if we take seriously Socrates' statement here that his argument for immortality is inadequate and if we assume that he has been aware of this all along, it seems reasonable to conclude that, when he claimed earlier that the immortality of the soul had been demonstrated, he was deliberately encouraging his friends to embrace a belief which he knew might be false and hence that he was deliberately deceiving his friends (see 63b5–c4; see also 91b7–c5).[25]

But why would Socrates, who declared at his trial that the pursuit of the truth is the greatest good for a human being,[26] encourage his own friends to embrace an opinion which he believes may be false? In his defense, we may first suggest that, even if the opinion that there is an afterlife is false, it may not be harmful for his friends to believe that this opinion is true, at least during the period surrounding Socrates' execution. Indeed, precisely insofar as philosophy is the greatest good for a human being, it may be good for Cebes, Simmias, and the others to believe even in the false opinion that the philosopher will be rewarded once he is dead. For inasmuch as Socrates is about to be executed and inasmuch as philosophers in general suffer from persecution, they must fear for their lives, especially on this day, and hence must feel tempted to abandon philosophy (see 64b1–6). And insofar as philosophy is the greatest good for a human being, by abandoning it they would be doing harm to themselves. By encouraging them to believe in the possibly false opinion that the philosopher will be rewarded in an afterlife, then, Socrates may be trying to save them from the evil of abandoning philosophy (see 114d1-115a5). And consequently, insofar as Socrates is deceiving them, he may be deceiving them for their own good.[27]

But this defense of Socrates is not altogether satisfactory. For even if we concede that it is good for Cebes and Simmias to believe in the soul's immortality during the period surrounding Socrates' death, would it not be harmful to them in the long run to believe in and to live according to such a false opinion (see 91b1–c5)? Precisely if the pursuit of the truth is the greatest good for a human being and the unexamined life is not worth living, would it not be bad for them to live according to the unexamined and possibly false opinion that the soul is immortal?

Yet, it is hard to know how Socrates could have encouraged Cebes and Simmias to examine the opinion that the soul is immortal more effectively than to proceed as he has. For, before we can genuinely examine an opinion, we must feel the desire or need to know whether or not that opinion is true. We must feel in our bones the importance for us of the possible truth or falsehood of this opinion. And this is precisely what Socrates has encouraged Cebes and Simmias to feel in the course of this conversation. He has shown them that their own belief that the goal of the philosophic life is the attainment of perfect wisdom depends on the belief in an afterlife in which that goal will be reached (see 63e8-67b6). He has shown them that the satisfaction of their own desire for perfect wisdom, and therewith of what they take to be their desire for happiness, is only possible if the individual soul is immortal (see 81a4-11). In this way, Socrates has allowed them to grasp and to feel what is at stake for them in the truth or falsehood of the opinion that the soul is immortal. By encouraging them, then, to long to believe that the soul is immortal, he has encouraged them to long to know the truth about the immortality of the soul (70a6–b4).

Now, once Cebes and Simmias feel all the power of their desire to believe that the individual soul is immortal, Socrates attempts to supply them with a convincing argument that the individual soul is, in truth, immortal. But Socrates' repeated and seemingly thorough attempts fail to prove the immortality of the individual soul. And precisely insofar as Cebes and Simmias long to be sure that the individual soul is truly immortal, they cannot help but sense the inadequacy of Socrates' arguments (see 77b1–c5, 84c1-4). Finally, just at the moment in which he divines that their doubt is most acute, Socrates acknowledges that they have good reason to doubt that the soul is immortal and urges them to express their doubts (84c5-85b9). By awakening in them the desire to know that the soul is immortal and by letting them see for themselves the reasons for doubting that the soul is immortal, then, Socrates encourages Cebes and Simmias most effectively to examine the question of the immortality of the soul for themselves and on their own.

In the light of these reflections, we may be able to see more clearly why Socrates has conversed with Cebes and Simmias in a somewhat deceptive manner rather than plainly revealing his true thoughts about the immortality of the soul. If Socrates were simply to level with his young friends, he would be, so to speak, doing their thinking for them. He would be giving to them what they would inevitably take to be his authoritative conclusions about the fate of the soul rather than allowing them to think their way through to those conclusions on their own. In this way, he would be reinforcing their tendency to believe that the pursuit of wisdom is not an active and independent pursuit but rather consists of the passive acceptance of the opinions of the wise (see 62c9–e7, 65d4-8, 70b8-10, 72e3-73a3, 74a9–b1; see also 58d5-6). And he would be deepening their sense of dependence on him on the day he is to abandon them (see 76b8-12, 77e8–78a2). On the other hand, by stirring up their desire to believe in the soul's immortality and by making clearly inadequate arguments for immortality, Socrates gives them the opportunity, at least, to question and to think for themselves and to attempt to see the truth for themselves.[28] In this way, he gives Cebes and Simmias the opportunity to have the ultimately independent experience of pursuing and seeing the truth for themselves.[29]

Our suggestion that Socrates is deceiving his friends in order to dissuade them from abandoning the philosophic life would only be plausible, however, if there is reason to think that he believes that the goodness of the philosophic life does not, in truth, depend on the existence of an afterlife in which the philosopher will acquire perfect wisdom. It would only be plausible, then, if there is reason to think that he believes that it is possible to acquire at least a kind of wisdom in this life by means of the senses. Yet it is important to note that, even in this discussion, he does not rule out this possibility. For, while he does say that what is perceptible is not "most clear" and "most true" and hence is not most intelligible, he does not say that what is perceptible is not at all clear, true, and intelligible (see 83c5-8; see also 67a6–b1, 73c1-74a8, 60b1–c7). Socrates does, then, leave open the possibility that we can acquire at least an imperfect or human wisdom in this life by means of our senses. And he thereby leaves open the possibility that the reasonableness of the life devoted to the pursuit of wisdom does not depend on the existence of an afterlife.[30]

One might still object that, insofar as philosophers are exposed to the threat of persecution and insofar as Socrates himself is about to be executed, the philosophic life cannot be a reasonable way of life unless there is an afterlife in which the philosopher is rewarded. Yet, inasmuch as Socrates has managed to live with the threat of persecution for seventy years, he may believe that a prudent philosopher can generally avoid the worst evils of persecution.[31] Furthermore, and more importantly, Socrates may not regard his imminent execution simply as an evil. For he suggests in both the *Apology* and the *Crito* that it may be better for him to die now rather than to die later, after suffering the evils of a drawn out and impoverished old age.[32]

It is important to note, however, that, even if Socrates does believe that the reasonableness of the philosophic life does not depend on the existence of an afterlife in which the philosopher is rewarded, it would still be necessary for him to address the question of whether or not there is an afterlife. For it is possible that there is an afterlife in which the philosopher is not rewarded but punished. Indeed, insofar as the pious Athenians have condemned Socrates to death for impiety and insofar as they believe that the philosophers are impious, they, at least, must believe that, if there is an afterlife, the philosophers will suffer there from the just wrath of the gods (see also 60d7–e3, 61a8–b1). In order, then, for Socrates to defend the reasonableness of the philosophic life, he would have to show that he can know, or at least be reasonably confident, that there is not an afterlife in which the philosopher will be punished. For how could the philosophic life be reasonable if those who led that life were condemned to everlasting torment in the hereafter?

Now, Socrates' investigation has pointed to the conclusion that we human beings cannot *deserve* to be rewarded with everlasting happiness. And insofar as he has shown that we cannot be justly rewarded by the gods with everlasting happiness, he has also shown that we cannot be justly punished by the gods with everlasting torment. For, if the gods' demands cannot possibly be fulfilled by any human being, then it would be manifestly unjust for them to punish us for our failure to do what we cannot do. It would seem, then, that, insofar as the gods are just, there cannot be an afterlife in which we will either be rewarded or punished and hence that there cannot be an afterlife at all.

Yet, inasmuch as Socrates has not shown that the gods are necessarily bound by justice—or at least by any human understanding of justice—it would seem that he has not shown that it is impossible for us either to enjoy an everlasting happiness or to suffer an everlasting misery. Indeed, the pious could object that their belief in an afterlife does not depend on the belief in just gods at all, but rather on the seemingly irrefutable belief in omnipotent and unfathomable gods who show mercy to some and who punish others in a way that is forever beyond our comprehension.[33] And if Socrates cannot refute the pious belief in an afterlife, how can he be reasonably confident that their belief is mistaken and hence that he and all philosophers will not be punished after death?

The case of Cebes and Simmias suggests, however, that it may be impossible for human beings to believe in personal immortality once they have recognized that it is impossible for a human being to deserve everlasting happiness.[34] For Simmias and Cebes go on to respond to Socrates' most obviously unfulfillable account of what the philosopher must do in order to deserve everlasting happiness not by affirming the possibility that there is an afterlife but rather by expressing their strongest objections in the dialogue to the claim that the soul is immortal (see 82b10-84b8, 84c1-7, 85b10-88b8). Furthermore, even though Cebes had only moments before given his strongest assent in the conversation up till now to the claim that the soul is immortal, he now goes so far as to suggest, for the first time, that it is foolish for any human being to be confident that his soul is immortal (compare 81a4-11 with 71e2-3, 72e3-73a3; 87e6-88b8 with 69e7–70b3, 77c1-5, 77e3-7). Once Cebes senses that no human being can genuinely transcend his concern for his own good and thereby deserve the reward of everlasting happiness, he becomes extremely doubtful that the soul is immortal. And once Cebes senses that it is impossible for us to purify ourselves of our merely human and mortal selves, once, that is, he senses that our truest selves are our human and mortal selves, he becomes positively unsympathetic to the very hope for immortality. The examples of Simmias and especially of Cebes suggest, then, that the very belief in personal immortality ultimately depends on the belief that we can purify ourselves of our desire to attain what is good for our selves. They suggest, in other words, that the very belief in an afterlife ultimately depends on the belief that everlasting happiness can be deserved. And insofar as Socrates has shown that it is impossible for us to deserve everlasting happiness, it would seem to be reasonable for him to be confident that there is no afterlife and hence that he will not be punished after death. Socrates' confidence that he will not be punished after death, then, would seem ultimately to rest on his contention that it is impossible for a human being to believe in personal immortality once he has recognized that it is impossible for any human being truly to deserve everlasting happiness.

In the *Phaedo*, then, Socrates defends the reasonableness of the philosophic life against the pious claim that such a life will provoke divine punishments after death by showing that the philosopher can be reasonably confident that he will suffer no such punishments after death.[35] And in this way, Socrates strengthens his broader case, a case which Plato has him make not only in the *Phaedo* but in all the dialogues, that the philosophic life is the best and wisest way of life for a human being. Yet it may be appropriate to point out that Socrates also appears to show in the *Phaedo* the limits of the philosopher's confidence that he will not be punished after death. For, to glance ahead, near the end of the dialogue, he says that even now, at the end of his life, he does not know what the causes of perishable things are. By saying this, he appears to admit that he does not know with perfect certainty that the soul is perishable or mortal and hence that he does not know with perfect certainty what will become of his soul once he is dead (see 96a6–c2, 97b3-7). And, to glance even further ahead, this lack of absolute certainty about the fate of the soul may shed light on the significance of Socrates' last words before he dies. For, just before his death, he tells Crito that they owe a sacrifice to Asclepius and urges him to attend to this, perhaps because, like old Cephalus in the *Republic*, he is afraid that he may be punished in Hades for owing sacrifices to the gods.[36] And it may be because he does not have the strength that absolutely certain knowledge of the ultimate fate of the soul would give him that, at the last moment of his life, Socrates, the very embodiment of the life of reason, appears to be overwhelmed by a fear of the gods.

Chapter 8

*The Objections of Simmias and Cebes to the
Argument for Immortality*

I. Socrates' Affirmation that He Believes in Immortality

Once Socrates tells his friends that they should not hesitate to speak up if they are perplexed by the argument for immortality, Simmias says that he and Cebes are, indeed, perplexed and that, since they desire to hear his response to their doubts, they have been urging one another to speak up. But, Simmias explains, they have been hesitating to trouble Socrates lest it be unpleasant for him to hear their objections on account of his present misfortune (84c8–d7). Simmias indicates here that, even though he and Cebes want to hear Socrates' response to their doubts about the argument for immortality, they do not, at this point, believe that he will be able to resolve those doubts. For, according to Simmias, they fear that Socrates will simply be troubled and pained by their objections to the argument. They evidently suspect, then, that Socrates will not be able to answer their objections by proving that the soul truly is immortal. And consequently, Simmias suggests, they wonder whether it would not be better to spare their friend the pain of doubting the immortality of the soul and allow him to enjoy, during his last hours of life, the pleasure of hoping for immortality.

Socrates responds to Simmias by laughing gently and remarking that it will be difficult for him to persuade "the other human beings" that he does not believe that his present fortune is a misfortune when he cannot even persuade his friends of this (84d8–e3). In this way, he tries to reassure his friends that he truly believes that he will be going to Hades on this day, that he will fare well there, and hence that his death is not a misfortune (see 58e1-59a1). But Socrates also reveals here that he wishes to persuade not only his friends but also "the other human beings," namely, his enemies who have condemned him to death for impiety and who believe that philosophers as a whole are impious men, that he embraces the pious belief in the afterlife (compare 84d9–e3 with 63b4–c7, 63e8-64a3, 64a4–b6; see also chapter 1). Indeed, by saying that he wishes to persuade those human beings that *he* believes in the afterlife rather than that he wishes to persuade

them that this belief is a reasonable one, Socrates suggests that he wishes
to persuade those human beings simply that *he* is pious. Socrates suggests
here, then, that, on the day he is to be executed for impiety, he wishes to
persuade not only his friends but, through them, his enemies and the
enemies of philosophy that he is a truly pious philosopher and hence that
the impiety charge against the philosophers and the religious persecution
of them are unjust (see 60d5–61c1; see also 89b2–c4).

Socrates proceeds to reassure his friends that he will not be troubled
at all by their objections to the argument for immortality. For just as the
swans, who sing with joy before they die, know through their prophetic art
that they will enjoy good things in Hades and that they will be with their
master Apollo, so too does he, their fellow slave to the god, know through
his prophetic art, which comes from the god, that he will be with his
master and will be happy when he dies (84d8–85b9). Socrates reveals to his
friends here that his belief in immortality is not based at all on the argument for immortality but rather on the knowledge of immortality revealed
to him by the god Apollo. He reveals to them, then, and through them, to
"the other human beings," that his belief that there is an afterlife and that
he will fare well there is based on a divine revelation and is therefore
unshakable (but see 63b9–c4). And he thereby reassures Simmias and Cebes
that they should not hesitate to state their objections to the argument for
immortality.

II. The Objection of Simmias

Apparently reassured by Socrates' speech, which he praises as a fine
one, Simmias says that he will first explain why he is perplexed by the
argument for immortality and then Cebes will explain why he does not
accept it (85b10–c1). Simmias indicates here that, even though he has
doubts about the argument, he does not necessarily reject it as, he claims,
Cebes does. In order to explain why, despite his doubts, he may yet accept
the argument for immortality, Simmias sets aside for a moment his specific
objection to that argument and proceeds to explain his general opinion
that perhaps all human arguments about such matters are subject to doubt
(see also 107a8–b3, 73b6–10).

Simmias says that, in his opinion, and perhaps in the opinion of
Socrates as well, it is either impossible or extremely difficult to know with
certainty "in this life" about such matters as the immortality of the soul
(85c1–3). Simmias doubts, then, that any human being can possess sure
knowledge about these important matters. And consequently, he doubts
that any human argument for, or indeed against, the immortality of the

soul can be altogether persuasive. On the other hand, Simmias is sure that, if it is possible to attain sure knowledge about this question, it is extremely difficult to do so, presumably because, in order to search for such knowledge, a man must make extraordinary efforts and must also expose himself to the pain of doubting the immortality of the soul (see 84d5-7). Nevertheless, he says, only a "very soft man" would not test "in every way" what is said about these things and would desist from searching for knowledge about them before he has first examined "every aspect" of these questions and then given up on this search (85c4-6). Simmias emphasizes, then, that, even though he doubts that it is possible to know with certainty about such questions as the question of immortality, he believes that it would be reprehensible to give up on the search for such knowledge too easily (see 85d4-7).

And yet Simmias has evidently thought about what he would do if it should prove to be impossible to acquire such knowledge. For he says that, if it is impossible either to learn from someone else or to discover for oneself the truth about such matters as the immortality of the soul, we ought to take the best and least refutable of human arguments and, being borne on it as though we were braving dangers on a raft, we ought to sail through life on it. And we ought to do this unless, he adds, we are able to go through life with greater safety and with less danger on a more stable raft or on some argument which is revealed by the gods (85c8–d4). Simmias suggests, then, that, if we should discover that it is impossible for us to discover the truth about the fate of the soul through human reason, we ought to abandon the philosophic quest for the truth and live our lives in accordance with that human argument which best protects us from our dangerous and painful doubts. And we ought to do this unless we receive a divine revelation which would presumably dispel our doubts altogether and thereby provide us with the security—the dry land—that we long for (see 85a8–b10).

Simmias does emphasize here that he does not yet believe that it is impossible to learn or to discover for himself the truth about the fate of the soul. Accordingly, he will explain why he thinks that the argument for immortality is inadequate, in the hope that he may yet learn from Socrates whether or not the soul is immortal. But he also suggests that, even if Socrates cannot resolve his doubts, he may nonetheless accept that argument in the future (see 85b10–c1). For Simmias may discover that it is impossible to know for sure whether or not the soul is immortal. He may, then, give up on his search for such knowledge, adopt the most plausible human argument, and live his life in accordance with it. And consequently, he may eventually accept Socrates' argument for immortality, despite his doubts, as the most plausible argument about the fate of the soul.

Now, notwithstanding Simmias' claim that he will, for the time being, persist in seeking for sure knowledge about the immortality of the
soul, he has evidently prepared himself for the day on which he may abandon that search. He is evidently inclined to believe, then, that the day will
come when he will abandon that search. And he is inclined to believe this,
it seems, because he holds the opinion that it may simply be impossible for
human beings to acquire sure knowledge about such matters as the fate of
the soul. But why does he hold this opinion? What is the reason for his
skepticism? Simmias never explains this. Even though he suggests that
Socrates may share this opinion, Simmias never asks him whether he does,
in fact, share it. While later on he urges Socrates to respond to the argument that the soul is necessarily mortal, Simmias never urges him to
respond to the claim that it may be impossible to know with certainty
whether or not the soul is immortal (86d1-4). Since Simmias never even
attempts to argue for his skepticism and never invites others to question
it, his skepticism would seem, then, to be a dogmatic skepticism. And the
dogmatic character of his skepticism is underscored by the fact that he is
a rather young man who has reflected on the question of immortality for
only a relatively short period of time under the guidance of only a handful
of teachers (see 89a1-4, 61d6-7, 78a3-7).[1]

It is true that Simmias does not rule out the possibility that he may
yet learn or discover the truth about the immortality of the soul. And he
does emphasize that one should abandon the search for the truth only if
it is impossible to complete that search and hence only if one knows with
certainty that it is impossible to know with certainty what the fate of the
soul is. To give up on the search for such knowledge before one is sure that
it is unattainable, he says, would be to give up too easily and to reveal that
one is a "very soft man." But it would seem to be impossible ever to be
certain that we can never know with certainty whether or not the soul is
immortal. For how can we ever be sure where the limits of our understanding lie? It would seem, then, that the day can never come when Simmias
can give up on the search for wisdom on the grounds that he is sure that
wisdom is unattainable. And consequently, the fact that Simmias looks
forward to the day when he will give up on the search for wisdom suggests
that he himself is inclined to give up too easily. It suggests that he himself
is a "very soft man." It suggests that he himself is unwilling to make the
efforts required by the "extremely difficult" search for knowledge about the
soul's ultimate fate and that he is unwilling to expose himself to the pain
of doubting that the soul is immortal.

To be sure, insofar as Simmias believes that it may be impossible to
be sure about the immortality or mortality of the soul, he must accept the
possibility that he will never be free of the pain of doubting that the soul

is immortal. For if we can never know with certainty whether or not the soul is immortal, we can never be sure that it is immortal. It is important to note, however, that, while Simmias' skepticism leaves room for doubt, it also leaves room for hope. For if we can never know with certainty whether or not the soul is immortal, we can never be sure that it is mortal. We can never be sure, then, that our hopes for immortality will not be justified. And consequently, Simmias' skepticism allows him to enjoy the pleasure of hoping that his soul may, after all, be immortal.

Indeed, Simmias' inclination to embrace skepticism may be especially strong now that he recognizes that the argument for immortality is so weak. For his awareness of the inadequacies of that argument leads him to feel quite doubtful about the immortality of the soul. It reminds him of an extremely powerful argument for the mortality of the soul (see 86b5–d4, 88c8–d8). And precisely insofar as Simmias is too soft to face what would be a painful truth and to deny himself the pleasure of hoping for immortality, he must be especially eager to believe, at this moment, that no human argument, including, above all, the argument for mortality, possesses the compelling power of the truth.

The case of Simmias suggests that there may be a certain softness at the very heart of skepticism itself. For his skepticism seems to reflect not a genuine doubt that we can know what death holds in store for us but rather a fear that we can know all too well what it holds in store for us. And it thereby reminds us that, while the skeptic most obviously and perhaps most impressively denies himself the comfort and the pleasure of contemplating beautiful and pleasant truths, he also protects himself from the full recognition of harsh and painful truths.

Yet Simmias is evidently not altogether satisfied with the prospect of living his life in accordance with the belief that it is impossible to know whether or not the soul is immortal. For, as we have noted, that belief would never free him entirely from the painful suspicion that his soul might be mortal. And while it would allow him the pleasure of hoping that his soul might be immortal, it would deny him the greater pleasure of being confident that this is so. Accordingly, Simmias leaves open the possibility that, even if he should discover that it is impossible to find a convincing human argument for immortality, he may still receive a divine revelation that will justify his hope for immortality. And while Simmias believes that the day may come when he can reasonably rule out the possibility of finding a convincing human argument for or against the immortality of the soul, he evidently believes that he can never—and hence need never—rule out the possibility, or abandon the hope, that the gods will reveal to him, as they seem to have revealed to Socrates, that his soul truly is immortal (see 84e3–85b10).

We may say, then, that Simmias' skepticism is a pious skepticism.[2] For he combines a distrust of human arguments with a trust or faith in the possibility of divine revelation. He combines a skepticism about human reason not only with the hope for immortality but also with the hope for a divine revelation which will justify his hope for immortality. And his hope for such a revelation may be another sign of the softness of his character. For, rather than attempt to justify his hope for immortality through his own efforts, rather than attempt to discover for himself whether reason truly vindicates or denies that hope, Simmias relies on the gods to justify his hope.

Simmias now goes on to explain why, in his opinion, Socrates' argument for the immortality of the soul is not an adequate one. He points out that someone could use this same argument about an attunement, a lyre, and its strings. For this person could say that the attunement in the attuned lyre is invisible, incorporeal, extremely beautiful, and divine and that the lyre and its strings are corporeal, composite, earthly, and akin to what is mortal. And once someone else shattered the lyre or cut its strings, this person would, using Socrates' argument, strongly affirm that the particular attunement in the attuned lyre "necessarily" still exists and has not perished. For, since the mortal lyre and strings still exist after they have been broken, the attunement, which is "similar by nature to what is divine and immortal," must also still exist somewhere and may perish only after the lyre and the strings have rotted away (85e3-86b5).

Simmias here addresses Socrates' argument that, since the soul is more similar to what is invisible than the body is, it must also be more similar to what is immortal than the body is and that, since the body continues to exist for a very long time after death, the soul must continue to exist for an even longer time after death (see 79a6-17, 80a10–e2; see also 79e8-80a9, 85e3-86b5). And by applying this very argument to the case of an attuned lyre, Simmias points to its inadequacy. For even though the attunement of an attuned lyre is invisible and incorporeal and even though the lyre itself is corporeal, that particular attunement clearly ceases to exist once the lyre is smashed, even though the bits and pieces of the lyre still exist. The fact, then, that the soul is more invisible than the body is does not prove that it "necessarily" continues to exist after death. For, just as the attunement of a lyre depends on the sound condition of that lyre for its very existence, so may the soul depend on the sound condition of the body for its very existence.

Simmias raises here a powerful objection to Socrates' argument for immortality.[3] He shows that the mere fact that the soul is more invisible than the body does not prove that it "necessarily" survives after death (see 86a4-6, b2-5). And he also raises the possibility that the soul depends on the healthy condition of the body for its very existence. But his objection here does not, by itself, prove that the soul is not immortal. Indeed, Simmias himself seems to leave open the possibility that, notwithstanding his objection, the soul may still be immortal. For, even though he is objecting to the argument for immortality, he persists in suggesting, throughout his speech, that the soul is somehow divine and hence might somehow be immortal (86a1, b1, c6). It would therefore seem reasonable for Simmias to stop here and to urge Socrates to respond to his objection by attempting to demonstrate yet again that the soul is immortal.

Yet Simmias does not ask Socrates to respond to his specific objection. Indeed, he does not even spell out what his objection is (compare 85e3-86b5 with 87c6ff.). Instead, Simmias abruptly breaks off—in midsentence (86a3–b5)—his specific objection to Socrates' argument that the soul is "necessarily" immortal and presents an argument that the soul is "necessarily" mortal (compare 86a3-6, b2-5 with c2-5). And once he has presented this argument for the mortality of the soul, he urges Socrates to respond to it and, it seems, to it alone (86d1-4). Rather than urge Socrates to present a new argument for immortality, Simmias seems to urge him to argue against an argument for mortality.[4]

Simmias' behavior here seems to reflect his eagerness to support his thesis that it is impossible to be sure whether or not the soul is immortal and thereby to protect his hope for immortality. Having seen Socrates fail in his three attempts to prove that the soul is immortal and admit his failure (84c6-7), Simmias seems to have given up hope that he will now prove that the soul is immortal in the few hours left to him. Yet he is concerned lest the argument he has heard from others—an argument evidently popular in certain philosophic circles—that the soul is an attunement of bodily elements prove to be a conclusive argument for the mortality of the soul (see 85b5–d1, 88d3-6). Accordingly, rather than urge Socrates to renew his attempt to argue for the immortality of the soul, Simmias presents this argument for the mortality of the soul and urges him to consider it in the hope that he will call that argument into question and thereby allow Simmias to continue to hope for immortality.

According to Simmias, the argument for the mortality of the soul goes as follows. The body is composed of various elements, such as heat, coldness, dryness, and wetness. And when these elements which make up the body are mixed together in a fine and measured way, the soul exists. For the soul is itself a certain attunement or arrangement of bodily elements. The soul, then, is not a separate being which may or may not depend on the body for its existence. But neither is it simply identical to the body. For when the body is attuned, but not in due measure, it still exists but the soul does not (86c2-5). The soul, then, is identical to that attunement or form which matter must possess in order for matter to be alive (see 91c7–d2). And therefore, if the individual soul is such an attunement of the body, then once our body is beset by diseases and other evils, our soul "necessarily" perishes immediately, "even though it is most divine," but our body and its elements continue to exist for a long time thereafter (86b5–d1). For, since the soul is not a separate being but rather a certain arrangement of matter, once that arrangement is upset, for example, by a mortal disease, the soul simply ceases to exist even though the material elements remain.

According to the argument Simmias presents here, then, since the soul is that attunement or form which matter must possess in order to be alive, the soul must be mortal. And by saying that "we suppose" the soul to be such an attunement, Simmias seems to indicate that he is convinced by this argument (86b5–7). But, at the end of his speech, Simmias distances himself from this argument by urging Socrates to consider what "we will say" in response to it (d1–4). While Simmias finds this argument to be very persuasive, he evidently hopes that Socrates will challenge it. For, should it go unchallenged, it would seem that Simmias would have to abandon all hope for immortality (see also 88d3–8).

Socrates does not, however, encourage Simmias or his other companions to hope that he will challenge the argument for the mortality of the soul. For he responds to Simmias' argument by praising it as a just one (86d5–6). He then turns to the others and asks them to respond to the argument, if anyone is more capable of responding to it than he is. But before anyone can reply to his request, he proposes that they all listen to Cebes' indictment of the argument for immortality so that they may deliberate as to whether they agree or disagree with the two youths' case against that argument (86d6–e4). Socrates here seems to go out of his way to convey to his companions the impression that he is incapable of responding to Simmias' argument for mortality. He even suggests that, after hearing Cebes' speech, he may agree that the soul is mortal (86d8–e4). Socrates, then, deliberately encourages his companions to feel the full weight of the argument against immortality and hence to feel the full power of their doubts about the immortality of the soul (compare 86d5–e4 with 77c6–e2; see also 88c1–d8).

III. The Objection of Cebes

Cebes begins his objection to Socrates' argument for immortality by saying that, in his view, it remains open to the same objection which he and Simmias made to the argument for the pre-existence of the soul (77b1–

c5). For while, in his opinion, Socrates has demonstrated quite successfully that our soul existed before it entered "this form," he has still failed to demonstrate that it continues to exist after we die (86e6-87a5). Now, Cebes stresses that this opinion places him at odds not only with Socrates but also with Simmias. For, since he believes that our soul existed before it entered the body, he cannot agree with Simmias' argument that the soul is an attunement of bodily elements and hence is not stronger and more long-lasting than the body (87a5-7). But furthermore, and more importantly, it would seem that, insofar as Cebes accepts Socrates' argument for the preexistence of the soul, his doubt that the soul is immortal cannot be as extreme as Simmias' is. For, insofar as Simmias has argued that the soul is an attunement of bodily elements, he has denied that it is at all separable from the body and consequently has denied that it is even possible for the soul to exist after death. This account of the soul, then, would seem to destroy all hope for immortality. But insofar as Cebes believes that our souls existed before we were born, he must believe that the soul can exist apart from the body and hence that it might continue to exist once it has been separated from the body in death. Moreover, insofar as Socrates' argument for the preexistence of the soul identifies the body with "the human form," it suggests that our true selves, our souls, are distinct from and higher than what is merely human and mortal. If, then, Cebes truly accepts this argument, he must leave open the possibility that we are divine and immortal beings (see 72e7-73a3, 76c11-13).

Cebes, however, emphasizes that he does nonetheless doubt the argument for immortality. And he anticipates that the argument will ask him why he persists in doubting that the soul of a dead man continues to exist. For, since he agrees that the soul is more long-lasting than the body is, and since he sees that the weaker part of the dead man continues to exist, is it not necessary for him to agree that the more long-lasting part of the man also continues to exist? Cebes responds by applying the same line of reasoning to an old weaver and his cloak. Someone might argue that, since the old weaver's cloak continues to exist after he dies, and since the species of human beings is more long-lasting than the species of used cloaks, then the weaver must also continue to exist. But everyone, Cebes says, would suppose that the man making such an argument is a simpleton. For this weaver has worn out many of his cloaks in the course of his life and has outlasted all but the last cloak. And therefore, Cebes suggests, the fact that the last cloak survives after his death proves neither that the old weaver still exists then nor that a human being is inferior to or weaker than a cloak (87a7–d3).

Cebes goes on to say that he is inclined to believe that the relation between the soul and the body is, in fact, similar to that between a weaver and his cloak. For the same body does not exist continuously throughout our lives but each soul wears out many bodies, especially if it should live for many years. And since the body flows and perishes while we are alive, the soul always reweaves what has been worn down. But when the soul perishes, it necessarily perishes after all the bodies it has woven have perished except for the last one. And once the soul has perished, that body will reveal its weak nature by quickly rotting away. Therefore, Cebes says, since he is inclined to accept this account of the soul, he believes it is "not yet" proper to trust in the argument for immortality and to be confident that, once we die, our soul will continue to exist (87d3–88a1).

Yet, precisely insofar as Cebes does accept this account of the soul, precisely insofar as he believes that the image of the weaver and his cloak accurately reflects the nature of the soul's relation to the body, it would seem that he must reject altogether the argument for immortality.[5] And it would seem that he must reject the argument for the preexistence of the soul as well. For the comparison of the soul to a weaver suggests that, just as a weaver needs his cloak in order to survive,[6] so does the soul need the body in order to survive. And if this is true, then it would be impossible for the soul to survive apart from the body either after we die or before we are born. Insofar, then, as Cebes accepts this account of the soul, and insofar as he understands fully and clearly the implications of that account, he must agree with Simmias that the soul cannot exist apart from the body. Indeed, Cebes' account of the soul suggests even more emphatically than Simmias' does that the soul cannot be immortal. For, by suggesting that the soul is similar to a human being, that account suggests that the soul itself is human and not, as Simmias has continued to suggest, divine (compare 87b3–d7 with 86a1, b1, c6). If, then, Cebes truly accepts this account, he must accept that our truest selves, our souls, are not distinct from and higher than what is human and mortal, that they are not divine and immortal in any way, but that they—or, rather, we—are, in fact, human and mortal beings.

Furthermore, insofar as Cebes accepts this account of the soul, he must reject not only the argument for immortality but also Socrates' exhortations to his companions to attempt to fulfill the duty of the philosopher. For Socrates has claimed that, in order to fulfill his duty and hence to deserve the divine reward of everlasting happiness, the philosopher must, at the very least, long to release his soul from the body that imprisons it and hence must long to escape from the human evils (see 82d1–84b8). Indeed, throughout this conversation, he has virtually defined the true philosopher as one who does not love his body or regard it as good in any way but who instead longs to be free of it (see 64d2–65a8, 65c11–d2, 66b1–67b5, 67d7–10, 68b8–c1, 80e2–82c8; but see also 73c1ff.). Socrates has emphasized to his companions, then, that, in order to fulfill his duty, the philosopher must, at the very least, regard his body, and therewith his human form, as an evil (see 66b1–d7, especially 66b5-6, 70a6–b1, 81a4-11, 84a2–b4; see also 72e7-73a2, 76c11-13; but see 79b1-2, 79e8-80a5). But, if Cebes accepts his account of the soul as true, he cannot regard the body as evil or long to be free of it. For if, as that account suggests, the soul depends on the body for its very survival, it must be impossible for a human being to release his soul from his body without destroying his soul altogether. Moreover, inasmuch as the body is necessary for the soul's very survival, the body cannot be evil but must rather be good for the soul. And insofar as the body is good for our souls and therefore good for us, it cannot be reasonable for us to regard the body as an evil or long to be free of it (see 62d8-e3). Furthermore, and more importantly, if, as Cebes' account of the soul suggests, our very souls are human, it cannot be reasonable for us to regard what is human as evil and to long to escape from it. For, since our very souls are human, all that we are is human (see 87a7–b2). And since we are thoroughly human, since we are human through and through, it cannot be evil or bad *for us* to be human. For anything that is bad for us can only be bad for us given what we are. It is what we are, it is our nature, that determines what is bad or good for us. And therefore, given our nature as human beings, it must be bad for us to regard our nature as bad and to seek to escape from or to rise above our humanity by, for example, fulfilling the duty of the philosopher. For it is only by recognizing and accepting what we are, it is only through self-knowledge, that we can ever know what is good for such beings as ourselves. If, then, Cebes accepts this account of the soul as true, he must regard the exhortation to fulfill the duty of the philosopher not only as impossible but also as evil or bad. For insofar as that exhortation calls on us to regard our humanity as an evil and to long to be free of it, insofar, that is, as it calls on us to long for and to hope for immortality, it encourages us to lose sight of what we are and therefore leads us away from what is good for beings such as ourselves. Insofar, then, as Cebes accepts this account of the soul as true, and insofar as he does so with a full and clear awareness of all that this account implies, he must reject not only the arguments for immortality and the preexistence of the soul but also the very hope for immortality.

Now, it is important to note that, even though Cebes says that he is inclined to accept this account of the soul, he evidently does not see all that it implies. For even though his account of the soul contradicts the argument for the preexistence of the soul, Cebes never retracts his earlier claim that he is convinced by that argument (see 87a1-4, 91e5-92a3). And while Socrates later points out to Simmias the contradiction between his account of the soul and the argument for the preexistence of the soul, he never points out to Cebes the contradiction between his account of the soul and that argument (see 92a6–c10). Furthermore, it seems that Cebes does not recognize that, if his account of the soul is true, it is impossible for the soul to be immortal. For he goes on to argue not that the soul is mortal but rather that Socrates has not demonstrated that the soul is altogether immortal. He says that, even if he were willing to grant that our souls exist not only before we are born but also after we die and that they return to life and survive death again, he would still not agree that Socrates has demonstrated the immortality of the soul. For the soul may still labor in its many births and in one of its deaths it may perish altogether (88a1–10). In other words, even though the soul may be able to exist apart from the body before it enters the body, once it enters the body, it may be doomed to perish sooner or later (see 95c9–d2). And since it is impossible for us to perceive and hence to know which of our deaths will bring destruction to our soul, it is foolish for anyone to be confident in the face of death, unless he is able to demonstrate that the soul is altogether immortal and indestructible. But if one is not able to do this, and if he is not a fool, it is always necessary for him to fear for his soul when he is about to die lest, in its separation from the body, it perish altogether (88a10–b8).

It appears, then, that Cebes objects to Socrates' argument for immortality by arguing that, even though the soul is more long-lasting than the body is and hence is more similar to what is immortal, that fact alone does not prove that the soul is altogether immortal and indestructible and therefore does not constitute sufficient grounds for being confident in the face of death (see 80a10–c10, 84a2–b8). And while this objection is a powerful one, it does not rule out the possibility that the soul may be immortal. It seems, then, that Cebes does not truly recognize that, if his account of the soul is true, our souls are necessarily mortal.

Yet Cebes does sense, if only vaguely, this implication of his account of the soul. For, in contrast with Simmias and in contrast with his own earlier objections to the argument for immortality, he does not urge Socrates to respond to his objection, and he does not attribute his objection to the many or to a childish part of himself (compare 86d1–4, 69e7–70a9, 77c1–5, e3–7, 78a10–b1 with 88b6–8, 87d3–7). Instead, he identifies himself almost unequivocally with the argument against immortality (see especially 87d3–7; but see 87e6–88a1). It seems, then, that Cebes is inclined to believe that his objection to the argument for immortality is decisive and hence that the soul is mortal.

Furthermore, at the conclusion of his speech, Cebes, for the first time in this conversation, speaks disparagingly of the hope for immortality and approvingly of the fear of death. He suggests that it is not at all admirable but simply foolish to hope for immortality in the face of death when there is no sufficient reason for such hope (compare 88b3-6 with 69e6-70b9). And, by saying that it is always necessary for the man who is not a fool to fear for his soul in the face of death, he suggests that the fear of death is a sign not of foolishness or childishness but rather of wisdom (compare 88b3-8 with 69a6–e7, 77e3-7, 81a4-11). It seems, then, that Cebes is not only inclined to believe that the soul is mortal but is also inclined to reject the very hope for immortality as a hope unbecoming a sensible man.[7]

When we recall, however, the reasons which led Socrates to argue for the immortality of the soul in the first place, we might expect that, insofar as Cebes rejects that argument, he must also reject the philosophic life itself. For Socrates has argued that the philosopher longs throughout his life for death because it is only in an afterlife that he can possess the perfect wisdom he seeks (see 64a4-9, 65a9-68b4, especially, 66b5-7, 67e6-68a3, 68b3-4; see also 80e2-81a10, 84a2–b4). Socrates has argued, then, that the reasonableness of the philosophic life depends on the existence of an afterlife in which the philosopher is rewarded with perfect wisdom. And insofar as Cebes rejects the belief in an afterlife, must he not reject the philosophic life as well?

Yet, in sharp contrast with Simmias, Cebes does not suggest at all that the philosophic quest for wisdom is an unreasonable quest or that he himself anticipates abandoning that quest. Indeed, by saying that it is foolish for anyone who is unable to demonstrate the immortality of the soul to be confident in the face of death, Cebes seems to insist that it is wise and therefore good for men to live strictly in accordance with their human reason and that it is foolish and therefore bad to indulge in hopes which cannot be justified by reason (compare 88b3-8 with 84e3-85b10, 85c7–d4). It seems, then, that Cebes' inclination to believe that the soul is mortal does not weaken at all his devotion to the philosophic life. Indeed, it may be that, precisely insofar as Cebes recognizes that he is truly a human being, he also recognizes that the attainment of an imperfect, human wisdom is a proper and even a necessary goal for a being such as himself. And since the attainment of such wisdom and progress in such wisdom are possible in this life, Cebes may conclude that the reasonableness of the philosophic life does not, in truth, depend on the existence of an afterlife.

Now, if, as we have argued, Socrates himself does not believe either that there is an afterlife or that the reasonableness of the philosophic life depends on the existence of an afterlife, we might expect that he would accept Cebes' argument for mortality and explain why it does not destroy the case for philosophy. Yet, even though Socrates has, as we have seen, encouraged his companions to doubt the argument for immortality and even though he never does specifically address Cebes' argument for mortality, he does proceed to urge Phaedo to fight against the arguments of both Simmias and Cebes (see 84c4–d3, 86d5–e5, 95e7ff., 88b2–c10). And Socrates then proceeds to argue against Simmias' argument for mortality, to argue yet again for the immortality of the soul, and to urge his companions to hope for immortality (see 91e2-95a2, 100b7-107a1, 107c1–d2, 114c2–115a3). In order to understand why Socrates proceeds in this way, we must examine his companions' immediate response to the arguments for mortality.

Chapter 9

Socrates' Warning Against Misology

I. The Distrust of Reason

The objections of Simmias and Cebes to Socrates' argument for immortality provoke a crisis in the conversation. According to Phaedo, all of those who were listening were pained by those objections. For they had found the argument for immortality extremely persuasive and the objections led them to distrust not only that particular argument but also all future ones, for fear that they were unworthy judges of anything or even that "the things themselves" were untrustworthy (88c1-7). The arguments of Simmias and Cebes against the immortality of the soul lead Socrates' companions, then, to lose their faith that there is any truth in arguments, that there is any truth that we can know through reason, and even, it seems, that there is any truth at all (see 65d4-66a6; but see 67b1-2).

Now, it makes sense that, having heard the arguments for the mortality of the soul put forth by Simmias and Cebes, Socrates' companions should come to distrust the argument for the immortality of the soul. But why do they go further and feel distrust toward all arguments? Why does the apparent fact that the argument for immortality is not true lead them to doubt that any argument can be true? Why do they not rather conclude that the evidently strong arguments for mortality are or may be true?

The extreme response of Socrates' companions to the arguments for mortality seems to reflect the power of their hope for immortality. For they evidently fear that those arguments are so strong that they destroy all hope for a true argument for immortality. They fear, then, that, if they continue to seek for the truth about the fate of the soul through argument or reason, they will be compelled to agree that the soul is mortal. And so powerful is their hope for immortality that they would rather believe that no argument can be true than accept as true an argument that the soul is mortal. They would rather believe, in other words, that there is no truth that we can know through reason than admit that their hope for immortality is deluded. And they would even rather believe that are no "things themselves," that is, that there is no permanent or stable truth at all, than believe that the soul is mortal. For, if there is nothing stable or true, if, that is, there is no stability in things but all is in flux, then at least they could cling to the belief in immortality, not as an absolute truth, but as a belief that is "true" for them, that is a relative or personal truth, and that is no less true than any other belief. So unyielding, then, is their desire to believe that the soul is immortal that, when faced with the apparent necessity of choosing between that belief and the belief that the truth is accessible to us through reason—the belief that lies at the heart of the philosophic life (see 90c8–91a3)—they deny the truthfulness of reason and thereby reject the philosophic life.[1]

At this point, Echecrates interrupts Phaedo's narrative and declares emphatically, with an oath to the gods, that he forgives Socrates' companions for their distrust of arguments. He explains that he, too, now wonders what argument they might still trust. For while he, too, found the argument for immortality persuasive, he now doubts it as well. And he also says that he now stands in need of another argument that will persuade him that the soul is immortal (88c8-d8; see also 70d1-5, 106c9–d1). By saying this, Echecrates implies that, if there is no argument that will satisfy his need to believe that the soul is immortal, he, too, may seek to satisfy this need by denying that there is any truth in arguments or reason. It seems, then, that, like Socrates' companions, Echecrates would sooner deny that we can know the truth through reason than accept that he is truly mortal.

The responses of Socrates' companions and of Echecrates to the argument for mortality reveal just how tenuous the human attachment to reason may be. For these men are friends of philosophy. At considerable risk to themselves, they have devoted their lives to the rational pursuit of wisdom. But they have evidently always assumed, perhaps half-consciously, that that pursuit was supportive of, or at least compatible with, their deepest hopes. And now, through this conversation, Socrates has rendered that implicit assumption explicit. He has encouraged them to identify the belief in immortality with the belief in the superiority of the philosophic life (see 63e8-64a9, 69a6–d2, 80e1-84b8). He has encouraged them to believe, or rather to hope, that the rational pursuit of the truth about the soul will culminate with the conclusion that their souls are immortal (see 72e3-73a3, 77c1ff.). He has encouraged them, then, to believe that reason will justify their hope for eternal happiness in the afterlife. But once they sense that reason may require them to abandon this hope, once, that is, they sense that the philosopher's practice of dying and being dead may consist precisely in his recognition and acceptance of his own mortality, they deny that there is any truth in reason and thereby turn against philosophy itself. For they see that philosophy, which had seemed to be the great defender of their hope for immortality, may be its deadliest foe. And we see that the very longing for immortality, which had seemed to be almost identical with the philosopher's longing for wisdom, may, in truth, be an enemy to philosophy.

The response of his companions to the argument for mortality suggests that Socrates cannot persuade them of the goodness of the philosophic life without somehow accommodating their hope for immortality. For, even though the conversation up till now points to the conclusion that the soul is mortal, their hope for immortality is evidently so powerful that, should Socrates argue that it is necessary to choose between that hope and the philosophic life, it is doubtful that they would, at least at this point in their lives, surrender their hope. Insofar, then, as Socrates seeks to persuade his companions that the philosophic life is the good life, it would seem that he must assure them that the philosophic life can, indeed, satisfy their need to believe in the immortality of the soul and hence that he must adorn the life of reason with the promise of immortality.

When Echecrates urges Phaedo, in the name of Zeus, to explain how Socrates responded to the argument of Simmias and Cebes, Phaedo describes that response with considerable precision. First, he says, Socrates "accepted the argument of the youths"—that is, the argument for the mortality of the soul—with pleasure, good will, and admiration. Far from being pained by that argument, as his companions were, Socrates was, according to Phaedo, pleased by it and even admired it. But Phaedo goes on to say that Socrates was also quite sensitive to what his companions were feeling in response to the argument for mortality. In other words, he sensed that they were pained by that argument and that they consequently felt a deep distrust of all arguments, of reason itself, and even of the things themselves (compare 89a4-5 with 88c1-7). And Socrates went on, Phaedo says, to cure them of this distrust and to rally them, as a general rallies his fleeing and beaten troops, to follow and examine the argument and hence, it seems, to persevere in the philosophic pursuit of the truth (88e4-89a7).

Now, it would seem that, in order to rally his companions, Socrates must provide them with a persuasive argument for the immortality of the soul. Yet, insofar as they have just had the experience of coming to distrust an argument for immortality which they had found to be extremely persuasive, and insofar as this experience has led them to distrust all arguments, they must be in no mood to place their trust in a new argument for immortality, no matter how persuasive it might seem to be. And since Socrates is aware of their mood, before he even attempts to make another argument for immortality, he first attempts to dispel their extreme distrust of all arguments.

II. Socrates' New Account of the Duty of the Philosopher

Phaedo says that, at this point in the conversation, Socrates turned to him, caressed his hair, and urged him not to cut his beautiful hair on the following day as a token of mourning. For if, he explained, "the argument (*ho logos*) should die for us and we should be unable to bring it back to life," then they should both cut their hair and mourn the death of the argument on this day. And he went on to say that, if he were Phaedo and the argument were to flee from him, he would swear an oath to the gods that he will not cut his hair until he has vanquished the argument of Simmias and Cebes (89a9–c4).

Socrates suggests here to Phaedo and to all of his companions that it is their sacred duty, and his as well, to persevere in trying to vindicate the argument for immortality and to refute the argument for mortality. And since Socrates has been attempting to persuade his companions of the immortality of the soul in order to persuade them of the goodness of the philosophic life, he seems to call on them here to persevere in the effort to vindicate the argument not only for immortality but also for philosophy (see 63e8–64a2). But furthermore, by urging them specifically to keep the argument *alive*, Socrates seems to urge them not only to defend the philosophic life but also to live that life. He seems to urge them, on this the day of his death, to keep reason alive in their very selves by living the life of reason. Socrates responds, then, to his companions' distrust of reason and of philosophy by emphasizing to them that it is their duty to dedicate themselves to the life of philosophy.

Socrates goes on to supplement his exhortation to his companions to keep reason alive by urging them to beware of misology—that is, the hatred of arguments or of reason. He tells them that they could not suffer an evil greater than succumbing to the temptation of misology (89c11–d3). And after explaining how misology comes into being, he exhorts his companions, and also himself, not to allow into their souls the thought that there is nothing sound in arguments but rather to believe that they themselves are not yet sound or healthy and that they must be courageous and zealous in their efforts to become sound (90d9–e3). Now, by saying, within the context of this discussion of immortality, that misology is an evil second to none, Socrates suggests that the hatred of reason and of philosophy is evil, at least in part, because it deprives human beings of their only chance of enjoying everlasting rewards after death (compare 89c11–d3 with 81b1–c2, 83b3–e3). And by urging his companions not to allow into their *souls* the thought there is nothing sound in arguments, he suggests that, by fulfilling this demand, they will purify their souls of the evil passion of misology and hence will render their souls worthy of divine rewards after death (compare 90d9–e2 with 66b1–d7, 67a2–b2, 80e1–81c2). Socrates suggests to his companions, then, that if they resist the temptation of misology and if they persevere in their efforts to defend the life of reason and to live that life, they will have fulfilled the duty of the philosopher and hence will deserve the reward of an everlasting happiness once they are dead. And from this we see that Socrates responds to his companions' distrust of reason by presenting them first not with a new argument for immortality but rather with a new account of the duty of the philosopher.

In order to understand why Socrates responds to his companions' distrust of reason in this way, it is necessary to recall how his companions came to feel distrust for arguments and for reason. According to Phaedo, their distrust arose in response to the objections of Simmias and Cebes to the argument for immortality (88c1-7). But the strong doubts of those two youths concerning that argument arose in immediate response to Socrates' argument that the philosopher can only deserve everlasting happiness in the afterlife if he believes that nothing perceptible is true and if he abstains from all pleasures and pains (83a1–e3). In other words, the doubts of Simmias and Cebes concerning the argument for immortality and, it seems, the doubts which Phaedo and the others came to feel later on, first arose in response to Socrates' most obviously unfulfillable account of the duty of the philosopher. It seems, then, that the source of their fear that there is no true argument for immortality and of their subsequent distrust of arguments is their sense that it is impossible for the philosopher to fulfill his duty and to deserve the divine reward of everlasting happiness after death.

Now, however, Socrates encourages his companions to believe that, in order to fulfill his duty, the philosopher need not disbelieve his senses entirely nor abstain from all pleasures and pains but must rather persevere in his efforts to defend and to live the life of reason and must also courageously and zealously resist the temptation of misology (compare 89b4–c4, 90d9–e3 with 83a1–e3; see also 67a2–b2, 69a6–d2). And while these demands would seem to be difficult, they are not, at least, impossible to meet. Socrates encourages them, then, to believe and to feel that they can fulfill the duty of the philosopher and hence can deserve everlasting happiness after death. And in this way, he encourages his companions to believe that they may reasonably hope for immortality and thereby reassures them that they need not fear that reason threatens that hope. For insofar as they believe that they can deserve everlasting happiness, they may plausibly hope that there are just gods who will reward them according to their desert. By reviving and strengthening their belief that they may deserve everlasting happiness, then, Socrates attempts to assuage their fear that the argument for mortality may be true and therewith their distrust of reason itself.[2]

The rest of the dialogue would seem to suggest that, by encouraging his companions to believe that they can deserve everlasting happiness, Socrates does, indeed, succeed both in encouraging them to believe in immortality and in curing them of their distrust of reason. For, while Simmias and especially Cebes had objected with increasing vehemence to

Socrates' first three arguments for immortality, once he gives his new account of the duty of the philosopher, they seem to become quite docile. Simmias goes on to abandon quite speedily his objection to the argument for immortality. And while he says that he cannot quite accept Socrates' final argument for immortality, he does not raise any specific objections to it (compare 77a10–b9, 85b10-86d4 with 91e1-95a3, 107a8–b3). Furthermore, Cebes appears to accept the final argument, even though it does not demonstrate that the individual soul is immortal and does not even claim to satisfy his original demand for reassurance that the soul possesses wisdom after death (compare 69e7-70b4, 86e6-88b8 with 106c9–107a7).[3] Finally, while Phaedo tells Echecrates that, in the middle of this conversation, he and his companions felt a distrust of reason and hence of philosophy, he goes on to say that Socrates cured them of this distrust, and he concludes his narrative by praising the philosopher Socrates, on behalf of his companions, as the best man they ever knew and especially as the wisest and the most just (compare 88c1-7 with 89a5-7, 118a15-17; see also 58d4-6, 58e1-59a7). It seems, then, that, it is above all by presenting his companions with an account of the duty of the philosopher which they can hope to fulfill and thereby reassuring them that they can deserve the reward of everlasting happiness that Socrates persuades them that the soul is immortal and that the philosophic life is the best and wisest way of life.

Yet, even though Socrates does strengthen his companions' hope for immortality by providing them with a new account of the duty of the philosopher, he also seems, at the same time, to warn them against an excessive attachment to that hope. For, by warning them, at the very moment that they feel an extreme distrust for all arguments, that the hatred of arguments is an evil second to none, Socrates suggests that it would be evil or bad for them to hate even and especially that argument which they may feel most tempted to hate, namely, the argument for mortality. Indeed, he suggests that to accept the argument for mortality as true and even actually to suffer the destruction of one's soul would, at the very least, not be a greater evil than to hate arguments or reason itself. Socrates suggests to his companions, then, that they should resist misology not only because it deprives one of the reward of everlasting happiness after death but also because it harms one in this life.

III. Socrates' Account of Misology

In order to explain to his companions how they may fulfill their duty to keep reason alive and to resist misology, Socrates explains to them, at some length, how misology comes into being and hence how they may avoid becoming haters of reason. He first says that both misology and misanthropy come into being out of the same disposition (*tropos*—89d3-4). And he then proceeds to explain how misanthropy comes into being, presumably in order to shed light on how misology comes into being. According to Socrates, misanthropy comes into being in the following way. A man trusts in someone in an extreme way and without art and believes that that human being is "altogether" true or truthful, sound, and trustworthy. But then, a little later, he discovers that this human being is bad and untrustworthy, though not, evidently, that he is "altogether" so. And when someone has this experience many times and especially when he experiences this with respect to those whom he believed were his nearest and dearest companions, he ends up hating all human beings and believing that there is nothing "at all" sound or healthy in any of them. It seems, then, that it is the misanthrope's repeatedly disappointed hope to find an altogether truthful, sound, and trustworthy human being that leads him eventually to hate all mankind (89d3–e3).

Now, at first glance, it seems difficult to see why the man Socrates describes here should end up hating all human beings. For he seems to portray that man as someone who simply longs to find a good companion or friend and hence one who is trustworthy and who can especially be counted on to tell the truth and to be of sound character and body. And, given this portrait, it is not immediately apparent why the misanthrope should be disappointed over and over again in his search for such a companion (see 78a3-7). Yet, upon closer examination, Socrates' portrait reveals a marked extremism in this man's longing for a companion. For, according to Socrates, this man longs to find a human companion who is not only truthful, sound, and trustworthy but rather one who is "altogether" (*pantapasin*) so (89d4-7). He longs, in other words, for a human companion who not only has many good qualities but who is good in every respect or perfectly good. Hence, by longing for a human companion who is altogether truthful, he must long not only for a perfectly honest companion but also for a perfectly wise one (see 76b8-12). For only a human being who knows the truth can be altogether capable, at least, of speaking the truth.[4] Similarly, by longing for an altogether trustworthy human companion, he must long not only for a loyal companion, who will always either sacrifice his interests for his companion or identify his interests with those of his companion, but also for an immortal companion. For, since a mortal being can always be snatched away from us by death and can therefore always be compelled to desert us, no mortal being can be an altogether trustworthy or loyal companion (see 63a4-9, 78a1-2).[5] By seeking, then, for an altogether truthful, sound, and trustworthy human companion, the misanthrope must be seeking for a human companion who is perfectly wise, good, and immortal and hence, it would seem, for a companion who is not human at all but who is rather a divine soul or a god (see 62c9–e4). And therefore this man is bound to be disappointed in his search for such a human companion.

Yet, it still seems strange that the misanthrope should conclude from his failure to find a perfectly good human companion that all human beings are perfectly bad and deserve to be hated. For it would seem to be more reasonable to conclude that human beings evidently cannot be perfectly good and hence that his hope to find such a perfect companion is unreasonable and that his hatred of human beings for not being what they cannot be is unjust. Furthermore, the belief that all human beings are altogether bad and deserve to be hated would seem to be not only unreasonable but also itself bad for the man who holds this belief. For inasmuch as the misanthrope is himself a human being, he must, if he is a thorough-going misanthrope, believe that he, too, is altogether bad and must hate himself. And such self-hatred might even lead him, at some point in his life, to consider seriously the possibility of killing himself (see 61d3–62a9; see also 81a4–c3, 70a6–b1). But why would any human being embrace and cling to such a seemingly unreasonable and depressing belief about human beings?

The misanthrope is evidently so attached to his hope for a perfect companion that he would rather believe that all human beings, including himself, are altogether bad and deserve to be hated than believe that his hope is deluded. But how can he hope to find such a companion, given his failure to find one among human beings? In order to answer this question, we must recall our earlier suggestion that, inasmuch as the misanthrope is seeking for a perfectly good companion, he must ultimately be seeking not for a human but rather a divine companion. He must be seeking for gods who are perfectly wise and good and who care for him (see 62c9–e7, 63b5–7). It seems, then, to be the misanthrope's love of such gods and longing to be with them that leads him to be disappointed with all human beings and to hate them all, including, insofar as he is a human being, himself.[6] But the misanthrope may still hope to satisfy his longing to dwell with the gods not in this life but in an afterlife. For, even though, insofar as he is a human being, he must hate himself, the misanthrope may not simply identify himself as a human being. He may rather identify his true self as a divine and immortal soul which is lodged in a human and mortal body (see 72e3–73a3, 80a10–b7, 81a4–11; see also 66b1–7). And consequently, he may cherish the hope that, once he is released from his body and thereby ceases to be at all human, he will dwell with the gods and hence finally find the perfect companions he seeks. Moreover, by hating the human part of himself, that is, his body, and by blaming it for all of what would seem to be his own all too human evils, he could hope all the more confidently that he will dwell with the gods after death. For, by blaming all his sins on that which is human in him, namely, the flesh, he could believe that his true self—his soul—is altogether good and hence deserves to dwell with the gods after death (see 66b1–67b2). The misanthrope's hatred of human beings or, more precisely, his hatred of that which is human, both in others and in himself, would seem, then, to reflect his desire to identify himself as a divine and immortal soul rather than as a human and mortal being and hence to reflect his hope that he will dwell with perfectly good companions, namely, the gods, after death.

By presenting this portrait of the misanthrope to his companions, Socrates is presenting them, albeit in a somewhat obscure way, with a portrait of a man who longs for immortality and hence with a portrait of themselves (compare also 88c1-7 with 89d3-4). Indeed, throughout this conversation, Socrates has suggested that the man who longs for immortality necessarily identifies his true self with his soul and his merely human and mortal self with his body and necessarily regards his human self as something evil and even perhaps as something hateful as well (compare 72e7-73a2, 76c11-13 with 66b3–d7, 83a1–e3; see also 80e2-81a10, 84a2–b4). Misanthropy, then, seems to be a passion that necessarily accompanies the longing for immortality. It is, we may say, the negative or dark side of the positive longing for immortality. And insofar as Socrates has urged his companions to admit to their longing for immortality, he himself has encouraged them, it seems, to admit to their hatred of that which is human (see 69e6-70b1; but see 79b1-2, 87a7–e5). But now, in addition to describing the misanthrope here, he also criticizes that man and hence, indirectly, his companions as well. He warns them against misanthropy. And he thereby seems to warn them against their own longing for immortality.

Socrates says, in the course of his account of the misanthrope, that he is artless and he says at the end of that account that it is base or ignoble of the misanthrope to attempt to deal with human beings without the art concerning human things. For, if he had possessed that art, Socrates explains, he would have believed that few are extremely good or extremely bad and that most are in between (89e5-90a2). The art concerning human things, then, consists, at least in part, of the knowledge that we human beings are, by and large, neither extremely good nor extremely bad. And we acquire such knowledge, according to Socrates, not by contemplating the pure and separate forms but rather by observing through our senses human beings and other visible beings (contrast 90a4-9 with 65a9-66a8, 83a1–c9). For since, he argues, we *perceive* that there is nothing rarer than a human being or a dog or any other thing that is extremely big or small, fast or slow, ugly or beautiful, and black or white, and hence since we perceive that, with respect to such qualities, the extremes are rare while the vast majority are in the middle, it is reasonable to conclude that, if there were a contest for wickedness, very few would win it (90a4–b2).[7] It seems, then, that the misanthrope is base or ignoble because he mistakenly believes that all human beings are extremely bad and because he unjustly hates most human beings, at least, for being what they cannot help being, namely, less than extremely good.

Socrates stresses to Phaedo and to his other companions here that it is only by acquiring knowledge of that which is human and by acquiring it through our senses that we can avoid the ignoble hatred of that which is human. And Phaedo's responses here indicate that this is a point worth stressing. For when Socrates states that a man who possessed the art concerning human things would believe that few human beings are extremely good or bad, Phaedo is perplexed and, it seems, taken aback (89e7–90a3). And even after Socrates has argued for the truth of this statement, Phaedo gives only a qualified assent (90b1-4).[8] Phaedo, then, is evidently inclined or tempted to share the misanthrope's belief that what is human is evil. Indeed, as we have suggested, insofar as they identify what is human with what is corporeal and evil, identify their true selves with their divine souls, and long to dwell with the gods after death, Socrates' companions as a whole resemble the misanthrope. Accordingly, by drawing their attention here to the misanthrope's ignoble ignorance of the human things, Socrates quietly draws their attention to their own ignorance.

At the same time, though, Socrates does not explicitly challenge here his companions' longing to find a perfectly good companion in the afterlife or in this life as well, even though this longing bears within it the seeds of misanthropy. For, according to his explicit criticism of the misanthrope, had he possessed the art concerning human things, he would have recognized that, since only a few human beings are extremely truthful, sound, and trustworthy or the opposite, his disappointment with most human beings, at least, was to be expected and, moreover, that his belief that all human beings deserve to be hated because they are altogether unsound is unreasonable. In this way, Socrates seems to criticize the misanthrope, not for hoping to find the companion that he seeks, but rather for failing to see that there is nothing rarer than an extremely good companion.

Yet, according to Socrates' own account of the misanthrope (89d3-e3), that man longs not merely for an "extremely" (*sphodra*) good companion but rather for an "altogether" (*pantapasin*) or perfectly good companion (compare 89e7-90b2 with 89d4-8). And while Socrates' claim that there is "nothing rarer" than an extremely good human being, dog, or "any other thing" leaves open the possibility that there is such an extremely good human being, it would seem to rule out the possibility that there is a perfectly good human being (see 89e7-90b2). It seems, then, that the art concerning human things which Socrates speaks of here entails not only the recognition that few human beings are extremely good but also the recognition that no human being is perfectly good, perfectly wise, or perfect in any way. Accordingly, Socrates' more precise criticism of the misanthrope would seem to be that, because of his ignorance of that which is human, he fails to see that his hope to find even a single human being who is altogether good and wise is unreasonable.

But furthermore, and more simply, Socrates criticizes the misanthrope here for his failure to recognize that he does not possess the art concerning human things, that he is ignorant about the human things, and that he needs to learn about them. And the reason that the misanthrope fails to recognize these things is not merely that he is blinded by his hatred for human beings but that he fails or refuses to see that he is a human being, that he is "altogether" human, and hence that he needs to learn about the human things. It is, then, his longing to believe that his truest self is higher than what is human, and hence his longing for immortality, that leads him both to hate and to ignore or misunderstand what is human. By criticizing the misanthrope for his ignorance of the art concerning human things, then, Socrates criticizes him for his refusal to recognize and to accept his humanity and hence his mortality (see 64a4-6).

Nevertheless, Socrates does not explicitly state this criticism of the misanthrope here. Nor does he explicitly criticize the misanthrope's longing for a perfectly good companion. Instead, he confines himself to criticizing that man's belief that all human beings are altogether bad and the ignorance on which that belief is based. And he thereby leaves the impression that the misanthrope's longing for a perfectly good companion is not altogether unreasonable. In this way, while he draws his companions' attention to the ignorance of the misanthrope and therewith, albeit indirectly, to their own ignorance, he still allows them to cherish the hope of finding a perfectly wise and good companion. For, given the depth of their hope for everlasting happiness in the company of the gods, were Socrates to argue directly against this hope, he would only deepen their distrust of arguments and might even provoke them to distrust himself.

After discussing the genesis of misanthropy, Socrates turns to explain to his companions how someone becomes a misologist and hence how they may avoid becoming misologists. According to him, the man who becomes a misologist begins by trusting, though not in an extreme way (compare 90b6-7 with 89d5), that a certain argument is true, but without the art concerning arguments. Then, a little later, this argument seems to him to be false, sometimes being false but sometimes not. And when he has had this experience a number of times and especially when he has been exposed to arguments that contradict one another, he ends up supposing that he is most wise and that he alone understands that there is nothing at all sound or stable in things or in arguments but that all the beings are simply in flux and do not remain in the same place for any time at all. Socrates then goes on to suggest to his companions that misology would be a pitiable experience, if there were, in fact, a true, stable, and intelligible argument. For if there were such an argument and if, because he has encountered certain arguments which seem to be true at one time but not at another, someone were not to blame himself or his own artlessness but were to end up, because of his pain, gladly thrusting responsibility away from himself and onto the arguments and were to live out the rest of his life hating and reviling the arguments, then he would be deprived of the truth and knowledge of the beings (90b4–d7).

Socrates' description of the misologist clearly resembles Phaedo's description of Socrates' companions at this point in the conversation. Like them, the misologist first believes that a certain argument is true but then, after hearing an opposing argument, rejects it as false (compare 90b6–c1 with 88c2–5). And like them, the misologist is led by this experience to believe that there is no truth that we can know through argument or reason and even that there is nothing true and stable at all (compare 90b9–c6 with 88c5–7). It would seem, then, that, even though Phaedo does not say that he and his companions had come to hate arguments or reason at this point in the conversation, Socrates believes that they are in danger of succumbing to such hatred. And it would also seem that, by giving this account of misology, he means to show his companions how they may overcome the temptation not only to distrust reason but to hate it.

Now, Socrates seems to emphasize to Phaedo that the misologist's primary failing is his failure to persevere in his search for a true argument. For, while he says to Phaedo that the misanthrope's longing to find a perfectly true or wise companion is at least somewhat unreasonable and hence that his hatred of all human beings is ignoble, he emphasizes to Phaedo the possibility, at least, that the misologist's longing to find a true argument is not at all unreasonable and hence the possibility that his hatred of arguments is pitiable (compare 89e5–7 with 90c8–d7). More precisely, he emphasizes to Phaedo and to his other companions as well the possibility that there may be an argument which is true, stable, and intelligible and hence the possibility that, by embracing the conclusion that there is no truth in the arguments, the misologist needlessly and foolishly deprives himself of the very knowledge or wisdom which he longs to possess. Socrates seems to suggest, then, that, if only the misologist had persevered in his search for a true argument, if only he had not been so very unmanly or soft, he might have been able to satisfy his desire to know the truth about the beings. And he thereby seems to suggest to his companions that, in order to overcome the temptation of hating arguments as a whole and the argument for mortality in particular, they should manfully and zealously persevere in their search for a true, stable, and intelligible argument and, specifically, for a true argument for immortality (compare 90c8–e3 with 85c1–d7).

It is important to note, however, that Socrates does not affirm here that there actually is such an argument. He only says that, "if" there were such an argument, if, that is, there were an argument that reveals "the truth" about "the beings," misology would be a pitiable experience. Socrates' criticism of the misologist for giving up on the search for such an argument is, then, a hypothetical criticism.[9] Yet, since Socrates has stated unequivocally that misology is an evil second to none, we must assume that, in his view, misology is evil even if there is no argument that reveals the truth about the beings. But what, then, exactly is Socrates' criticism of misology?

In his account of misology, Socrates says that the man who becomes a misologist begins by trusting that an argument is true without the art concerning arguments. And since Socrates says unequivocally that the misologist lacks this art, we may surmise that his principal criticism of that man is that he is somehow ignorant about the nature of arguments. It seems, then, that just as the misanthrope ends up hating human beings because he initially trusted them without the art concerning human things, so does the misologist end up hating arguments because he initially trusted them without the art concerning arguments. And consequently, it would seem that, in order to fulfill their duty to resist misology, Socrates' companions must acquire or learn the art concerning arguments. Yet, amazingly, Socrates does not spell out what that crucial art is or entails. While he explains, at least somewhat, what the art concerning human things entails, he does not explain at all what the art concerning arguments entails (compare 89e5-90b2 with 90b7). And he thereby leaves us wondering what that art might be and how it might help us to fulfill the duty to resist misology.

In order to address these questions, let us examine Socrates' account of misology more carefully. That account suggests that the man who becomes a misologist seeks an argument that reveals "the truth" about "the beings" (see 90c8–d7). It would seem, then, that he seeks not merely a true argument but a true account or doctrine about all the beings and hence a doctrine that reveals the whole truth about things. And this man, to begin with, places his trust in an argument which claims to reveal the complete truth about the beings. He begins, then, by believing that he knows the complete truth and hence is completely wise. But then he comes to see that

that argument is not completely true and rejects it as false. And when he has placed his trust in other arguments that claim to reveal the complete truth, he has the same experience. Now, these experiences suggest that this man is ignorant not only about the truth of the beings but also about the nature of arguments. For inasmuch as the arguments he trusts in turn out to be false, inasmuch as his trust proves, time and time again, to have been unwarranted, it seems that his belief or hope that there can be an argument that reveals the complete truth about the beings is itself unreasonable. This man's artlessness concerning arguments seems to consist, then, in his belief that some human argument could be completely true and hence that a human being could be completely or perfectly wise. And consequently, it seems that the art concerning arguments entails the belief that no argument can be altogether or perfectly true and hence entails the distrust of those arguments or speeches which claim to reveal the complete truth about the beings (see, for example, 63b9–c4, 65b1-4, 76d7–e5). It seems that, like the art concerning human things, this art entails the belief that no human being can be perfectly wise and hence that our arguments or speeches inevitably reflect our imperfect nature (see 76b5-12). Accordingly, the man who approaches arguments in an artful way will hope to discover in them as much of the truth as is available to such imperfect beings as ourselves. Through examining arguments, he will hope to attain as much wisdom as is humanly possible. But he will not place his trust in those arguments which claim to reveal the complete truth about the whole, he will not hate them for failing to be as true as they claim to be, and he will not hate reason when it shows the inadequacies of such arguments.

The misologist, however, does not learn from his experiences the art concerning arguments. Indeed, in the aftermath of those experiences, he concludes not that he is ignorant about arguments or about the beings but rather that he is "most wise" and that he "alone" understands that there is nothing at all sound or true in arguments and that "all the beings" are in flux. He continues to believe, then, as he had at the beginning, that he is completely or perfectly wise. And so strong is his attachment to the belief that he is perfectly wise that he would sooner believe that there is nothing at all sound or true in arguments or in reason than believe that he cannot attain perfect wisdom.

In order to see why the misologist ends up denying that there is any truth in arguments, let us consider his longing for a completely true argument in the light of the dialogue as a whole. The clearest example in the *Phaedo* of an argument that claims to reveal the complete truth about the beings is the argument for immortality. All three of Socrates' arguments for immortality claim to reveal the truth not only about the soul but also about the beings as a whole. The first argument, for example, claims to reveal the truth about all beings that come into being and that have opposites (see 70d7–e6, 71a9–b2, 71e8-72d3). The second argument claims to reveal the truth about the things themselves or forms and also about perceptible things (74d9–e4, 75b4-8, c10–d5). And the third argument claims to reveal the truth about all things visible and invisible, changing and unchanging, mortal and immortal (see 78b4-80b6). Furthermore, the accounts of the afterlife in the *Phaedo* claim to reveal not only that our souls are immortal but also that there are gods who reward the good and punish the wicked in an afterlife, who consequently rule over human beings, and who also rule over the other beings as well (see 62b6–d6, especially d5-6, 63b5-7, 69c3–d2, 80e2-84b8). The dialogue suggests, then, that the argument for immortality is necessarily an argument about the whole, about all the beings, and hence that it necessarily claims to reveal the complete or perfect truth about the beings.[10] And it thereby suggests that the human longing for perfect wisdom necessarily entails the longing to escape from our imperfect, human selves and hence entails the longing for immortality (see 66d7-67b2, 68a7–b6, 80e2-81a10).

Let us assume, then, that the man who becomes a misologist begins by trusting in an argument for immortality and hence begins by believing in immortality. But then he comes to see that that argument is inadequate and rejects it as false. And when he has this experience a number of times, when his hopes to find a genuinely trustworthy argument for immortality are repeatedly raised and dashed, he ends up believing that there is nothing at all true in arguments, that there is no truth that we can know through reason, and even that there is no truth at all.

Yet, the inadequacies of the argument for immortality do not, in fact, show that arguments cannot provide us with at least some access to the truth. Cebes, for example, is led by the inadequacies of Socrates' arguments for immortality to consider the possibility that the argument for mortality may be true (see 86e6-88b8, especially 87b2-88a1). To be sure, the argument that Cebes presents is quite limited in its scope. It does not claim to reveal the whole truth about the beings. Indeed, inasmuch as that argument explicitly makes use of an image of the soul to explain the nature of the soul and thereby necessarily abstracts from certain aspects of the soul, it does not even claim to present the whole truth about the soul. Yet, it does plausibly claim to reveal the truth about one crucial aspect of the soul, namely, its mortality. In this way, the limited or imperfect scope of the argument reflects the mortal and imperfect nature of the soul that it describes. The example of his argument suggests, then, that the examination of the inadequate arguments for immortality can assist us in our search for the truth about the soul. And precisely insofar as Cebes' argument for mortality is limited in its claims, precisely insofar as it does not claim to present the complete and definitive truth about all the beings and even about the soul, it itself points to the need for a further investigation of the arguments in our search for wisdom.

In contrast with Cebes, however, the misologist responds to the inadequacies of the arguments for immortality by embracing the conclusion that he is most wise and that he alone understands that there is no truth that can be known through arguments or reason, that there is no truth at all, and that all the beings are in flux. And it seems that he is led to embrace this conclusion by his attachment to the belief in immortality. For, by claiming to know that there is no truth and hence that there are no true or false beliefs, he can cling to the belief in immortality as a belief which is true for him, which is a wholly personal truth, and which is no less true than any other belief. Furthermore, by claiming to know that "all the beings" are in flux, the misologist can claim, in some sense, that he is perfectly wise. He can cling to the belief that he is, in some sense, a perfect being. And he can thereby reassure himself that he is not, in truth, an imperfect, and hence a mortal, being. It appears, however, that the misologist never succeeds in freeing himself entirely from the fear that he is, in truth, a mortal being. For, according to Socrates, the misologist does not simply ignore or dismiss reason but rather spends his life reviling and hating it. And the fact that the misologist devotes his life to silencing, or trying to silence, the voice of reason suggests that he fears, throughout his life, the threat that reason poses to his belief in immortality.[11]

It seems, then, that what prevents the misologist from acquiring the art concerning arguments is not simply his hope for perfect wisdom but rather his hope for immortality.[12] He is led by that hope to deny that there is any truth that can be known through reason and to hate reason. And consequently, he is led by his longing for everlasting happiness after death to deny himself that portion of wisdom which truly is available to us in this life and hence to suffer, at least according to Socrates, an evil which is second to none.

Socrates' account of the genesis of misology suggests, then, that the roots of misology, like the roots of misanthropy, lie in the hope for immortality (see 89d3-4). And if this is true, then, in order to overcome the temptation of misology, one must first free oneself from that hope. Yet, as we have seen, Socrates concludes his account of misology by actually encouraging his companions in their hope for immortality. In the first place, he encourages them to persevere in the search for a true argument for immortality and hence to hope that they may find one. And by giving them an account of the duty of the philosopher which they can hope to fulfill, he also encourages them to believe that, if they fulfill it, they will deserve the reward of everlasting happiness. But, if misology is itself a consequence of the hope for immortality, is Socrates not deliberately exposing them to the temptation of misology by encouraging them in their hope?

It would indeed seem that, by encouraging his companions to seek for a true argument for immortality, Socrates is leading them into temptation. For insofar as his companions continue to seek for a true argument for immortality, they are bound to be disappointed in that search. And insofar as they remain attached to the belief in immortality, they are bound to feel tempted to hate reason for revealing the weakness of the case for immortality. Yet, precisely by emphasizing to them, in this most memorable conversation, that it is their duty to resist misology throughout their lives and to keep reason alive in their very selves, Socrates tries, at least, to forestall the possibility that they will be led by their hope for immortality to succumb to the temptation of misology. He tries, that is, to take away from them the excuse that misology seems to provide for refusing to face the weakness of the argument for immortality. And if they succeed in resisting the temptation to deny that there is any truth in arguments, they may, at least, come to appreciate the evident weakness of the argument for immortality and the evident strength of the argument for mortality. And they may thereby overcome their attachment to the belief in immortality. By both encouraging them to hope for a true argument for immortality and forbidding them to succumb to misology, then, Socrates tries to lead them to where they might see for themselves why there cannot be a true argument for immortality. And he thereby points them along the path to the true salvation from misology.

It is still true that, by providing his companions with an account of the duty of the philosopher which they can hope to fulfill, Socrates does encourage them to believe that they can deserve everlasting happiness. But, on the other hand, once he has given that account, Socrates immediately proceeds to suggest to them, albeit in a somewhat playful tone, that he himself does not actually take seriously the duty of the philosopher and hence that he does not actually believe that the philosopher who fulfills his duty will be rewarded after death. After exhorting his companions and himself to be courageous and zealous in their efforts to resist misology and to be philosophic, Socrates says that he fears that he himself is not being philosophic in this discussion of immortality but rather that, like those who are completely uneducated, he is in love with victory. For those people, he explains, do not care about the truth of their arguments but are instead eager to persuade their interlocutors that the argument they are making is true. And he goes on to say that he *will* differ from those *only* inasmuch as he will be eager to persuade himself rather than his companions that his argument, namely, the argument for immortality, is true (91d9-92b1).[13]

Socrates appears to confess to his companions here that he is not being genuinely philosophic in his discussion of the question of immortality—that is, that he does not genuinely care whether or not the argument for immortality is true—but that he cares only about indulging his own desire for immortality by persuading himself that this argument is true. And by speaking in the future tense, he appears to predict that he will fail in his efforts to be philosophic in the time that remains before his death. Socrates seems to anticipate here that he will succumb not precisely to a hatred of reason but rather to an indifference to reason and, consequently, that he will fail to fulfill his duty to be philosophic during his last few hours of life.

But then Socrates goes on to argue that it is *reasonable* for him not to be philosophic and not even to try to be philosophic under the present circumstances. He argues specifically that it is in his self-interest to disregard his duty to be philosophic. And he thereby reveals to his companions that, notwithstanding his repeated claims on this day that the philosopher who fulfills his duty may reasonably hope for everlasting rewards in Hades, he will not even try to fulfill his duty during the few hours before his death and that it is reasonable for him not to try.[14]

Socrates explains to Phaedo, whom he addresses here as his "dear friend," the reasoning behind his decision to be unphilosophic and urges him to observe how selfish it is. He says that, if the soul truly is immortal, it is a fine thing to be persuaded that this is so. But if it is not immortal and there is nothing for the man who has died, he will at least spare his companions the unpleasant experience of seeing him lament his fate during the time before his death. And furthermore, he adds, the foolish belief in immortality will not continue to exist with him—for that would be evil—but will perish a little later (91b1-7).

Now, it is true that Socrates here expresses the desire to spare his companions the pain of seeing him suffer and therefore does not appear to be simply selfish. But it is also true that he surely wishes to spare himself the pain of lamenting his fate during his final hours of life. Furthermore, Socrates is evidently willing to expose his companions as a whole and even his "dear friend" Phaedo to the lasting evil of holding a false belief about the fate of the soul. And although he goes on to urge Simmias and Cebes to resist him with every argument if they are not persuaded by what he is saying and to beware lest he deceive both himself and them, it is still true that, while his deliberately unphilosophic zeal to argue for the immortality of the soul is, by his own account, good for him, it is also, by his own account, potentially harmful to them. Socrates suggests here, then, both that it is reasonable to place one's self-interest above one's duty and that it is reasonable to place one's self-interest above the interests of one's friends.[15]

Socrates' claim here that he will argue for the immortality of the soul out of an unphilosophic selfishness is surely somewhat playful. At the very least, it is simply implausible that his discussion of the question of immortality up till now has been motivated solely by the "uneducated" desire to persuade himself that the soul is immortal. As we have seen, Socrates has throughout this discussion carefully and consistently pointed to the difficulties that bedevil and even undermine the arguments for immortality (see, for example, 80b8-10, 83a1–e3, 84c5-7, 86d5–e5; see also 107a8–b9). But, on the other hand, there is evidence in the dialogue to support Socrates' suggestion that he does not think it reasonable for him to be zealous in his efforts to be philosophic in the face of death and that he does not think it unreasonable for him, during the time before his death, to indulge at least somewhat his desire to believe that the soul is immortal. For he has been devoting his time in prison not to philosophizing but to composing music, something he never did before (60c8-61b1). Furthermore, when his wife, Xanthippe, who may be more sensitive to her husband's feelings on this day than his young companions are, laments the fact that this is the last time he will converse with his companions, Socrates has her removed from his cell and taken home, perhaps out of a desire not to be so directly reminded of this painful truth (60a3–b1; compare also 117c5–e2 with 116d2-7). Finally, by spending his last day discussing the immortality of the soul with his friends, Socrates may not only be rethinking the whole question of immortality but also may be indulging himself, at least somewhat, by telling tales about the afterlife not only to his friends but also to himself (see 61d10–e4, 70b5-7, 84d8-85b7, 108c3-115a3, especially 114d1-7, 115d2-6). In these ways, Socrates may have sought to charm and calm his own fear of death during the time before his death (see 88b3-8). Indeed, the philosopher's practice of dying and being dead may consist not only of learning how to accept the necessity of death but also of learning how and when to spare oneself the unnecessary pain of relentlessly thinking about one's own death.

Yet, while Socrates' statement here constitutes a plausible account of his own state of mind during this period before his death, it may also reflect his own efforts to help his companions to cure themselves of misology. For, by stating quite plainly that he will disregard his duty to be philosophic and that he believes that it is in his self-interest to do so, Socrates seems to suggest to his companions that, in his opinion, at least, no harm will come to him after death from his failure to do his duty and that no benefit would come to him after death should he fulfill his duty. He seems to suggest that he is calculating his self-interest solely in terms of this life. And he thereby seems to imply not only that he does not believe in an afterlife but also, and more specifically, that he does not believe that it is possible for a human being to deserve everlasting happiness. Indeed, unless Socrates were quite confident that there is no afterlife, his neglect of his duty here would be extremely foolish. For if he were not so confident, how could it be reasonable for him to run the terrible risk of forfeiting divine rewards and of incurring divine punishments after death by leaving his duty unfulfilled in this life? How could it be in his self-interest not even to try, on the day of his death, to fulfill his duty to philosophize? Indeed, how could it be reasonable for any human being to place his self-interest above his duty unless he were reasonably confident that there is no afterlife? Socrates' avowed intention to abandon all efforts to fulfill his duty and to do so for selfish reasons makes sense only if he is reasonably confident that the soul is mortal. By telling his companions, then, that he will disregard his duty to be philosophic during the final hours of his life and by telling them this in so playful a tone, Socrates gives them reason to wonder, at least, whether he seriously believes that the soul is immortal. And consequently, even though he does strengthen their belief in immortality by providing them with a fulfillable account of the duty of the philosopher, by suggesting that he does not take that duty seriously Socrates also invites them to question the reasonableness of that belief.

Throughout the rest of this conversation, Socrates will continue to support his companions' hope for immortality. He will do so most obviously by making yet another argument for the immortality of the soul. But, more importantly, he will also support their hope by leaving unchallenged his suggestion that, in order to fulfill his duty, the philosopher must keep reason alive, resist misology, and pursue the truth with courage and zeal. In other words, Socrates will never again present an unfulfillable account of the duty of the philosopher and hence will never again call into question whether the philosopher, or any human being, can deserve everlasting happiness. On the other hand, though, Socrates will also continue to point to reasons for questioning the reasonableness of their hope for immortality (see, for example, 107a8–b9). He will, to borrow his simile, leave in his companions a sting of doubt before he departs (91b8–c5). While Socrates, then, will shore up his companions' resistance to misology by strengthening their hope for immortality, he will also point them along the path of true salvation from misology by giving them reason to wonder about that hope.

Chapter 10

Socrates' Response to Simmias' Argument
Against Immortality

Before responding directly to the arguments of Simmias and Cebes against the immortality of the soul, Socrates has presented his companions with a new account of the duty of the philosopher and has exhorted them to be zealous in their efforts to pursue the truth, to keep reason alive, and to resist the temptation to hate reason (see 89b9–d3, 90d9–e3). But he has also told them that, in the ensuing discussion, he himself will not be zealous in the pursuit of the truth but will rather be eager to persuade himself that the soul is immortal (see 91a1–b7). He has suggested, then, that if his companions are to fulfill their duty to pursue the truth, they cannot simply rely on his opinions and on his guidance as they have in the past but must regard what he will say with considerable caution and even with skepticism (see 69e6-7, 70b8-9, 76b8-12, 78a1-9, 89c5-11). Accordingly, Socrates now explains to Simmias and Cebes in particular that, in the discussion that follows, they must care little for him and much more for the truth. If what he says does not seem to be true, they must resist him with every argument. And they must especially be on guard lest he be led by his eagerness to persuade himself of the soul's immortality to deceive them and also himself into embracing what might be a false belief about the fate of the soul (91b3–c5). We see, then, that Socrates prepares Simmias and Cebes for his final discussion about the soul by urging them to beware of and even to resist his argument for immortality. And we also see that he prepares his young friends for his imminent death by emphasizing to them that even now they cannot look to him for guidance, that their pursuit of wisdom must be an independent pursuit, and that their primary concern must be, now and always, not for him but for the truth.

Socrates now turns to address directly the arguments of Simmias and Cebes. Simmias, he says, seems to him to be distrustful and afraid lest the soul be a kind of attunement and lest it perish before the body does, even though it is more divine and noble than the body is. Socrates suggests here that Simmias is not truly opposed to the argument for immortality, that he would like to see it vindicated, but that he fears that the soul might be a kind of attunement and hence might be mortal (see 91c7–d2, 86d1-4; but see also b5–d1). On the other hand, he suggests that Cebes is altogether unpersuaded by the argument for immortality because, even though the soul is more long-lasting than the body is, it may still perish in death after it has worn out many bodies but before the last one has perished (91d2-7).

Socrates now asks the two whether they accept the earlier argument that learning is recollection and that, this being so, our souls necessarily existed before they were imprisoned in the body. When they both say that they do accept this argument, Socrates says to Simmias that it is necessary for him to reject it if he is to continue to think that an attunement is a composite thing and that the soul is a certain attunement of bodily elements. For, he explains, Simmias cannot maintain both that the soul is an attunement of bodily elements and that it existed before those elements out of which it is constituted existed (91e2–92c7). Socrates argues here, then, that Simmias cannot, without contradicting himself, believe both that the soul is a composite of bodily elements and hence cannot exist apart from the body and also that it existed, apart from the body, before we were born. It is important to note, however, that Socrates does not present any reasons here for believing either that the attunement argument is false or that the preexistence argument is true.

Yet, when Socrates asks Simmias which of the two he chooses, he not only chooses the argument for the preexistence of the soul but emphatically denounces the argument that the soul is an attunement. He says that the argument is not a demonstration, that it is boastful, and that it is deceptive. On the other hand, the argument for preexistence, he says, is based on the "worthy hypothesis" that there are perfectly intelligible beings—the things themselves or forms—that exist apart from the sensible world and that our souls knew when they existed apart from our bodies. And since Simmias, as he persuades himself, has rightly accepted that hypothesis, it is, he says, probably necessary for him not to allow himself or anyone else to say that the soul is an attunement (92c7–e3; compare c11–d5 with 90c8–d5).

Now, it seems strange that Simmias should abandon so easily an argument which, only a short while before, he had set forth so forcefully. After all, that argument seems to be a persuasive one, as Socrates has seemed to acknowledge, as Echecrates has acknowledged, and as Cebes will go on to acknowledge (86d6–e4, 88d3-6, 95a7–b3; see also 88c1-7). Furthermore, Simmias does not explain here why he now thinks that the attunement argument is deceptive and hence false. And while he claims that the preexistence argument is based on a worthy hypothesis, he does not explain why that hypothesis is worthy and he does not even claim that it is actually true. Why, then, does Simmias abandon the attunement argument so speedily?

Inasmuch as Simmias does not offer a clear explanation of his easy abandonment of the attunement argument, his abandonment seems to reflect not a reevaluation on his part of the merits of that argument but rather a renewed confidence on his part that the soul is immortal. For he had presented the argument that the soul is an attunement of bodily elements and is therefore necessarily mortal in response to Socrates' most clearly unfulfillable account of the duty the philosopher must fulfill in order to deserve everlasting happiness. That account, then, seems to have shaken Simmias' confidence that everlasting happiness can be deserved and therewith his confidence that the soul is immortal (compare 63c4–d2, 64c2-9 with 83a1–e3, 85e3-86d4). It seems to have inspired in him that fear that the soul is mortal which, according to Socrates, lies behind Simmias' attunement argument (91c7–d2). Now, however, Socrates has reinterpreted for his companions the duty of the philosopher and has thereby restored Simmias' confidence that he can fulfill that duty and thereby render himself worthy of rewards from the gods after death. And since the argument that the soul is an attunement of bodily elements would seem to rule out all hope for immortality, while the argument that the soul exists before it enters the body is at least compatible with that hope, Simmias eagerly chooses the pre-existence argument over the attunement argument.

But Simmias' abandonment of the attunement argument also seems to reflect his tendency to give up too easily in his examination of arguments (see 85b1–d4; compare with 63a1-2). For notwithstanding his suggestion that the attunement argument is deceptive and hence false, he clearly cannot know, even before it has been discussed or examined, that it is, in fact, false. And, if he were truly eager to know whether or not this argument for the mortality of the soul is false, he would surely press Socrates to address it. As we have seen, however, Simmias is doubtful that he can learn the truth about the fate of the soul from any human argument but rather seems to hope to learn the truth from a divine argument or revelation (see 85b10–d4, 107a8–b3). And consequently, the moment that the attunement argument seems at all doubtful to him, he simply rejects it as false (see 90b4-9).

Now, even though Socrates has, so to speak, vanquished in battle Simmias' argument that the soul is "necessarily" mortal, he has not yet resurrected the argument for immortality (see 89b8–c4, 95a9–b3). Indeed, he has not even addressed what had seemed to be Simmias' specific objection to the argument for immortality, namely, that the fact that the soul is more invisible than the body is does not, by itself, prove that the soul necessarily continues to exist after death (compare 85e3-86b5 with 80c2–e2). By inducing Simmias to abandon the argument for mortality, Socrates has at most reopened the question of the immortality of the soul. Accordingly, we would expect him to attempt, at least, to answer that question by attempting to prove, once again, that the soul is immortal.

Socrates, however, does not, at this point, attempt to argue for the immortality of the soul. Nor does he address, here or elsewhere in the dialogue, Simmias' specific objection to the argument for immortality.[1] Instead, he returns to the now forsaken argument that the soul is an attunement and proceeds to examine it with considerable care. In this way, Socrates encourages Simmias, and his other companions as well, to think more seriously about the attunement argument, and therewith about the argument for the mortality of the soul, rather than simply reject it on the grounds that it is contradicted by the argument for preexistence.[2] And he also encourages Simmias in particular to be more persistent in his pursuit of the truth in arguments.

In what follows, Socrates argues against the hypothesis that the soul is an attunement or a composite being on the grounds that this hypothesis cannot explain either the common sense distinction between good and bad souls or the apparent capacity of the soul to rule over the body (see 93b8-94b3, 94b4–d7). He seems to urge Simmias to reject that argument not merely because it is contradicted by the admittedly hypothetical doctrine of the preexistence of the soul but also because it is contradicted by common sense and by his own perception of the workings of the soul. Socrates seems, then, to encourage Simmias to rely on his own common sense and his own perceptions of things rather than simply rely on doctrines he has accepted from others in his appraisal of the argument for mortality. Yet, while Socrates appears to refute the claim that the soul is an attunement and thereby appears to strengthen the case for immortality (see 78c1–5), he also indicates that it might be possible to defend that claim against the very objections he raises. He indicates, that is, that it might be possible both to maintain that the soul is a composite being and to account for the distinction between good and bad souls and the soul's rule over the body (see especially 93c3-8). In this way, Socrates suggests, albeit quietly, that the attunement argument may not be deceptive but may rather point toward a true account of the nature of the soul.

Socrates begins by asking Simmias to explain more precisely what his understanding is of the argument that the soul is an attunement of bodily elements.[3] Specifically, he asks Simmias whether, in his opinion, it is fitting for an attunement or any other composite to possess any characteristics other than those which its elements possess (92e4-93a2). Socrates asks him, then, whether, in his opinion, the soul can be a composite of bodily elements and also possess characteristics which are not bodily or whether, if the soul is such a composite, it must simply be corporeal. Now, by asking this question, Socrates asks Simmias to clarify a certain ambiguity in his earlier speech about the soul. In that speech, Simmias had first suggested that, while the soul cannot exist unless the body is properly attuned or ordered, it does possess certain characteristics which the body does not and cannot possess. Specifically, he had said that the soul is invisible and incorporeal (see 85e3-86b5). Simmias had suggested, then, that, even though the soul is inseparable from the body, it is also distinct from the body. For even though it is, in a certain sense, an attunement or composite of bodily elements, it is not simply reducible to those elements but possesses certain characteristics that its bodily elements do not possess and hence that are "psychic" rather than "somatic." And this suggestion seems plausible. For there are a number of examples of composite beings which possess characteristics other than those possessed by their elements. To cite an example which Socrates discusses later, the number two is even, while its elements—the numbers one and one—when taken separately, are not (see 96e6-97b3). Similarly, we might add, water is wet while hydrogen and oxygen are not, and green is green while blue and yellow are not. It would seem, then, plausible to suggest that, while the soul cannot exist unless the body is properly attuned, once the soul comes into being, it comes into its own and possesses certain characteristics which the body does not and cannot possess.

Simmias, however, went on to speak of the soul which is an attunement of bodily elements as though it were simply corporeal (see 86b5–d1). And now, in response to Socrates' question, he says that, in his opinion, it is "in no way" fitting for an attunement or any other composite to possess any characteristics other than those which its elements possess. By saying this, he reveals that, in his opinion, the characteristics a thing possesses are determined by its material elements. Indeed, he suggests that the necessary and sufficient cause of what a thing is is to be found in its elements (see 92e4-93a3; see also 96a6ff.). And he thereby reveals that, in his view, if the soul is an attunement of bodily elements, it must simply be corporeal.[4]

In response to a series of questions from Socrates, Simmias spells out the implications of his materialistic understanding of the attunement argument. He says that, since an attunement or composite being cannot possess any characteristics other than those which its elements possess, it cannot do or experience anything beyond what its elements do or experience, it also cannot lead but must follow its elements, and consequently it cannot be opposed in any way to its own parts. He also says that, if the soul is an attunement, one soul cannot, even in the least degree, be more or less of a soul than another soul (93a4–b7). For if, he seems to imply, the soul is simply that attunement or arrangement of bodily elements which they must possess in order to be alive or animate, then, insofar as all souls that exist exist, they must all be equal to one another.

Socrates now proceeds to suggest an alternative interpretation of the attunement argument. He first reminds Simmias that it is said, and said truly, that the good soul possesses intelligence and virtue and that the bad one possesses folly and vice (93b8–c2). At this point, we might expect Socrates to argue that since, according to Simmias' interpretation of the attunement argument, all souls are equal, and since it is truly said, as Simmias agrees, that souls are not equal with respect to intelligence and virtue, the attunement argument must be false. Instead, however, Socrates asks how "those who maintain that the soul is an attunement" will account for the distinction between virtuous and vicious souls. He suggests that they will say that virtue is also an attunement and that vice is a lack of attunement. He also suggests that they will say that, consequently, the good soul is attuned and hence possesses in itself, that is, in its attunement of bodily elements, another attunement, presumably of other, noncorporeal, elements, and that the unattuned or bad soul does not possess in itself another attunement (93c3-8).[5] Socrates, then, presents here, albeit somewhat tersely, a version of the attunement argument that seems to account for the distinction between good and bad souls and that differs from Simmias' version of that argument by suggesting that the soul is not simply corporeal.[6]

According to this version of the attunement argument, since the soul cannot exist unless the body is attuned, it is an attunement of bodily elements. But once the soul comes into being, it possesses characteristics or elements, such as intelligence, which are psychic rather than somatic. And it seems that, when these psychic elements are attuned or properly ordered, when, that is, intelligence rules over the other elements or parts of the soul, it possesses virtue and is good. But when the psychic elements are out of tune, when intelligence is missing or is ruled by the other parts of the soul, the soul is vicious and bad. And since this version of the attunement argument, in contrast with Simmias' materialistic version, can take into account the existence of virtue and vice and can distinguish between good and bad souls, it would seem to be a more plausible and hence a superior version of that argument.

Now, insofar as this account of the soul maintains that the soul possesses characteristics which are distinctively psychic, it differs from Simmias' view that, if the soul is an attunement, it must be altogether corporeal. But this account also differs from the account of the soul which Socrates has presented in the conversation up until now. For up until now Socrates has seemed to identify the soul simply with intelligence (see especially 65e6-66a8, 67b7–d2). He has suggested that, insofar as the soul possesses elements other than intelligence, such as passions, it has been corrupted by the body. Accordingly, he has suggested that the soul is virtuous only insofar as it has purified itself of the body and its passions (see, for example, 66c2-67b2, 69a6–c3, 80e2-81a9). But according to the version of the attunement argument which Socrates sketches here, the soul naturally possesses elements or parts other than intelligence, the soul is a composite of psychic elements, and consequently the soul is virtuous only when its elements are attuned or properly ordered and hence when intelligence rules over its other parts. It is important to note, however, that, while this account does suggest that the soul is higher and hence more divine than a simply corporeal being and consequently does differ from Simmias' account of the soul (see 94e2–6), it does seem to agree with that account in one crucial respect. For insofar as, according to this account, the soul is a composite being, it must, it seems, be a mortal being as well (see 92a7-8, 78c1-4).[7]

Having sketched a version of the attunement argument which might distinguish between good and bad souls, Socrates asks Simmias whether those who maintain that the soul is an attunement will make such an argument. In this way, he seems to invite Simmias to consider further this nonmaterialistic and seemingly superior version of the attunement argument. Simmias, however, does not seem to be interested in the possibility that the attunement argument which he has now abandoned might be defensible or even true. He only says that those who maintain that the soul is an attunement will make some such argument (93c9-10). Accordingly, Socrates now proceeds to show Simmias that his materialistic version of that argument cannot make any distinction at all between good and bad souls.

Socrates points out that, if, as Simmias has agreed, the soul is simply that attunement or arrangement which bodily elements must have in order to be alive or animate, then no soul can be more or less of a soul or be more or less attuned than any other soul. For either the bodily elements are attuned and the soul exists, or they are not attuned and it does not exist. Accordingly, Socrates suggests, the soul cannot exist and be out of tune at all. And consequently, if the argument is correct, all souls that exist must be perfectly and equally attuned and, if virtue is an attunement, the souls not only of human beings but of all living things must be equally good (93d1-94a11). In other words, if the soul is simply that characteristic of bodies by virtue of which bodies are alive or animate, then it is impossible to distinguish between good and bad souls, intelligent and foolish souls, and even human and nonhuman souls. Now, an account of the soul which cannot make such fundamental distinctions is evidently flawed. Yet it is only Simmias' materialistic interpretation of the attunement argument that leads to the absurd conclusion that all souls are equally good. For if, as Socrates has suggested, the soul has a noncorporeal dimension, if it contains elements which are psychic rather than somatic—such as intelligence and passions—then it would be possible to maintain that, insofar as all souls that exist have properly attuned bodily elements, they are equal but that, insofar as only some have their psychic elements properly attuned or ordered, insofar, that is, as only some souls are ruled by intelligence, they are unequal. Socrates' argument here, then, does not constitute a refutation of the attunement hypothesis as such but only of Simmias' materialistic interpretation of it. Nevertheless, when Socrates asks him whether, in his opinion, the argument would suffer these things if the hypothesis that the soul is an attunement were correct, Simmias says that it would in no way suffer these things and thereby suggests that the hypothesis itself is not correct. It seems, then, that, rather than follow Socrates' lead and attempt to refine the attunement hypothesis, Simmias continues to reject that hypothesis as simply false.

Socrates now examines whether the attunement hypothesis can account for the soul's capacity to rule over the body. He first suggests to Simmias that, of all the elements in a human being, it is possible only for the soul, and especially the wise soul, to rule. He then suggests that the soul does not agree with "the passions of the body," such as the desire for drink or food, but rather opposes them and "drags" the body away from following them. And once Simmias has agreed to these suggestions, Socrates reminds him of his opinion that, if the soul is an attunement and hence a composite of bodily elements, it cannot oppose the body or lead it but must rather follow it (94b4–c8). In this way, Socrates emphasizes to Simmias that, at least according to his interpretation of the attunement hypothesis, it is impossible to account for the soul's capacity to oppose and to rule the body.

Socrates here appears not only to argue against the view that the soul is an attunement or a composite of bodily elements but also to reaffirm the view which he has expressed earlier that the soul is identical to intelligence, that the body is the seat of the passions, and that the soul naturally rules the body (compare 94b4–c2 with 65b9-66d7, 79e8-80b6, 80e2-81a10). He seems to reaffirm the view, then, that the soul is a noncomposite being and hence is immortal (see 78c1-4). Yet, upon closer examination, Socrates' account of the soul here actually seems to depart from the view that it is a noncomposite being. In the first place, by distinguishing the soul as such from the wise soul, he implies that wisdom or intelligence is only a part of the soul. For since the wise soul is presumably ruled by intelligence, the unwise soul must be ruled by some other part of the soul. Furthermore, even though Socrates does say here that the passions, such as the desire for food or drink, are elements or parts of the body, he seems to imply that the passions may actually be parts of the soul. For since, as he suggests, the soul always rules the body and since all souls are not wise, the unwise soul must itself be ruled by the passions. For example, while the wise soul may oppose the desire for drink, the unwise soul presumably would not. But then the unwise soul would itself be ruled by the desire for drink. And consequently, that desire, and the other passions as well, must be lodged not in the body but in the soul. Finally, Socrates' example of the wise soul opposing the body's desire for drink implies that the wise soul will care for the body and hence that it will recognize its dependence on the body's well-being. For the wise soul presumably opposes the desire for drink when that desire would do harm to the body. And it presumably is concerned about the body's well-being because it itself would suffer or perish if the body were to suffer or perish. Socrates' account of the soul here implies, then, that the soul is indeed a composite being, that it is composed of intelligence, on the one hand, and of the passions on the other, and that it is also dependent on the body for its well-being and indeed for its being as well. And in this way his account implies that, on the one hand, the soul cannot exist unless the body is properly attuned, and, on the other hand, that the soul possesses virtue only when its passions are properly ordered and hence when intelligence rules the passions.

Socrates goes on to give a somewhat more detailed account of the soul's rule over the body. He suggests that the soul leads all those things that are said to be its elements, that it opposes almost all of them throughout life, and that it masters them in every way. The soul, he explains, is harsh with some of its supposed elements and punishes them by inflicting pain in accordance with the medical and gymnastic arts. But with others, he continues, it is gentle, threatening, admonishing, and conversing with the desires, angers, and fears (94c9–d6). Now, Socrates appears here to be continuing his argument against the claim that the soul is a composite being. But he actually indicates here that the soul may, in fact, be a composite being. To begin with, even though he does not say so, the soul Socrates describes here is clearly the wise soul, that is, the soul ruled by intelligence. For it is only such a soul that would know how to rule the body in accordance with the medical and gymnastic arts and that would know how to persuade the passions. But furthermore, and more importantly, Socrates here seems to draw a sharp distinction between the body and the passions and to suggest that the passions are elements or parts of the soul rather than of the body. For he suggests that, while the wise soul rules the body in accordance with arts that deal with the body, namely, medicine and gymnastics, and that it rules the body by using physical force, namely, punishments that are physically painful, it rules the passions through speech, that is, through threats, criticisms, and persuasion. The wise soul, then, does not rule the passions in accordance with the arts that deal with the body and it does not use physical force against them. And it does not do so, it seems, because the passions are not themselves parts of the body but rather parts of the soul itself. It seems, then, that what rules the passions must be not the soul as such but rather a part of the soul, namely, intelligence or reason.[8]

Socrates concludes his discussion of the attunement hypothesis by citing as an example of the soul's rule of the passions the lines in the *Odyssey* in which Homer says that Odysseus beat his breast and told his heart to endure, since it had endured an even greater outrage once before. He then asks Simmias whether he supposes that Homer would have composed those lines if he had thought that the soul is an attunement and that it is something which is led by the passions of the body rather than thinking that the soul leads those passions, masters them, and is a much more divine thing than an attunement. Socrates asks Simmias, then, whether it is possible to maintain that the soul is an attunement or a composite thing and to account for Odysseus' mastery of his anger and, more generally, for the soul's rule over the passions. And Simmias suggests that, in his view, it is not possible. For he says emphatically that, in his opinion, Homer would not have composed those lines about Odysseus' rule over his bodily passions if he had thought that the soul is an attunement. And consequently, he agrees with Socrates' suggestion that they should therefore not say that the soul is an attunement, for, as is likely, they would agree neither with the divine poet Homer nor with themselves (94d6–95a3).

Yet if we examine Homer's lines,[9] we find that he may well have thought that the soul is, if not an attunement, at least a composite thing. (Indeed, in the *Republic*, Socrates cites these very lines as evidence that the soul is composed of three parts: reason, desire, and anger or spiritedness— see 441b3–c8; but see also 611a10–d8).[10] To be sure, the fact that Odysseus strikes his breast and addresses his "heart" does suggest that he believes that his passions, and specifically his anger, are lodged in his body. Yet, the fact that he speaks to and argues with his anger rather than simply using force against it suggests that his anger is actually a part not of his body but of his soul. It seems, then, that his reason is struggling with his anger over which will rule in his soul and hence which will determine his course of action. And it would also seem that Odysseus' anger is no more lodged in his breast than his reason is lodged in the hand with which he strikes his breast.

We see, then, that while Socrates does argue here against the hypothesis that the soul is an attunement of bodily elements, he also suggests that that hypothesis might, upon further examination, prove to be true. Specifically, he suggests that, if the soul may be composed of but not reducible to its bodily elements, then it might be possible to defend the attunement hypothesis against the objections that it cannot account either for the soul's capacity to rule the body or for the distinction between good and bad souls. For, if the soul is not simply bodily but rather has a nature of its own, then it might have a life and a will of its own and hence might have the capacity to oppose the body. And if the soul contains elements or parts that are psychic rather than somatic, such as intelligence and the passions, then it might be possible to account for virtue as the attunement or proper ordering of the parts of the soul and hence as the rule within the soul of reason. Now, in this discussion, Socrates does no more than hint at this line of investigation and give Simmias the opportunity to question him about it. But when Simmias fails to seize this opportunity, when, that is, he fails repeatedly to reconsider his opinion that, if the soul is a composite of bodily elements, it must be itself simply bodily, Socrates allows and even encourages him simply to reject the hypothesis that the soul is a composite and therefore a mortal being. Yet, in the ensuing discussion, Socrates does not simply drop the question of whether the soul might be a composite of bodily elements even if it is not simply corporeal. For, in his response to Cebes' argument against immortality, Socrates addresses and argues against the general opinion that a (composite) thing may be understood simply and fully in terms of its material elements. In this way, he goes on to challenge the basis of Simmias' materialistic interpretation of the attunement hypothesis: namely, his belief that something that is composed of material elements is simply reducible to those elements (compare 86b5–c1, 92e4-93a3 with 96a6-97b7, 98b7-99b4). And he may thereby give his companions reason to wonder, as they think back on this conversation, whether the soul might not be something more divine than a merely corporeal being and still be a composite of bodily elements (see 58d5-6, 88c2, 116a4-5).

Chapter 11

Socrates' Response to Cebes' Argument Against Immortality

I. Socrates' Account of His Experiences

As we have seen, Socrates' efforts to prove the immortality of the soul in the *Phaedo* grow out of his attempt to persuade his companions, on the day of his death, that, notwithstanding their doubts, the philosophic life remains the best way of life for a human being. Socrates says, near the beginning of this conversation, that he will attempt to persuade them that the man who has led the philosophic life may be reasonably confident that he will be rewarded with wisdom and everlasting happiness once he is dead (63b4–c7, 63e8-64a3; see also 66d7-67b2, 67e6-68b4, 69c3–d6, 70b1-4, 72d9–e2, 80e2-81a11, 82b10–c1). And, later on, when pressed by Cebes to reassure them that the soul of a dead human being continues to exist and possesses wisdom, Socrates offers a number of arguments for the immortality of the soul (69e6-70b4). Now, Socrates' response to Cebes' argument against the immortality of the soul would seem to be the culmination, and indeed the successful culmination, of his efforts to prove the immortality of the soul and thereby vindicate the philosophic life. For in his response, Socrates presents his final argument for the immortality of the soul. And Cebes, who is said by Simmias to be the mightiest of human beings in distrusting the arguments and who has directly or indirectly challenged each of Socrates' previous arguments for immortality, says that he, at least, is unable to distrust this final argument (see 77a8-9; compare 107a2-7 with 69e7-70b4, 72e3-73a3, 77c1-5, 86e6-88b8; see also 62e8-63a3). Socrates' efforts to persuade his companions that the soul is immortal and hence that the philosophic life is the good life appear, then, to be successful (see 58a3-59a1, 118a15-17; but see 107a8–b3).

Yet Socrates' final argument for immortality is clearly inadequate. In the first place, it ends not with a demonstration but with an assertion that the soul never perishes (see 106c9-d4).[1] Moreover, Socrates does not even claim, in the course of making this argument, that the individual soul—that is, that his soul or Cebes' soul or any human soul—is imperishable and immortal. He concludes the argument by affirming only that "The god himself, the form itself of life, and anything else that may be immortal" will never perish (106d5-7; see also e1-7; but see 106e9-107a1).[2] Finally, he does not claim that this argument shows that the philosopher's soul, in particular, will be rewarded in an afterlife. The final argument for immortality, then, clearly does not show either that our individual souls will never perish or that the philosopher will attain wisdom and happiness after death and hence does not show what Socrates seems to have promised he would show or what Cebes has urged him to show (see 63b4–c7, 63e8-64a2, 70b1-4, 77c1-5, 95b7–e6). Yet Cebes, in particular, appears to be largely persuaded by this argument. In order to understand why, we must consider as a whole Socrates' response to Cebes' objection to the argument for immortality.

After Socrates has persuaded Simmias to abandon his argument against the immortality of the soul, Cebes predicts that he will be persuaded to abandon his argument against immortality as well. He explains that, since Simmias' argument did not withstand Socrates' first attack, he will not be surprised if his argument is also defeated (95a7–b4). Yet Cebes' confidence that his argument will suffer the same fate as Simmias' is itself surprising. For Cebes had already explicitly rejected Simmias' argument that the soul is an attunement even before Socrates "attacked" it (see 87a1-7). Furthermore, in contrast with Simmias, Cebes had identified himself almost unequivocally with the argument against immortality (compare 86d1-4 with 87d3-7, 88b3-8). He had seemed to suggest that the soul is necessarily mortal and even that the very hope for immortality is foolish. Why, then, does he now expect to abandon his argument against immortality?

Cebes' words here suggest that, since he set forth his argument against immortality, he has become predisposed, even before hearing Socrates' specific response, to abandon that argument and to embrace the hope for immortality. This suggestion is strengthened by the fact that Cebes accepts wholeheartedly Socrates' account of his objection to the argument for immortality. For even though Socrates claims that he is simply summarizing Cebes' earlier speech about the soul, his account actually differs from that speech in certain crucial ways and specifically suggests that Cebes (now) longs to see the hope for immortality vindicated (compare 95b9–e6 with 86e6-88b8).

In his earlier speech about the soul, Cebes had suggested that the relation between the soul and the body is similar to the relation between a weaver and his cloak (see 87b4-88a1, especially 87d3-7). And, as we have noted, that account implies that the soul is necessarily mortal. In the first place, it implies that, just as the weaver needs his cloak in order to survive, so does the soul need the body in order to survive. But furthermore, by comparing the soul to a human being, that account implies that the soul is itself human rather than divine and hence that our truest selves, our souls, are not higher than what is merely human and mortal but are altogether human and mortal. Now, it is true that Cebes went on to argue not that the soul is mortal but only that Socrates had not yet demonstrated that it is altogether immortal and imperishable (88a1–b8). Yet, in the conclusion of his speech, he did not urge Socrates to provide such a demonstration but, instead, seemed to reject the very hope for immortality as foolish and hence unbecoming a sensible man (compare 88b3-8 with, for example, 77c1-5). Furthermore, inasmuch as Cebes did not speak at all against the philosophic life but only against the argument for immortality, it had seemed that his inclination to believe that the soul is mortal had not weakened his devotion to the philosophic life. Cebes' objection to the argument for immortality suggested, then, that he believes that the soul is mortal, that he rejects altogether the hope for immortality, and also that he may not believe that the reasonableness of the philosophic life depends on the existence of an afterlife.

In his "summary" of that speech, however, Socrates makes a number of crucial subtractions and additions. In the first place, he leaves out altogether Cebes' comparison of the soul to a weaver and thereby leaves out his suggestion that the soul needs the body in order to survive, that it is human rather than divine, and hence that it is necessarily mortal (compare 95b9–e1, 91d2-7 with c7–d2). Furthermore, Socrates attributes to Cebes the belief that the soul is divine and hence that it might very well be immortal (compare 95c4-5 with 87a5-7). Finally, he suggests that, according to Cebes, the reasonableness of the philosophic life does depend on the existence of an afterlife. He claims that Cebes has argued that, unless the soul is shown to be imperishable and immortal, the philosopher who is about to die and who is confident that he will fare better in an afterlife than if he had lived another way of life must be a fool (compare 95b8–c4 with 88b3-8). According to Socrates, then, Cebes believes that the philosophic life, in particular, would be a foolish way of life if there is no afterlife. And he believes this apparently because he believes that the philosophic life is intrinsically unsatisfying and that, unless there is an afterlife in which the philosopher is compensated for his unhappiness in this life with greater rewards than other human beings receive, his must be a foolish way of life. Socrates suggests, then, that Cebes has not argued at all for the mortality of the soul, that he hopes for immortality, and that he wants Socrates to vindicate that hope and therewith the belief in the wisdom and the goodness of the philosophic life (compare also 95b9–c1 with 88b3-8). And Cebes accepts this suggestion by saying that, "at the present time," he does not wish to take anything away or to add anything to Socrates' "summary" of his objection to the argument for immortality (95e4-6).

It seems, then, that, since he expressed his objection to the argument for immortality, Cebes has come to embrace, once again, the hope for immortality. And the reason for this change of heart would seem to be the new account of the duty of the philosopher which Socrates has given since Cebes made his argument against immortality. For Cebes' most vehement objection to the argument for immortality immediately followed Socrates' most clearly unfulfillable account of the duty of the philosopher. And this suggests that it was Cebes' sense that it is impossible for the philosopher or for any human being to do what is demanded of him by the gods and hence to deserve everlasting happiness that led him, for the first time in the dialogue, not only to doubt the immortality of the soul but also to believe and to feel that the soul must be mortal (compare 86b6-8, 87d3-7, 88a1–b8 with 70b1-4, 77c1-5). In other words, once Socrates made Cebes feel that it is impossible for any human being to rise above his merely human and mortal self and to transcend his concern for his own good by fulfilling his duty, he, so to speak, persuaded Cebes that the soul is mortal.

But now Socrates has offered a new account of the philosopher's duty—namely, the duty to resist misology and to pursue the truth in arguments with courage and zeal—which Cebes may plausibly hope to fulfill. In this way, even before responding to Cebes' argument against immortality, he has restored Cebes' belief that everlasting happiness can be deserved, that we can rise above our merely human selves and self-concern, and hence that the soul may truly be immortal. And it may be above all because of Cebes' renewed belief that everlasting happiness can be deserved and his renewed hope for immortality that he will go on to accept Socrates' final argument for immortality.

At this point, however, Socrates emphasizes to Cebes that his argument against immortality is a powerful one. For, after completing his summary of that argument, Socrates retreats for a long time from the conversation and reflects in silence. He then tells Cebes that his argument is not at all insignificant but requires them to consider thoroughly the cause of coming-into-being and perishing. In these ways, he stresses to Cebes that his argument against immortality is not as vulnerable to attack as Simmias' apparently was (95e7-96a4; see also 95b5-6).

Nevertheless, Socrates does propose to respond to that argument by giving an account of his own experiences in examining the cause of coming-into-being and perishing. Now, such an account would seem to address Cebes' concerns in two ways. In the first place, by explaining what the cause of perishing is, Socrates may show that there is nothing that can cause the soul to perish. In this way, he may fulfill Cebes' specific demand that he show that the soul is imperishable and immortal and hence that the philosopher's confidence that he will fare better after death than other human beings is at least plausible (see 95b9–c4). But furthermore, and more generally, by recounting his own philosophic experiences and, indeed, his own philosophic life as a whole, Socrates would seem to be addressing Cebes' belief or fear that the philosophic life is intrinsically unsatisfying and unhappy. Indeed, it may be that, by showing that his own philosophic life has not been unhappy, Socrates hopes to persuade Cebes that the philosopher fares better than other human beings in this life and hence that the reasonableness of the philosophic life does not depend on the existence of an afterlife.[3] And, in this way, he may hope to ease, at least somewhat, Cebes' longing and need to believe in immortality and therewith his demand for a proof of the immortality of the soul.[4]

Cebes welcomes Socrates' proposal to recount his own experiences, and it would seem that he does so in the hope that Socrates will explain how he discovered the cause of coming-into-being and of perishing and will then explain that the soul never perishes. In other words, Cebes must hope, especially now that the conversation is drawing to a close, that Socrates will reveal that he has acquired wisdom in this life, will prove that the soul is imperishable and immortal, and will thereby vindicate the philosophic life. Yet, insofar as Cebes has such hopes, he must be disappointed, at least initially, by Socrates' account here. For Socrates gives an account of his life which begins by highlighting his setbacks, his disappointments, and, above all, his failure to become wise and which appears to culminate with the admission that even now, on the last day of his life, he does not know a single account of the cause of the coming-into-being, the perishing, or the being of *anything* and hence, it would seem, that he does not know whether or not our souls perish when we die (see especially 97b3-6; compare with 95d6–e1, 95e8-96a4).

Socrates explains that, when he was young, he felt a "wonderful" desire for this wisdom which people call natural science. For he thought that it would be grand to know the causes of each thing, that is, why each thing comes into being, why it perishes, and why it is. The young Socrates evidently expected, then, that he would be able to acquire a complete knowledge of each thing and hence would be able to acquire a complete knowledge about the whole of nature. However, after some time, he ended up believing that he had no natural gift for this type of inquiry. For, while there had been a number of things which he had known clearly, not only in his own opinion but in the opinion of others, he was "so extremely blinded by this inquiry" that he "unlearned" even those things which he had previously thought he knew. And Socrates goes on to reveal to Cebes that, even now that he is an old man on the very threshold of death, he does not know a single account which explains why anything, much less each thing, comes into being, perishes, or is (96a6-97b7; compare 97b3-6 with 96a6-10).

The account Socrates offers here must be especially dispiriting to Cebes, in particular. For the youthful Cebes must identify with the youthful Socrates' "wonderful" desire to know the causes of each thing and hence to become completely wise (compare 96a6-10 with 89a2-4). But Socrates seems to go out of his way to suggest to Cebes that his life-long quest for such wisdom, or indeed for any wisdom at all, has been all for naught. For example, rather than portray his discovery that he did not know what he thought he knew as an important step forward in his quest for wisdom, Socrates tells Cebes that he was "blinded" and that he "unlearned" what he thought he knew and thereby suggests that, as a result of his efforts to become wise, he actually became more and not less ignorant.[5] Furthermore, by stating so emphatically that even now, presumably after some fifty years of searching for wisdom, he still does not know a single account which explains why anything comes into being, perishes, or is, Socrates seems to suggest to Cebes that his search has been entirely fruitless and hence that his philosophic life has been a complete failure (see 96e5). And he seems to say quite specifically that he does not know that the soul is imperishable and hence does not know that there is an afterlife in which the philosopher is rewarded with the wisdom he seeks. In this way, Socrates seems to admit that he cannot offer that demonstration or proof which, Cebes evidently believes, is necessary in order to vindicate the philosophic life (compare 97b3-7 with 70b1-4, 80e2-81a11, 95b8–e5). Socrates' account here of his philosophic life, then, would seem to justify Cebes' fear that it truly is a foolish way of life (see 95b8–c4, c9–e1; see also 62c9–e7).

Socrates does go on to tell Cebes that he once cherished the "wonderful" hope of learning from Anaxagoras an account which would explain the cause of each being in terms of a beneficent and ruling intelligence which has ordered each being as is best for itself as well as for the common good (97b8-98b6). And, in this way, he may arouse Cebes' own hopes for an account which explains the cause of each being in terms of the gods, whom he earlier described as "the best commanders of the beings," and which explains that it is best for the philosopher to be rewarded with everlasting happiness (see 62d3-6, e3-4). Yet Socrates goes on to explain that Anaxagoras dashed his "wonderful" hope and that he has been unable either to discover for himself or to learn from someone else an account which explains all the beings in terms of a beneficent intelligence who rules over all the (other) beings (98b7-99c9). Socrates' account of his disappointment with Anaxagoras, then, would seem only to add to the bleakness of the portrait of the philosophic life he offers here to Cebes. For, according to this portrait, it seems that, if Cebes is to devote his life to the pursuit of wisdom, or, at least, to the pursuit of that complete wisdom about all the beings which he longs to possess, he must expect nothing but the pain of unfulfilled longing and the heartache of disappointed hope.

Yet, Socrates' account of his own experiences in his pursuit of wisdom, even before he explains his second sailing in search of wisdom, must be heartening to Cebes in at least one important respect. According to this account, even though he experienced setbacks and disappointments in his pursuit of the truth through reason, Socrates never abandoned that pursuit. Despite the fact that he first trusted in and was then disappointed by the seemingly true arguments of the natural scientists and of Anaxagoras, it seems that he never allowed into his soul the thought that there is nothing at all sound or true in the arguments. In other words, in spite of the apparent similarity between Socrates' own experiences and those he ascribes to the misologist and specifically in spite of his "wonderful" desire and hope to find an argument which will reveal the complete truth about all the beings, he never succumbed to the temptation of misology (compare 90b6-9, c8–e3 with 96a8-99d2). Indeed, Socrates goes on to explain that, after his disappointments with the arguments or speeches (*logoi*) of the natural scientists and of Anaxagoras, he turned to the arguments or speeches as a whole in order to examine the truth of the beings (see 96a6–b8, 97b8–c6, d1, 99e4-6). Far from leading him to believe that there is nothing at all sound or true in the speeches, his disappointments seem to have led him to believe all the more strongly in the soundness of and the truth in speeches. Socrates' account here, then, seems to suggest that he has, throughout his life, fulfilled his duty to persevere in seeking for the truth through reason and to resist the temptation of succumbing to the hatred of reason. And consequently, by hearing this account, Cebes must feel encouraged in his belief that it is possible to fulfill the duty of the philosopher as Socrates has described it and hence that it is possible to deserve the reward of everlasting happiness.

It is important to note, however, that Socrates does not say in this account that he ever felt tempted to deny that there is anything true in the arguments and to hate the arguments. But if he never felt this temptation and hence never had to struggle to overcome it, it is not clear that he truly exhibited a virtuous sense of duty in his life.[6] Furthermore, Socrates never ascribes to himself in this account a desire or hope to be rewarded by the gods with wisdom after death and hence a desire to fulfill his duty in order to be so rewarded. Indeed, as we have seen, Socrates has already admitted to his companions that, now that he no longer believes it to be in his self-interest to be philosophic, he will ignore his duty to be philosophic (91a1–b7). It would seem, then, that Socrates persevered in his quest for wisdom throughout the greater part of his life not out of a desire to fulfill his duty in the hope of winning for himself the reward of wisdom in the hereafter but rather out of a self-interested desire to acquire wisdom for himself in the here and now.

II. Socrates' Second Sailing

After describing how he failed to discover the cause of all the beings either through natural science or from the books of Anaxagoras, Socrates tells Cebes that he embarked on a "second sailing" in search of the cause, a sailing which has occupied the rest of his life.[7] He explains that, once he gave up examining the beings, it seemed to him that he ought to beware lest he suffer what those who gaze at an eclipse of the sun suffer. For some of them destroy their eyes unless they examine the image of the eclipsing sun as it is reflected in water or in something of that sort. And he feared that, by looking directly at the beings and by attempting to grasp them through his senses, he would blind his soul altogether. Accordingly, it seemed to him that he ought to flee into the speeches or arguments in order to examine in them the truth of the beings (99c8–e6). And he goes on to suggest that he attempted to explain the cause of things in terms of their forms or ideas (100a3–b7; see also 102a10–b2, 104d1-3). It seems, then, that Socrates' new approach to the study of all things entailed the attempt to seek for the truth in speeches and to understand things in terms of their ideas.

Socrates' explanation of his second sailing here raises a number of questions. In the first place, it is not immediately clear in what sense Socrates' effort to search for the truth of the beings, or the true cause of the beings, in the speeches or arguments (*logoi*) constitutes a break from his previous way of searching for the truth. For, according to his account, he hoped to find the true cause of the beings in the written speech or argument (*logos*) of Anaxagoras (see especially 97b8–c6, d1-5, 98b1-6). Furthermore, Socrates also at one point hoped to find the true cause of the beings, it seems, in the speech or argument of the natural scientists (see 96b2-8). What, then, does Socrates mean by his fleeing to the speeches and how does it differ from his earlier search for the truth in the speeches?

Socrates' discussion here of the ideas is also perplexing. Up until now, he has suggested that we can only acquire knowledge of the ideas either by releasing our souls from our bodies or by recollecting the knowledge our souls acquired when they existed apart from our bodies before we were born (see 65d4-66a8, 74a9–76e7). Now, however, Socrates seems to suggest that we can acquire knowledge of the ideas in this life by examining speeches (see 99e4-6, 100b3-7).[8] But what is the connection between the ideas and speeches? And what is the connection between Socrates' turn to the ideas and his turn to speeches?

In order to address these questions, let us examine more carefully why Socrates rejected the arguments of the natural scientists and Anaxagoras. When he was young, he sought to discover the necessary and sufficient causes of the coming-into-being, the perishing, and the being of each and every being by attempting to explain all the beings in terms of what seem to be the material elements of the universe. In other words, the young Socrates adopted as a hypothesis what would seem to be the hypothesis of natural science, namely, that the necessary and sufficient causes of all things may be found in the material elements of the universe. And he attempted to explain in this way why there are living beings, why there is intelligence, why living beings and intelligent beings perish, and why the heaven and the earth possess the characteristics they do (96a6–c1).

Nevertheless, Socrates was (and still is) unable to explain the necessary and sufficient causes of beings in terms of their material elements. To take the example which he discusses most thoroughly, he was unable to explain the number two as *the* effect of adding one unit to another. For, while this explanation is sometimes true, it is sometimes not true (compare 96e6-97b3 with 90b6-9, d1-3). After all, two may also result from dividing one unit into two. And therefore the addition of one unit to another cannot be the necessary cause of two. As Socrates suggests, it seems rather that it is the character of being two or the idea of two that determines the number that a unit, when put together with another unit, must be (see 101b9–c6). In other words, it seems that it is the idea or the nature of two (see 104a7–b1, d9–10), rather than the elements of two, that determine or cause the coming-into-being of two. And consequently, in order to understand why two comes into being, it is necessary to examine, above all, two itself or the idea of two rather than the elements of two. Furthermore, we cannot understand why two necessarily is what it is, that is, why it necessarily possesses all the characteristics that it does, simply in terms of its elements. For example, we cannot understand why two is necessarily even in terms of single units which are not themselves even. It seems rather that it is the idea or the nature of two which determines why it must be even (see 104a7–b4). Similarly, to take an example which Socrates goes on to use, we cannot fully understand why a beautiful flower is necessarily beautiful in terms of its elements which are not themselves beautiful but must consider rather the character or idea of beauty (100c3-e3). And, as we might add, we cannot fully understand why water is necessarily wet in terms of hydrogen and oxygen which are not themselves wet or why green is necessarily green in terms of blue and yellow which are not themselves green but must examine instead the characters or ideas of water and green.[9]

Socrates discovered, then, that it is impossible to understand two adequately in terms of what is not two, or beauty in terms of what is not beautiful, or, more generally, the coming-into-being, the perishing, and the being of any being by breaking it up into its material elements. For, by doing so, we are "blinded" to the full or whole character of that being and hence to what that being fully is (see 96c4-5, 99d4–e4).[10] Hence, for example, if we try to understand human beings, as the young Socrates and Anaxagoras tried to do, in terms of the hot and the cold, blood and air, flesh and bones, we blind ourselves to the full character of a human being (see 96b2-4, c2–d5, 98c2–d6). For, if we "see" nothing but flesh and bones when we see a human being, we will not see what is distinctively human about that being and hence will not truly see that being.[11] More generally, if we see nothing but the parts of a thing when we see a thing, we are blinded to the sum of those parts, to the whole thing, and hence to the full character of that thing. By attempting to understand things in terms of their elements, then, we miss the wood for the trees and the trees for the molecules. We do not see things as they naturally present themselves to us. And precisely because he recognized that it led him to lose sight of the whole character of each of the beings, Socrates abandoned the hypothesis or account of the natural scientists according to which every being can be explained in terms of its material elements. But furthermore, his experience with this hypothesis seems to have revealed to him the importance of studying things on their own terms. It seems to have led him to see that it is more important to ask what a thing is than to ask what its material elements are. And it seems to have pointed out to him the importance of examining the form or the idea of each being in order to understand the fundamental causes of the coming-into-being, the perishing, and the being of each being.

Now, as Socrates indicates by saying that he was "blinded" by his attempt to understand things in terms of their material elements, his new approach to the study of all things led him to return, so to speak, to his senses (see 96c4-5, 99e1-4; see also b4-5). For, while we do not immediately perceive the material elements of things when we see things, while we do not immediately see, for example, "the hot" and "the cold" or even blood, air, and fire when we see human beings, we do, in some sense at least, see their "form" (see 96b2-4, 73d7-8; see also a1-2, 76c11-13, 92b5-6). After all, the form of a thing means, in the first place, the look or the appearance of that thing.[12] Accordingly, if we seek to understand the forms of things, we must begin by examining them as they are revealed to us by our senses.

Yet, as Socrates also indicates, an understanding of the form or idea of a thing is not accessible to us simply by looking at a particular thing (see 99e1-100a3). For, in order to understand the idea of a thing or what a thing is, it is necessary to identify to what class of things it belongs. To take an example from earlier in the dialogue, we cannot see or recognize that a painting of Simmias is a painting of Simmias in particular and not of someone else unless we know who Simmias is and can thereby identify those characteristics which the painting shares with Simmias and hence which make it a painting of Simmias in particular (see 73e9-10 and context). But furthermore, we cannot see, simply by looking at a particular painting, that it is a painting, as opposed, say, to a canvas splashed with paint, unless we can recognize to what distinctive group or class of things it belongs and thereby see what its distinctive and defining character is. Similarly, we cannot see that Simmias is a human being by observing only him, since we cannot, from this experience alone, identify those characteristics which he shares with all human beings (for example, the ability to speak or to reason) and hence which distinguish him from other beings (for example, apes) with whom he also shares characteristics (for example, the ability to perceive or to move his body). In other words, we cannot know what the distinctive character of a human being is and hence what a distinctively human being is unless we can identify to what class of beings it belongs (and hence to what class of beings it does not belong). It seems, then, necessary to identify the class-characteristics of things or to classify things simply in order to see the distinctive character of the thing we are looking at. And the class-characters or ideas of things (see 79e6-7) are most apparent to us through speeches or language. For in speech we naturally group particular things together and also distinguish groups of things from one another. Simply by using words, words like "painting" or "human being" or "beautiful," we classify the things around us and thereby point, at least, toward an understanding of the class-character or idea of each thing (see 102a10–b2). Hence, for example, which beings we call human and what we say about them enables us to see and to begin to examine what the distinctive character of a human being is. It would seem, then, that when Socrates says that he is turning to the speeches or the arguments (*logoi*) in order to examine the truth of the beings, he means not that he is seeking for one speech or account which will reveal the complete truth about all the beings, as he had hoped to find, for example, in the books of Anaxagoras, but rather that he is turning to the speeches, that is, to what we say about things and to how we distinguish or classify things in our speech in order to examine the class-character or idea of each being and therewith, it seems, the truth of the beings (99e4-6).[13]

It is important, however, to remember Socrates' claim that he does not, even now, know a *single* account which completely explains the cause of anything (97b3-6). For that claim suggests that, even after examining the ideas as they are revealed in the speeches for a great part of his life, he still has not been able to understand fully and with certainty "the truth of the beings" or even the truth of any single being. Moreover, by calling his new way of studying things a "fleeing into the speeches," Socrates suggests that the study of what human beings say about the character of each class of beings cannot enable us to understand the beings in a full or complete way (99e4-6). For the speeches of human beings necessarily reflect the limits of human experience and hence of human knowledge. It might seem, for example, to be impossible for us, either through examining speeches or in any other way, to know with certainty whether or not we possess immortal souls. For, even though we may perhaps become reasonably confident that we are mortal beings, our inability, as long as we are embodied souls and hence as long as we are human beings, to peer beyond the threshold of death may limit our knowledge of what death holds in store for us. But if we cannot know with certainty whether or not we are mortal beings, then we cannot know fully and with certainty what we are, and hence even our knowledge of ourselves can never be complete and certain but must always be limited. Hence, when Socrates says that he will seek for the truth of the beings in the speeches, he seems to mean that he will seek to know the truth in the speeches but not with the hope of becoming completely or perfectly wise. And this seems to explain what is new and distinctive about his turn to the speeches. For Socrates does not turn to the speeches with the hope of finding a single speech which reveals the whole truth about all things, as he had hoped to find in the books of Anaxagoras, but rather flees into the speeches with the hope of understanding all things, and especially the character or idea of each thing, only as far as is humanly possible (see 107b6-9).

It is true that, at some point before he embarked on his second sailing, Socrates attempted to discover the cause of each being in the books of Anaxagoras. For he heard that, according to that man, there is a ruling intelligence which orders all things in the universe. Socrates was pleased by this claim and thought that it would be good if there were such a ruling intelligence. Moreover, he believed that, if there were such an intelligence, it must order each being as is best for itself and for the common good and hence that what is best for each being as well as for the common good must be the necessary and sufficient cause of each being (see 97b8–d1, 98a6–b3). Consequently, Socrates thought that, according to Anaxagoras' argument, "it is fitting" (or good) for a human being to examine, in order to understand both himself and the other things in the world, nothing but what is best (97d1-3). And, accordingly, he expected Anaxagoras to explain in what way each thing is ordered as is best for itself and for the common good (97d4-98b6).

However, Anaxagoras actually explained things not in terms of what is best for them but in terms of their material elements. Accordingly, Socrates rejected his teachings and eventually turned to the speeches in order to study the character or idea of each of the beings. But even if Anaxagoras had, in fact, demonstrated that there is a ruling intelligence which orders each being in the universe as is best for itself and for the common good, it seems that Socrates still would have had to turn to the speeches in order to understand the beings. For what is best or good *for* any being is determined by the nature of that being. And consequently, in order to know what is good for a being, we must know what the nature of that being is. Hence, even if we somehow knew that there is a ruling intelligence or god who orders all the beings, we still would not know whether he orders each being as is best for itself until we knew the nature or the idea of each being.[14] Accordingly, since Socrates discovered that it is impossible to understand things fully either in terms of their material elements or in terms of a ruling intelligence or god who orders all things for the best, he turned to the speeches in order to understand the idea of each of the beings.

Socrates' account of his life also suggests that he turned to study the beings as they come to sight in human speeches in order to understand, in particular, whether or not the philosophic life is good for a human being. It suggests this in the following way. In this account, Socrates openly admits, for the only time in the dialogues of Plato, that he did pursue wisdom, at least in his youth, in the manner of the natural scientists. He admits here that, notwithstanding what he said at his trial, he did investigate the heavenly things.[15] And consequently, he admits that he once attempted to understand the world solely in terms of material elements and thereby seems to confirm what his Athenian accusers claimed, namely, that he was, at least in his youth, guilty of impiety.[16] Furthermore, when Socrates discusses Anaxagoras' apparent claim that there is a ruling intelligence who orders all things in the world for the good, he seems, as we have suggested, to discuss the possibility that there is a god who rules the world for the best (see 97b8–98b6, 62c9–e7). And by mentioning, also in his discussion of Anaxagoras, that the Athenians have condemned him to death because they thought it good to do so, Socrates seems to allude to their belief that there is a god who does not believe that it is good for human beings to pursue wisdom and who consequently punishes the philosophers (see 98d1–3; see also 97c4–d3). For the Athenians thought it good to condemn Socrates to death because they thought him guilty of impiety. More precisely, they thought that, by refusing to accept the authority of the priests and religious poets and by pursuing wisdom on his own and through reason alone, Socrates was opposing the will of the gods and consequently deserved to be punished by gods and men alike. The pious Athenians believed, then, that it is not good for human beings to pursue wisdom as the philosophers do because, by doing so, they oppose the will and incur the wrath of the gods (see 62c9–e7, b6–c4).[17]

Now, when he was young, Socrates was evidently confident that the philosophic life is a grand and hence a good way of life. His confidence seems to have been based, at least in part, on his assumption that it is possible to know the causes of each thing, why it comes into being, why it perishes, and why it is and hence that it is possible to attain a complete knowledge of all things. Furthermore, by saying that he desired to know why each thing perishes, Socrates suggests that, when he was young, he simply assumed that all things are perishable (see 96a6–c2). And he thereby implies that he believed, at that time, that there are no imperishable or immortal beings and hence that there is no afterlife for us and that there are no gods. It would seem, then, that, when he was young, Socrates simply dismissed the pious claim that the philosophic life is an impious and hence a bad way of life and that he did so because he was confident that the goal of the philosophic life is reachable in this life and also because he believed that he knew that there cannot be an afterlife in which gods will punish the philosopher.

Yet Socrates has gone on to explain that his youthful hopes for attaining a complete knowledge of all things have gone unfulfilled. Furthermore, since he has suggested, at least, that he still does not know what causes anything to perish (97b3-7), it would seem that he can no longer be confident that all things are perishable, that there are no gods, and that there is no afterlife. It would seem, then, that Socrates can no longer retain his youthful confidence that the philosophic life is an unquestionably grand way of life and that there cannot be an afterlife in which the gods punish the souls of the philosophers. And consequently, it would seem to be reasonable and even necessary for him to take seriously and to examine the claim of the pious that the philosophic life is not good but rather bad for human beings (see 60d8-61b3, 63b1-5).

But, in order to investigate whether or not there are gods who punish the souls of the philosophers in an afterlife, Socrates would have to turn to the speeches of human beings. For, perhaps unless we are prophets, we only know what we know about the gods and the afterlife from what is said about these things by human beings (see, for example, 61c10, d10–e2, 62b2-8, 67b2, 69c3–d1, 70c5-7, 81a4-10, 107dff.).[18] Our eyes may reveal to us the lifeless corpse of Socrates but only human speeches can possibly reveal to us the fate of Socrates after his death. It seems, then, that the gods and the afterlife are things which may become visible to us only insofar as they are reflected in human speeches. And therefore, in order to discover the truth about these things and thereby to know whether or not the philosophic life is good for human beings, it seems that we must turn to the speeches and arguments about these things. Socrates may, then, have turned to the speeches not only in order to discover the truth about the beings as a whole but also to discover the truth about the gods, in particular, in order to determine whether or not the philosophic life is truly good for him.

III. Socrates' Explanation of His Second Sailing to Cebes

After explaining that he embarked on his second sailing in search for wisdom by fleeing to the speeches in order to examine in them the truth about the beings, Socrates (rightly) supposes that Cebes does not understand what he is saying (100a7–10). Yet he emphasizes to Cebes that his new approach to the pursuit of wisdom should not be at all unfamiliar to him. He claims that he is not speaking about anything new but rather about those things he has never ceased speaking about both at other times and in the previous conversation: namely, the beautiful itself, the good, the big, and the other things themselves or ideas. And he says that, if Cebes will grant that these beings exist, he will explain the cause of all things and will also show that the soul is immortal (100b1-9). Socrates suggests here that his new approach to the study of all things is based on the hypothesis which has been repeatedly invoked throughout the dialogue, the hypothesis which we have come to know as the doctrine of the ideas, according to which the ideas are divine, immortal, and imperishable beings that exist apart from the sensible world (see 65d4–e5, 76e7-77a5, 80a10–b6, 92d7–e3). He suggests to his friends, then, that his second sailing is based on that account of the ideas which is not only familiar to them but which they appear to accept unquestioningly. And he thereby suggests to them that, while his new approach to the pursuit of wisdom is dramatically different from his own youthful approach, it is not at all different from their own understanding of that pursuit.

Yet, Socrates' account of the ideas here is, in fact, quite different from the way he and his friends have spoken of the ideas in the conversation up until now. Up until now, it has seemed that the ideas are invisible, incorporeal beings that exist entirely apart from the world our senses reveal to us. Accordingly, Socrates and his friends have suggested that we can only acquire knowledge of the ideas if we shun our senses and release our souls entirely from our bodies or if we recollect the knowledge our souls acquired before we were born and hence when they were entirely separate from our bodies (see 65d4-66a8, 74a9–77a5, 78c10-79d8). And consequently, it has seemed that, insofar as it is impossible to acquire a full and complete knowledge of the ideas in this life, the philosopher can only acquire the wisdom that he seeks in an afterlife.

Now, however, Socrates reveals to Cebes that the ideas are not wholly separate from the sensible world. He says, for example, that the idea of the beautiful is what "makes" all beautiful things, that is, all the beautiful things we perceive, beautiful (100d3-6). He suggests, more generally, that the ideas are what cause perceptible things to be what they are (100b3-9). And he also suggests that the ideas cause particular things to be what they are by being present or embodied "in" them.[19] Hence, he suggests that the idea of the beautiful may cause a particular flower to be beautiful by "being present" in it, that bigness may cause a man to be big by being "in" him, and that the idea of the cold causes snow to be cold because snow always possesses that idea (100c9-d9, 102b1-d2, 103c10-e5). It now seems, then, that the invisible ideas have visible effects and that the disembodied ideas may, in fact, be embodied in particular things.[20] And consequently, it seems that it is possible to acquire knowledge of, for example, the beautiful, by examining, in this life and through our senses, those particular things which it causes to be beautiful. Indeed, it would seem to be positively necessary to study the embodiments of the ideas in particular things in order to acquire a full knowledge of the ideas. For, insofar as to be an idea is to be a kind of cause of particular things, we cannot understand how it causes particular things to be what they are or even that it causes things to be what they are unless we understand its effects. And we can only understand the effects of the ideas by studying their embodiments in particular things. Socrates' account of the ideas here suggests, then, that it is not only possible but necessary to study particular things, and hence to study them by means of our senses, in order to acquire a full knowledge of the ideas. It suggests that the ideas do not simply exist apart from the sensible world but also exist in this world, in the things of this world, and hence that, to know them fully and completely, we must study the things of this world.[21] And consequently, by giving this new account of the ideas to Cebes, Socrates suggests that he can and even must pursue wisdom in this life rather than simply pin his hopes for the attainment of wisdom on the existence of an afterlife (see 101e6-102a1).

Furthermore, while Socrates' companions have spoken of the ideas as though they were certain that they exist apart from particular things, Socrates now emphasizes to them that the claim that the ideas exist apart from the sensible world is a hypothetical claim (compare 65d4-e5, 69e7, 74a9-b3, 76e8-77a5, 92d6-e2 with 100b3-7).[22] He emphasizes to them that he himself would not affirm strongly what the relation is between the ideas and particular things[23] and thereby suggests that he is not even sure that the ideas are separate beings (100d3-8). And he also encourages both Cebes and Simmias to examine the hypothesis that the ideas are separate beings rather than simply accept that hypothesis on faith (see 101d5-e1, 107b4-

9). In this way, Socrates encourages his friends to rethink their entire understanding of the so-called doctrine of separate ideas.[24] He invites them to consider the possibility that, for example, the idea of the beautiful is not a separate being but is simply that characteristic which all beautiful things share and by virtue of which they belong to the class of things that are beautiful.[25] More generally, he invites them to consider the possibility that the ideas are not separate beings at all, that they do not exist apart from their embodiments in particular things, and hence that they themselves are not divine but rather perishable things.

Yet Socrates does, as we have seen, suggest to Cebes that his present account of the ideas is not fundamentally different from his previous accounts, and he does persist in speaking of the ideas as though they were separate beings (100b1-9). In this way, he encourages his companions in their belief that the ideas are divine and imperishable beings which can, at least, exist apart from the sensible world. And he does so, it seems, in order to persuade them that the soul is immortal. For if, he says, Cebes will grant that the ideas are separate beings, he will show that the soul is immortal (see also 106d5-7). It seems, then, that Socrates persists in suggesting that the ideas are separate and divine beings in order to persuade his companions that their souls are separate and divine beings which will continue to exist once they are dead.

IV. The Final Argument for Immortality

Once Socrates completes his account of his second sailing, he returns to the question of immortality and proceeds to make his final argument for the immortality of the soul. Before we turn to that argument, however, let us consider what implications his account of his new approach to the study of all things may have for the question of immortality. Throughout the conversation that has preceded Socrates' account of the second sailing, the question of whether or not there is an afterlife for us has been identified with the question of whether or not our souls are immortal (see, for example, 63c4-7, 64c2-9, 66d7-67a2, 70b1-4). Throughout this conversation, then, we have been understood in terms of our elements, namely, our bodies and our souls, our human and mortal selves have been identified with our bodies, and our true selves have been identified with our souls (see, for example, 64c4-9, 66b1-67b6, 72e7-73a2, 79b1-2). Accordingly, the discussion has focused on the question, are our souls immortal?

Socrates' account of his second sailing suggests, however, that this is not the proper way to approach the question of immortality. For he has explained that it is a mistake to understand things primarily in terms of their elements. He has explained that, by trying to understand things in this way, we are blinded to their full or whole character. Accordingly, he has suggested that in order to understand, for example, the number two, one must try to understand the idea of two or the nature of two rather than break it up into its elements. It would seem, then, that, in order to understand human beings properly, one must understand them above all in terms of their whole character, in terms of their idea or nature as whole human beings rather than in terms of their bodies and souls (see 72e7-73a2, 76c11-13, 92b4-7). Consequently, it would seem that, in order to answer the question of the afterlife, we must focus on the question of what our nature is as human beings and whether we are by nature immortal rather than focus on the question of whether a part of us, our soul, is immortal. Now, it is true that Socrates does not explicitly raise the question of whether human beings are by nature immortal in his final argument for immortality. Nevertheless, as we will see, this question does make itself felt throughout this argument (see, for example, 102c1-2, 106e5-7).[26]

Socrates' final argument for immortality, like his third argument, addresses the question of what the relation is between the seemingly divine and immortal ideas and the soul (compare 78c10–d9, 80a10–b5 with 100b3-9, 102a10–b2, 105b9-106d7). In this argument, however, Socrates will argue that the soul is not merely similar to the immortal ideas but that soul always possesses within itself the immortal idea of life (compare 80a10–b5 with 105b9-12; see also 106d5-7). Accordingly, he will conclude that the soul is not merely "altogether" immortal or "nearly so" but that "soul is immortal" (compare 80a8–c1 with 105e4-9).

Socrates begins his final argument for immortality by suggesting to Cebes that, if he agrees that each of the ideas exist and that the particulars participate in them by possessing their name, then when he says that Simmias is bigger than Socrates but smaller than Phaedo, he is saying that there is both bigness and smallness in Simmias. Socrates immediately suggests, however, that it is not quite true to say that Simmias is bigger than Socrates. For it is not "by nature," that is, it is not by virtue of being Simmias, that Simmias is bigger than Socrates, but rather by virtue of his happening to possess bigness in him. Socrates suggests here, then, that bigness is not a necessary or defining characteristic of Simmias, that Simmias can cease to be big and still be what he is "by nature," and that, consequently, he may or may not participate in the idea of bigness and still continue to be what he is "by nature" (102a10-c9).[27]

Socrates seems to point here to a way in which one can understand the question of immortality, that is, the question of whether we continue to exist after death, in terms of the ideas. For he distinguishes here between ideas, such as bigness and smallness, which human beings need not possess in order to continue to be what they are by nature, and ideas which we must possess in order to continue to exist as human beings and hence in the absence of which we cannot exist. It would seem, then, that, in order to determine whether a human being may continue to exist after death, we must first determine what characteristics or ideas he must possess in order to continue to exist "by nature" and hence what characteristics or ideas are essential to our human nature. And then we must determine whether it is possible for a human being to continue to possess those characteristics or ideas once he is dead or whether he loses them then.

Socrates now proceeds to examine what causes any particular thing to lose its characteristics or its ideas. Socrates tells Cebes that, in his opinion, it is not only "bigness itself" that is never willing to be both big and small but also "the bigness in us" that is never willing to accept the small. Consequently, when the idea of smallness approaches us, the idea of bigness in us either flees and withdraws or perishes. Socrates suggests here that two ideas that are opposite to one another, such as bigness and smallness, cannot exist in the same thing, such as Simmias, at the same time (see 102d5-103a2; see also 103a4–c2, especially b7–c1; compare with 102a10–b2). Accordingly, when the idea of the small approaches Simmias, it drives out or destroys the idea of the big that is in him. It seems, then, that a human being loses an idea that is within him when the opposite idea enters him. And consequently, it would seem that, in order to determine whether a human being continues to exist after death, we must determine first what ideas are essential to our nature as human beings, then what the opposite ideas are, and finally whether those ideas drive out of us or destroy, when we die, the ideas without which we cannot continue to be what we are.

Socrates now turns to discuss an idea that is essential to the existence, not of human beings, but of snow. He says that snow will never accept the idea of heat and still continue to be what it is, presumably, by nature. While the ideas of bigness and smallness, then, are not essential to the existence of a human being, the idea of coldness is essential to the existence of snow. And consequently, we would expect Socrates to go on to explain that, when a particular thing loses that idea or characteristic which it must possess in order to continue to be what it is by nature, it ceases to be what is and hence perishes. Furthermore, since Socrates had said that, when smallness approaches Simmias, the bigness in him withdraws or perishes, we would expect him to say here that, when the idea of heat approaches snow, the snow perishes but the idea of coldness in it withdraws or perishes. We would expect him, in other words, to draw a distinction between the idea of the cold, which is presumably a divine and imperishable being, and the snow, which shares in that idea but which is itself clearly a perishable thing. Socrates, however, does not make any such distinction but says instead that, when heat approaches snow, the snow either withdraws or perishes (compare 103d5-9 with 102d6–e2, 102e6-103a2). By saying this, he introduces the suggestion, or the argument, that, if the idea of the cold withdraws, so must the snow, and that, if the idea of the cold is imperishable, snow must be imperishable as well (see 105e10-106a10). He suggests that, if snow "always" possesses the idea of the cold as long as it exists and if that idea is imperishable, then snow itself must be imperishable as well (see 103e2-5). He suggests, more generally, that if the ideas truly are divine and imperishable beings, and if particular things always possess certain ideas as long as they exist, then those particular things must be imperishable as well. And in this way Socrates implies that we, too, may be imperishable beings. For if all the ideas are imperishable, and if there are ideas which we human beings always possess as long as we continue to exist, then it would seem that, according to Socrates' suggestion here, we must be imperishable as well.

Socrates does also suggest, however, that, if snow perishes when heat approaches, then the idea of the cold that is in it must perish as well (compare 103d7-8 with 102d6–e2). He seems to suggest, then, that the idea of the cold cannot exist apart from its embodiment in particular cold things and hence that either the idea of the cold and snow both withdraw when heat approaches or they both perish. More generally, he suggests that none of the ideas can exist apart from their embodiments in particular things and hence that either the ideas and the particular things that always possess them are both imperishable or they are both perishable. Yet it is clearly impossible for snow to withdraw unmelted when it is approached by heat. We see that snow ceases to be snow and hence perishes when it is approached by heat. This example suggests, then, that particular things are perishable. Accordingly, if, as Socrates seems to suggest, the ideas cannot exist apart from their embodiments in particular things, it seems to follow that the ideas themselves must be perishable beings.[28] But if the seemingly divine and imperishable ideas are themselves perishable, if they cannot exist apart from their embodiments in particular things, how can we or our souls continue to exist, apart from our bodies, once we have died?

Socrates proceeds to suggest that it is the idea or the nature of a particular thing that determines what characteristic or idea it must possess in order to continue to exist. He suggests, for example, that it is the idea or the nature of three that determines that the number three must be odd in order to continue to exist (see 103e5-104b1, 104d5-7). Similarly, it seems to be the nature of snow that determines that it must be cold in order to continue to exist. But Socrates also suggests that the idea or the nature of a thing determines what characteristics or ideas cause that thing to perish. The idea of three, for example, determines that if three should become even, it would cease to be what it is. The idea of three, then, causes three to be odd and also to be incapable of becoming even and hence causes three to be both odd and uneven (see 104d8–e6). Similarly, it seems that the nature of snow determines that, if snow should become hot, it would cease to be what it is. The nature of snow, then, causes snow to be cold and also to be incapable of becoming hot (see 106a3-6). Accordingly, it would seem that it is our human nature that determines what ideas we must possess in order to continue to exist and also what ideas would cause us to perish (see 102c1-2, d5–e6).

Socrates now, at last, appears to identify what idea or characteristic we humans must possess in order to continue to be what we are "by nature." He suggests that, whenever "soul" is present in a body, it always brings to that body the idea of life and thereby causes the body to be alive (105c9–d5). Socrates seems to suggest here that, while it is possible for a human being to continue to be what he is by nature without being big, it is impossible for a human being to continue to be what he is by nature without being alive (see 102c1–e5). It would seem, then, that, just as snow cannot continue to be what it is unless it possesses the idea of the cold, we cannot continue to be what we are unless we possess "soul" and therewith the idea of life.

Socrates then goes on to suggest that death, or the idea of death, is the opposite of life, or the idea of life (105d6-9; see 106d5-7). It would seem, then, that, in accordance with his previous argument about snow, just as snow withdraws or perishes when heat approaches, so must we human beings withdraw or perish when death approaches. But in the case of snow, it is clear that it perishes when heat approaches it. It would seem, then, that, insofar as Socrates is trying to argue that we are immortal, he must argue that the case of human beings is somehow different, that the idea of life is imperishable, and that, since we always possess the idea of life, we must be imperishable as well.

Rather than argue that we are imperishable, however, Socrates, at this point, argues instead that "soul" is "immortal." He first gets Cebes to agree that, since soul "always" possesses the idea of life, it will never accept the idea of death. In this way, he implies that soul is not simply that which brings life to the body but is itself a living being and that, consequently, it cannot be dead and continue to be what it is any more than snow can be hot and continue to be what it is.[29] Socrates then suggests that, just as we call an odd number, which cannot continue to be what it is and be even (*artios*), uneven (*anartios*), so must we call soul, which cannot accept death (*thanatos*) or be dead, deathless or "immortal" (*athanatos*). Therefore, he concludes, soul is immortal. And when he asks Cebes whether they may say that the immortality of "soul" has been demonstrated, Cebes says that it has been demonstrated quite sufficiently (105d10–e9).

Now, Socrates does, in fact, show here that, insofar as soul is a living being, it cannot *be* dead. For, insofar as life is an essential characteristic of soul, that is, insofar as it cannot be what it is by nature unless it is alive, it cannot be what it is and be dead. Indeed, Socrates shows here that, insofar as to be a human being is to be a living being, that is, insofar as we cannot be what we are by nature—for example, living beings who possess speech or reason—unless we are alive, we, too, cannot be what we are and be dead any more than snow can be what it is and be hot.[30] In this way, he shows not only that soul is "immortal" but that all living beings, including himself, are "immortal."

Yet Socrates does not show here that either soul or human beings or living beings as a whole do not simply perish when death approaches just as snow perishes when heat approaches. He does not show that we continue to exist once we have died. Indeed, it would seem that, precisely insofar as we are "immortal," we cannot continue to exist once we have died. For insofar as we are "immortal," insofar, that is, as we cannot be the living beings we are and also be dead, when we die, as we clearly must (see 71e5-6), we must simply cease to be. It would seem, then, that, once Socrates dies, he, that is, the speaking, reasoning, and living being that he by nature is, will simply cease to be (see 115c3–d2). And it would also seem that the philosopher's practice of "dying and being dead" must consist of living as befits an "immortal" and hence a perishable being.

Yet, notwithstanding the specific limits and implications of Socrates' argument for immortality, Cebes is evidently impressed by the conclusion that "soul is immortal." After all, Socrates has apparently shown here that the soul is not only similar to the divine and immortal ideas but that it always possesses the idea of life within itself and hence is itself immortal (compare 80a10–c1 with 105e6-7). Furthermore, Cebes evidently assumes, as Socrates has seemed to assumed in his previous arguments for immortality, that the immortal ideas are imperishable or eternal beings and that, if soul is immortal, it must be imperishable as well (see 78d1-9, 80a10-81a11, 106d2-4). He also evidently assumes, as Socrates has seemed to assume in his previous arguments, that the ideas are separate beings that exist, or at least can exist, apart from their embodiments in particular things (see 65d4-66a10, 74a9–b1, 100b1-9). Accordingly, Cebes seems to understand Socrates to be arguing now that, since soul always possesses the immortal and imperishable idea of life within it, it must itself be immortal and imperishable. He seems to understand Socrates to be arguing that, since soul always possesses the idea of life within it, it, too, must be able to exist apart from its embodiment in particular things and hence once it is separated from the body. And Cebes evidently finds the argument, thus understood, to be persuasive. It seems, then, that Cebes' acceptance of the argument for immortality is based on his assumption that the ideas are separate and imperishable beings.

Now, however, Socrates explicitly calls that assumption into question. He first suggests to Cebes that, if the idea of the uneven were imperishable, then the number three, which always possesses this idea, would be imperishable as well. Similarly, he suggests that, if the idea of the "non-hot," that is, of the cold, and the idea of the "non-cold," that is, of the hot, were imperishable, then, snow and fire would be imperishable as well (105e10–106a11). Socrates returns here to his earlier suggestion or argument that the ideas cannot exist apart from their embodiments in particular things, that they are not, in truth, separate beings, and that, consequently, either both the ideas and the particular things that possess them are imperishable or both are not. Furthermore, he suggests here, through his examples of snow and fire, that the ideas of the cold and the hot are not imperishable, and he explicitly states that the idea of the uneven, that is, the idea of the odd, is not imperishable (106c3). It seems, then, that the ideas are neither separate nor necessarily imperishable beings. And consequently, it seems that the answer to the question of whether soul is imperishable depends on the answer to the question of whether the idea of life, in particular, is imperishable. Accordingly, Socrates now says to Cebes that, if they agree that "the immortal," that is, the idea of life, is also imperishable, then soul, in addition to being "immortal," would be imperishable as well. But, if they do not agree that this is so, then they would need another argument (106b1–d1). In this way, Socrates leaves the question of whether "immortal" soul is also imperishable entirely open.[31]

Cebes, however, says that, since it could hardly be that anything else would be imperishable if the immortal, which is everlasting, is not, there is no need for another argument (106d2–4). He implies here that, if the immortal were perishable, then all things would be perishable. He also implies that, since the conclusion that all things must perish is simply unacceptable, he must agree that the immortal idea of life and therewith (the) soul, must be imperishable (compare 106d2–4 with 71e8–72d5). But furthermore, Cebes simply assumes here that the immortal must be everlasting.[32] After all, he knows, in a way, that the immortal gods are everlasting. If, then, he presumes, soul is immortal, it must be everlasting as well.

Yet, once Cebes asserts that the immortal is everlasting, Socrates suddenly stops saying that soul is immortal. He formally concludes his final argument for the immortality of soul by saying only that the god, the idea of life itself, and anything else that may be immortal will never perish. He then suggests that, *if* the soul is immortal, it must be imperishable as well. And he also says that, when death attacks the human being, the mortal probably perishes, but "the immortal" survives, undestroyed, and departs (106d5–e8). Socrates implies, then, that, insofar as his argument has shown that soul is immortal, it has shown that it is "immortal" only in the sense that it cannot be what it is by nature, namely, a living being, and also be dead.

Furthermore, by suggesting that, while soul may or may not be immortal and imperishable, the idea of life definitely is immortal and imperishable, Socrates seems to call into question his entire argument for the imperishability of soul. For Socrates has seemed to argue that, if soul always possesses the idea of life, and if that idea is imperishable, soul must be imperishable as well (see 105e10-106d1). He has seemed to identify the question of the imperishability of soul with the question of the imperishability of the idea of life. But now he draws a distinction between those two questions. Now he distinguishes between the fate of the idea and the fate of soul. He thereby seems to suggest that the question of the immortality of the soul is entirely independent from the question of whether the ideas are divine and imperishable beings.

The conclusion of Socrates' argument leaves us wondering, then, whether, when we die, we will not cease to exist, even if we, or our souls, are "immortal." It leaves us wondering whether, when death attacks us, we will not perish, even if the idea of life continues to survive, undestroyed, and departs from us.[33] And it also leaves us wondering what connection, if any, there is between the question of the immortality of the soul and the question of the imperishability of the ideas. Nevertheless, Socrates goes on to add to this perplexing conclusion the emphatic statement that soul is immortal and imperishable and that our souls really will be in Hades (106e9-107a1). In this way, he ends his final argument for immortality on a note, not of doubt, but of certainty. And he encourages his friends to believe, when, in a little while, they see and even feel (118a1-2) death attacking him, that his soul will not perish but rather survive, undestroyed, and depart to the gods in Hades.

Cebes responds to Socrates' conclusion by saying that he, at least, has nothing further to say and that he is unable to distrust this argument for immortality in any way. But if, he adds, Simmias or anyone else (see 103a4-10) has anything more to say, he should not pass up this precious opportunity to speak or to hear Socrates speak about the question at hand (107a2-7). Cebes suggests here that he is satisfied that Socrates has met his demand for a demonstration that the soul is both immortal and imperishable (see 88b3-8). And consequently, it would seem that he is persuaded as well that the philosopher has plausible reasons for believing that, if he fulfills his duty in this life, when he dies, he will fare better than other men in Hades and will attain wisdom (see 95b8–c4, 63e8-64a2). Cebes seems, then, to accept Socrates' final argument for immortality, and therewith his final defense of the philosophic life, without reservations (but see 103c2-6, 107a3-7).

Simmias now speaks up and says that he, too, is unable to distrust the argument for immortality in any way. Nevertheless, he adds, given the magnitude of the question at hand and given his contempt for human weakness, he compels himself to maintain a certain distrust for the argument (107a8–b3). Simmias suggests that, while he does not distrust this argument in particular, he continues to doubt the power of any (merely) human argument and hence of human reason itself to reveal the truth about such questions as the fate of the soul after death (see 85c1–d4). His distrust of Socrates' argument for immortality, then, is rooted in his distrust of human reason itself and hence in his doubts about the philosopher's very attempt to discover the truth, or at least the most important truths, through reason. And consequently, unlike Cebes, Simmias does not encourage his friends to speak up and to investigate further the argument for immortality. In contrast with Cebes, then, Simmias is evidently not persuaded by Socrates' final argument for the immortality of the soul or by his defense of the goodness of the philosophic life.

Simmias' distrust of human reason seems to be based on his belief that the truth, or at least the most important truth, is inaccessible to us as long as we are human beings. It seems to be based, in other words, on his belief that the true objects of knowledge, the divine ideas, exist apart from the sensible world and hence that we cannot attain genuine knowledge or wisdom by reflecting on or reasoning about our perceptions of things in this life (see 65d4-67b6, 76d7-77a7, 92d7–e2). But Simmias' distrust of human reason also seems to reflect his implicit belief in the separateness and the immortality of the soul. For, by saying, misanthropically, that *he* contemns human weakness and therewith, it seems, human reason as well, he implies that he, that is, his soul, is not human, that it is separate from and superior to that which is merely human and mortal, and hence that it is divine and immortal. It seems, then, that Simmias distrusts Socrates' argument for immortality not because he doubts that the soul is immortal or that the ideas exist but rather because he doubts that any human being can know, through reason, the truth about such divine beings as the ideas and the soul.

Now, Socrates approves of Simmias' distrust of the argument for immortality. But he evidently does not approve of Simmias' distrust of and contempt for human reason.[34] For, while Socrates praises what Simmias says, he does not urge him to abandon the attempt to discover the truth about the soul through human reason. Instead, he tells Simmias, and Cebes as well, that the argument for immortality, and specifically the first things presupposed in the argument, namely, the separate ideas, must be examined more clearly, no matter how trustworthy they may seem to be (see 100b3-9). He tells them that, if they distinguish those things adequately, they will follow the argument as much as is possible for a human being. And he also tells them that should this, that is, the true nature of the ideas, become clear, then there will be nothing further for them to investigate (107b4-9). In this way, Socrates exhorts his friends to persist in seeking for the truth through argument and reason and hence to persevere in their efforts to live the philosophic life. And he suggests that they should do so, not because it is their duty to do so nor for the sake of rewards in an afterlife, but rather in order to attain wisdom in this life. We see, then, that, while Socrates responds to Simmias' distrust of the particular argument for immortality by encouraging him in his distrust, he responds to Simmias' doubt that it is possible for us, in this life, to attain clear knowledge or wisdom about such questions as the fate of the soul by affirming that such knowledge and such wisdom are indeed available to us in this life.

By urging Simmias and Cebes to reexamine the argument for immortality, Socrates urges them to consider the possibility that the soul is mortal, that it cannot exist apart from the body, and hence that our true selves are not separate from and higher than what is merely human and mortal but are themselves human and mortal. But, as we have seen, Socrates urges them to examine not only the argument for immortality as a whole but the hypothesis of the separate ideas in particular. And it is not immediately clear why he should urge them to examine that hypothesis in particular. For he has concluded his argument for immortality by suggesting that, while the idea of life is immortal and imperishable, the soul may or may not be immortal and imperishable (see 106d5–e7). He has suggested, then, that the question of whether or not the ideas are divine beings that can exist apart from their embodiments in particular things is distinct from the question of whether the soul is an immortal being that can exist apart from the body. Why, then, does Socrates urge his friends so emphatically to examine not only the question of whether the soul is immortal but also the question of whether or not the ideas are divine and separate beings?

In order to see the connection between these two questions, it is important to keep in mind that the argument in the *Phaedo* is not primarily about the immortality of the soul but rather about the goodness of the philosophic life. And while the question of whether or not the ideas are divine and separate beings may not bear directly on the question of whether or not we are immortal, it does bear directly on the question of whether the philosophic life is a good way of life. More precisely, it bears directly on the question of whether the belief in the goodness of the philosophic life depends on the belief in the immortality of the soul. If the ideas are separate beings, if, that is, they are divine beings who exist apart from the sensible world, then it would seem to be impossible for the philosopher to attain full knowledge of those beings and therewith true wisdom as long as he dwells in this world and hence as long as he is alive. It would seem, then, that the philosopher could only attain the wisdom he seeks if his truest self, his soul, is itself a divine and immortal being and if it receives the divine reward or gift of wisdom after death. If the ideas are separate beings, then, the philosophic life must consist of longing for and preparing for the afterlife. But if the ideas are not divine and separate beings, if, that is, they do not exist apart from their embodiments in particular things, then knowledge of them and therewith wisdom itself would be attainable in this life. For, in that case, wisdom would mean the greatest possible knowledge of the beings as they present themselves to our senses. And such wisdom is indeed attainable here. To put this another way, if there is no realm of being that exists beyond the sensible world, if there are no divine beings that exist apart from this world, then this world would be the only world. It would be the true world. And consequently, wisdom would consist of the greatest possible knowledge of the world as it is revealed to us by our senses. By urging his friends, then, to examine more clearly the hypothesis that the ideas are separate beings, Socrates urges them to reexamine their fundamental beliefs about what philosophy is. He urges them to consider the possibility that the seemingly divine beings, the ideas, cannot, in truth, exist apart from their embodiments in the sensible world, that it is possible to know them through perception, and hence that it is possible for us to attain wisdom in this life. He urges them to consider the possibility that the belief in the goodness of the philosophic life is not dependent on the belief that our truest selves, our souls, are divine and immortal beings. He urges them, in sum, to consider the possibility that the philosophic life is the best way of life for a specifically human, and hence mortal, being.

Chapter 12

The Ending of the Dialogue

I. Socrates' Myth about the True Home of the Soul

As we have seen, Socrates responds to Simmias' distrust of the final argument for immortality by urging both him and Cebes to examine further not only whether or not the soul is immortal but also whether or not the ideas are divine beings that dwell apart from the sensible world (107b4-9; see 100a3-9, 78c9-79a11, 80a10–b5). He thereby urges them to examine whether or not wisdom is attainable, by means of our senses, in this life and hence whether or not the goodness of the philosophic life depends on the existence of an afterlife in which the philosopher is rewarded (see 65d4-66e6). Yet Socrates does not propose to Simmias and Cebes that they examine these questions together with him during the time that remains before his execution (compare 107b4-9 with 84c8–d3). Instead, he turns to his friends as a whole, calls on them to embrace the belief in immortality, and proceeds to tell them a myth about the fate of the soul after death (see 107c1ff.). In this way, Socrates appears to leave the philosophic discussion behind and to turn to the poets' mythical accounts of Hades in order to gratify his wish to persuade himself that the soul is immortal (compare 61b3-7, d10–e4, 70b1-9, 91a1–b7 with 107c8–e2, 110b1-2, 111e6-112a5, 112e4-113c8, 114d1-7).[1]

Yet, within the myth that he tells, Socrates does address, albeit in mythic fashion, the questions that he has urged Simmias and Cebes to examine.[2] For, in his myth, he gives to his friends, and especially to Simmias, an account of the "idea" or nature of the earth and hence of the sensible world (see 108d9–e2, 111c4-5).[3] And in that account, Socrates claims that the gods dwell on the earth and that there are human beings on the earth who attain wisdom by means of perception and thereby attain happiness as well (see 111a1–c3). Through this myth, then, Socrates reveals to his friends, and especially to Simmias, that, notwithstanding what the poets say and notwithstanding what, according to Homer, Zeus himself says, the divine beings do not dwell in heaven but on earth and hence do not exist apart from the sensible world.[4] He reveals to his friends, and especially to Simmias, that, notwithstanding what "the poets are always babbling to us," human beings may, indeed, attain genuine knowledge of the divine beings, and of the other beings as well, by means of their senses (compare 65b1-4 with 111b1-c1). And he thereby suggests to his friends, and especially to the misanthropic Simmias, that, notwithstanding "human weakness," human beings may indeed attain wisdom, and happiness as well, in this life and hence that the belief in the goodness of the philosophic life is not, in truth, dependent on the belief in an afterlife (compare 85b10-d4, 107a9-b3 with 111a1-c3).

Nevertheless, notwithstanding this suggestion of his and notwithstanding his emphatic statement to Simmias and Cebes that the argument for immortality must be examined more clearly, Socrates does encourage his friends as a whole to believe that there is an afterlife and that the good fare better there than the bad. In order to understand why he does this, let us consider this section of the discussion more carefully. After urging Simmias and Cebes to examine further the argument for immortality, Socrates turns to his friends as a whole and tells them that this, at least, is a just thing to believe: namely, that, if indeed the soul is immortal, it is in need of care not only for the sake of this time that we call life but also for the sake of all time (107c1-4). Now, Socrates does not, at this point, say either that there is an afterlife or even that it is just to believe that there is one but only that it is just to believe that, if there is an afterlife, those who care for their souls—presumably, the philosophers—will fare well there. Furthermore, by saying that one should care for the soul for the sake of this life as well as the afterlife, he implies that, even if there is no afterlife, the philosopher will still fare well in this life. Socrates begins, then, by suggesting to his friends that they ought to believe not that there is or must be an afterlife in which the philosopher will be rewarded but only that, if there is an afterlife, it does not pose any threat to the earthly happiness of the philosopher but rather supplements or crowns that happiness with eternal life.

Socrates immediately suggests, however, that it is, in fact, just or at least good for his friends to believe that there is an afterlife. For if, he explains, death were a release from everything, if, that is, there were no afterlife at all, then it would be a godsend, or a divine reward, for the wicked, when they die, to be released from both the body and their own wickedness together with their soul (107c5-8). Socrates here suggests to his friends that it would be unjust and therefore intolerable to believe that the wicked could ever enjoy even the limited blessing of having their miserable existence come to an end. He suggests that, if there are just gods, they would never reward the wicked by allowing them ever to escape from their miseries. And, apparently on the basis of this suggestion, he now suddenly declares that, *since* the soul is apparently (or manifestly) immortal, there would be no escape for the soul from evils nor salvation except to become as good and as wise as is possible. For the soul, he adds, goes into Hades taking nothing with it but its education and rearing, and these are said to do the greatest benefit or harm to the one who has died at the very beginning of his journey to Hades (compare 107c8–d5, especially c8, with c2). In this way, Socrates urges his friends to believe that there is an afterlife, that the wise and the good enjoy the greatest benefits there, and that the wicked suffer the greatest harm.

Now, it is true that, by urging his friends to embrace this belief about the afterlife, Socrates encourages them to hope for a better future for themselves and for all those who live the philosophic life. But it is also true that he here urges them to believe that there truly is an afterlife only after he has spoken of the blessing death would be for the wicked if there were no afterlife. This suggests that, in Socrates' opinion, it is good for his friends to believe that there is an afterlife above all because it is good for them to believe that the wicked will suffer everlasting torment. And this suggestion is confirmed by the fact that, while Socrates does go on to describe to his friends the happy fate of the good souls after death, he describes at much greater length the unhappy fate of the bad souls (compare 108a6-7, c3-5, 114b6–c6 with 108a7–c3, 112e4-114b6).

It is not immediately clear why Socrates should think that his friends need to believe that the wicked will suffer evils for all time once they are dead. After all, he has not emphasized the sufferings of the wicked in his previous accounts of the fate of the soul (see 81b1-82a9; but see 61a8–b1, 62b6–c8, 63c4-7, 69c3-7, 72d9–e2). Furthermore, he suggests to his friends here that, just as the good fare well in this life as a consequence of their goodness, the wicked already suffer in this life as a consequence of their wickedness (see 107c1-8). And, finally, Socrates characteristically expresses the view that just punishments for the wicked do not harm but rather benefit them.[5] Why, then, does he now encourage his friends to believe that the wicked will not only be punished after death but will suffer quite specifically everlasting "evils" and the greatest "harm" (see 107c9–d5)?

In order to answer this question, we need only consider Socrates' examples of those who will suffer the greatest harm after they die. For the most prominent example he gives of such men are those who have committed "unjust homicides" in this life. It is those who have committed unjust homicides and other such things who will be abandoned by all souls, daemons, and gods when they first come to Hades and who will then be punished (108b3–c5). It is those who have committed either many great temple robberies, unjust homicides and many lawless acts, or other such things who will be hurled by fate into Tartarus and who will never escape from there (see 113e1-6, 111c5-113c8). And it is those who have committed homicides or other such crimes in anger and have then repented for the rest of their lives who must suffer forever after death unless they can persuade their victims, by shouting and calling to them, to allow them to escape from "the evils" they are suffering (see 113e6-114b6; see also 113d1-4). By encouraging his friends to believe, then, that there is an afterlife in which the wicked, and especially those who kill unjustly, suffer everlasting evil, Socrates attempts to prepare them for the sight of his own execution. He anticipates that, when they see him die, they will inevitably feel the anger and the pain of witnessing helplessly the unjust execution of a friend. And he also anticipates that they will inevitably wonder how it can be wise or good for a man to live the philosophic life when it renders him incapable of defending himself against his enemies.[6] Through his myth, Socrates reassures his friends that his death will not go unavenged and that his enemies will not go unpunished (see 62c1-5). He reassures them that his persecutors and indeed all those who persecute the philosophers will themselves suffer everlasting evil and the greatest harm (see 64b1-6). And he even suggests to them that he himself may ultimately sit in judgment of those responsible for his death (compare 113e6-114b6 with 98e2-3, 116c1-8, 117a4–b2; but see also 62c6-8, 98e5-99b4).[7] Socrates, then, assuages, in advance, the anger and fear his companions will feel when they see him executed (see 94c9–e1). But furthermore, he reassures them that the philosophic life remains the best way of life, despite the threat of persecution. For he reveals to them not only that the philosophers will enjoy the greatest of rewards for all time after death but also that their persecutors will suffer the greatest evils for all time unless, of course, the philosophers themselves have mercy on them.

Socrates' myth about the fate of the soul after death constitutes the formal conclusion of his defense of the philosophic life against the impiety charge of Cebes and Simmias (see 62c9-63b5; see also 60c8-61b1). Having argued for the immortality of the soul, he describes, through this myth, the great goods the philosopher will enjoy in Hades (see 63b5-7, 63e8-64a3, 107c8–d5). Accordingly, Socrates concludes his myth by emphasizing to his friends the piety of the philosopher (compare 113d1-4, 114b2–c6 with 107d2-5, 108a6–c5). He tells them that the souls of the pious will go to a pure home on the earth and that those among the pious who have purified themselves sufficiently through philosophy will live without bodies for the rest of time and will go to homes still more beautiful than those of the merely pious. Socrates, then, encourages his friends to believe that the philosophers are indeed pious and that, consequently, they will be rewarded by the gods once they are dead. For the sake of these rewards, he tells Simmias, he ought to do everything to partake of virtue and wisdom in this life. And for the sake of these rewards, he tells his friends as a whole, any man who has been serious in his life about the pleasures of learning rather than those of the body and who has adorned his soul with virtue and truth ought to be confident for his soul as he awaits the journey to Hades (114c6-115a5). Socrates concludes his defense of the philosophic life, then, by encouraging his friends to live that pious way of life for the sake of divine rewards in Hades.

Yet, if we examine Socrates' myth closely, we see that it actually calls into question the beliefs of the pious and specifically their belief that, when they die, their immortal souls will depart from this world and go to another, invisible world—the true Hades—where they will dwell with the gods (see 80d5-8, 69c3-7). For, according to that myth, when they die, the souls of the pious go to a place beneath the heaven and *on the earth* (compare 108c3-e2, 114b6-c6 with 110b1-111c3, 113d1-4). They go to a place where there are, for example, trees, flowers, and mountains, where the gods dwell and are visible to human beings, and where human beings attain wisdom by means of their senses, attain happiness, live much longer than we do, but then, it seems, die. Socrates' myth suggests, then, that while the souls of the pious and of the philosophers among them, do go to paradise once they are dead, they go to an earthly paradise. It suggests that the final and true home of the soul is not in heaven but on earth. And it thereby suggests that an intelligent man will not live for the sake of divine rewards in an other world but will rather live for the sake of a human happiness in this, our only world (see 114d1-7).

II. The Death of Socrates

Once he has completed his speeches in defense of his readiness, as a philosopher, to die and of his philosophic life as a whole, Socrates turns to the business of his own death. He points out to Simmias, Cebes, and the others that, while each of them will make his journey to Hades at some future time, he, as a tragic man would say, is already being summoned by fate to his journey and also it is just about time for him to take a bath. For, as Socrates explains, it is, in his opinion, better to bathe himself before he drinks the drug—that is, the poison—and to spare the women the trouble of washing a corpse (115a3-8). And with this abrupt reference to his corpse, Socrates seems to bring to an end his discussion of the immortality of the soul. For it seems that, having completed his defense of his philosophic life, Socrates now intends to bathe and then, immediately, to end his own life by drinking the hemlock (see 116b6, 116d7-117a3).

Crito, however, who has been silent throughout Socrates' defense of philosophy, now speaks up and asks him to tell his friends what they should do, either concerning his children or anything else, so that they may gratify him (115b1-4). The father Crito (58b7) naturally assumes that the father Socrates is at least somewhat concerned about the future of his soon-to-be-orphaned sons and that he would like to be reassured that they will be taken care of once he is dead.[8] But Crito may also believe that, whatever happens to their souls once they have died, human beings do in some sense live on after death through those who bear their name and who are the flesh of their flesh, namely their offspring.[9] And consequently, he may believe that, by caring for Socrates' sons in the future, his friends will, in some sense, be caring for and gratifying their friend as well.

Socrates, however, shows no concern whatsoever for the future lives of his sons. But he does express concern for the future lives of his friends. For he tells them that, by caring for themselves, they will gratify him, his own, and also themselves, even if they should not now make any promises. But if they neglect themselves and are not willing to live in accordance with what he has said, both in the present conversation and in the past, then even if they now make many vehement promises, they will accomplish nothing more (115b5–c1). Socrates suggests here that, if his friends truly wish to gratify him and his own, they should care for themselves by living in accordance with his arguments on behalf of the philosophic life. And in this way he implies that, insofar as his friends are capable of living that way of life (and insofar as his sons are not), he cares more deeply for them and even regards them more truly as his own than he does the sons Xanthippe has borne for him (see also 116a5-7).

Now, by urging his friends to care for themselves by living out their lives in accordance with his arguments, Socrates seems simply to repeat his earlier exhortation to them to fulfill their philosophic duty to keep the argument or reason itself alive by living the philosophic life (see 89b4–c1). Yet, by emphasizing to his friends here that he, in particular, will be gratified if they live the philosophic life, Socrates suggests that they ought to live that life not only for duty's sake or for their own sake but also for his sake. He suggests, in other words, that their future devotion to philosophy will be an act not only of duty or self-interest but also of friendship for him. And he thereby supplies his friends with an additional motive for living the philosophic, or Socratic, way of life. Furthermore, by saying that his friends *will* gratify him, regardless of what they say now, if they live in accordance with his argument for philosophy, Socrates suggests that he will know, even after his death, whether or not they devote their future lives to philosophy. He seems to suggest that, if they devote their lives to philosophy, they will gratify him because he will be aware, even in Hades, of their devotion to philosophy and to him. But he may also suggest here that, as long as his friends are living their lives in accordance with his speeches, as long, that is, as they are living the Socratic way of life, they will be gratifying him by keeping his speeches alive, by keeping his spirit alive, and thereby keeping him, in some sense, alive through them.

Crito now asks Socrates, in what way are we to bury you (115c2-3)? He naturally assumes that Socrates cares how his body will be buried. And it would seem that Crito makes this assumption because he assumes that Socrates will somehow continue to live on, at least for a while, through his body even after he has been executed. For, if the body of Socrates will become a merely lifeless thing once he is executed, why should he, or anyone else, care what will become of it (see 80c2–d2)? Now, insofar as Socrates and his friends have, throughout this conversation, identified the truest self of a human being with his soul, we might expect him simply to dismiss as absurd Crito's identification of his self not only with his body but with his corpse. Yet Socrates does not simply dismiss what Crito says here. Instead, he proceeds to give a somewhat extensive speech about his death to Crito and his friends. And while he begins that speech playfully and even laughingly, near the end of his speech he warns Crito that, by suggesting that he will continue to live on in his corpse, he is implanting "a certain evil in the souls" of those present (115e4-6). Socrates seems to imply here that, by identifying him with his corpse, Crito threatens to undermine his efforts to persuade his companions of the goodness of the philosophic life. And consequently, it seems that, notwithstanding Socrates' laughter here, he actually regards what Crito says here quite seriously.

In order to understand why Socrates takes so seriously Crito's suggestion that he will continue to live on, at least for a time, in his corpse, it is important to see in what way that suggestion might appear to be plausible. The lifeless body that Crito and his other friends will see immediately after the execution will not appear to be a merely lifeless thing (see 80c2–d2). It will still look like Socrates. It will still bear his image or form (see 72e7-73a3, d5-8). Consequently, the sight of that corpse will naturally tempt his friends to believe that, while Socrates has in some sense died and left them, he has not yet entirely died and left them. And these men will feel especially tempted to believe this because, being as attached to Socrates as they are, they will naturally long to believe that he has not yet left them altogether.[10] Yet the belief that Socrates is in any sense still alive in his body after his execution will inevitably lead them to imagine that he is suffering truly terrible things (see 115d8–e4). For, when they touch his cold and rigid body, they will imagine that their friend is trapped within it (see 117e4-118a14). When they see his corpse burned or buried, they will imagine that Socrates is feeling the heat of those flames or the horror of being buried beneath the earth. And when they consider that his body is slowly rotting away (see 80b8–d2, 86c2–d1, 87d7–e5), they will imagine that

Socrates himself is experiencing the pain and the terror of slowly rotting away. Crito's suggestion, then, that Socrates will not immediately perish or depart when he is executed may tempt his friends to imagine that his death and, indeed, any death is an unimaginably terrible thing. It threatens to intensify their fear of death. And it consequently threatens to lead them to fear all the more the persecution that attends the philosophic life. In this way, then, Crito's seemingly innocent question does indeed threaten to undermine Socrates' argument that the philosophic life is, despite the threat of persecution, the best way of life.[11]

Accordingly, Socrates responds to that question by gently ridiculing Crito. He tells his friends that he is not persuading Crito that he is this Socrates, who is now conversing and arranging each of the speeches, but Crito supposes that he is that corpse which he will see in a little while and consequently asks how he should bury "him." As for the very long argument he has made, that once he drinks the hemlock he will no longer remain with his friends but will depart to the happy condition of blessed men, Socrates supposes that, while he has given encouragement to his other friends and also to himself, to Crito he has spoken these things in vain. Nevertheless, he urges his friends to reassure Crito that, once he is executed, he will have departed, so that Crito will bear it more easily when he sees the body of Socrates burned or buried. And he urges Crito to be confident, to say that he is burying Socrates' body, and to bury it in whatever way is dear to him and he believes to be lawful (115c4–116a1). Socrates urges his friends, then, to believe that, once he has been executed, he will immediately depart from his body and also from them and that he will enjoy an everlasting happiness in Hades. And he thereby reassures them that, by dying, he will not be suffering anything frightful or pitiable.

Yet while Socrates' speech here would seem to assuage his friends' fear of death, it would also seem to intensify their feeling of being abandoned. For he emphasizes here that, when he dies, he will leave them immediately and forever. And consequently, once he gives this speech and goes off to take his bath, Socrates' friends are overwhelmed by the misfortune they themselves are about to suffer and by the prospect of living out the rest of their lives deprived of the man they love as a father (116a2-7). In this speech, Socrates does, however, suggest to his friends a way in which they may ease their sense of abandonment, if not immediately, at least in the long run. For by saying quite emphatically that he is this Socrates, who is now conversing and arranging each of the speeches, he suggests that, as long as his friends discuss his conversations with one another and repeat his conversations to one another, he will in some sense be present among them. He suggests that, as long as they do not abandon his speeches, he will not entirely abandon them. And while repeating and listening to others repeat the speeches of Socrates cannot ease their painful sense of loss on this day, we know, at least from the example of Phaedo, that it may indeed ease the pain of these orphans of Socrates, and may even give them the greatest pleasure, throughout the rest of their lives (compare 116a2-7, 117c5–d1 with 58d5-6). For, by recounting Socrates' conversation, Phaedo not only allows Echecrates and his companions to enjoy the company of the true Socrates but also allows himself to enjoy the company of his dearest friend. By bequeathing his speeches to his friends, then, and by urging them to identify him with his speeches, Socrates shows them how they might continue to be with him even after he has abandoned them.

After Socrates has spent a very long time away from his cell, bathing, seeing his sons, and conversing with the women of his household, he returns to his friends. Shortly thereafter, the jailer enters the cell to announce that Socrates must now drink the hemlock. And after praising Socrates as the noblest, the gentlest, and best of those who have ever been imprisoned in his jail and after urging him to try to bear his death as easily as he can, the jailer bursts into tears and departs (116a7–d2). Now, by weeping for Socrates here, just as Xanthippe had wept for him at the beginning of this day, the jailer shows that, like Xanthippe, he is convinced that Socrates is not happy but sad that he is dying (see 60a3-6). Yet whereas Socrates had indicated in no uncertain terms that he disapproved of his wife's outburst, he now praises the jailer for weeping so nobly for him (compare 116d3-7 with 60a6–b1; see also 117d7–e2). Perhaps he believes that, insofar as he has now persuaded his friends that he is confident, and has reason to be confident, that he and all philosophers will enjoy the greatest goods after death, he can afford to praise the jailer's expression of compassion without undermining their confidence in the goodness of the philosophic life (see 58e1-59a7, 107c1–d5, 114d8-115a3). But it is also possible that, as the moment of his death draws near, Socrates cannot help but express his appreciation for the jailer's recognition of the sadness Socrates himself feels in the face of his own death (see 91a6–b7, 106c9–d7, 107a8–b10).

Be that as it may, Socrates now tells Crito to tell the executioner to bring in the poison. Crito, however, pleads with Socrates to wait a bit longer. He points out that others drink the poison long after the jailer makes his announcement, that they have one last meal, and that some even have intercourse with those whom they desire. Crito does not, however, mention the possibility that Socrates may continue to converse with his friends. Even he seems to acknowledge that the time for conversation has passed (see 115c7-8). And consequently, once Socrates points out that he sees no profit in postponing his execution any longer and urges Crito to obey him, Crito relents and gives the signal for the execution to proceed (116e1-117a7).

Throughout this conversation, Socrates has given speeches to his friends about his death. According to those speeches, when he dies, Socrates' soul will leave his body and go to Hades where it will enjoy an everlasting happiness. Now, however, his friends are able to witness the death itself. What light does his death shed on his speeches? What light does it shed on his argument for the philosophic life and on the ultimate fate of the philosopher? What light does it shed on the wisdom and the goodness of the philosophic way of living and dying? According to Phaedo, Socrates drank the hemlock readily and calmly. He then walked around and, when his legs began to feel heavy, he lay down. Gradually his body became cold and rigid, first his feet, then his legs, and then his midsection. And finally, a little later, his friends saw that he moved and, when the executioner uncovered him, they saw that his eyes and his mouth were open. This, as Phaedo tells Echecrates, was the end of his companion (117b3-118a15). But this death does not disclose what has become of Socrates. It does not reveal whether he has perished or gone to Hades or whether, if he has gone there, he will fare well. It does not reveal whether he was right to drink the hemlock readily and calmly or, as Phaedo had said earlier, happily and without fear (117c3-5, 58e3-4). It seems, then, that the sight of the death itself does not shed light on Socrates' speeches, for it does not reveal whether he died wisely or whether he lived wisely.

Perhaps it is for this reason that Socrates does not simply let his friends see his death. In the first place, he covers himself during his final moment (118a5-13). But furthermore, and perhaps more importantly, Socrates continues, both immediately before and during his death, to speak about his death. Once he accepts from the executioner's hand the cup containing the hemlock, he prays to the gods for good fortune on his migration from this world to the next (117c1-3). Then, once he has drained the cup and his friends begin to weep violently and loudly, Socrates silences them and thereby ensures that they will be able to hear his last words (c5–e4; but see also 91b1-7). And finally, at almost the very last moment, he tells Crito that they owe a sacrifice—a cock—to Asclepius and that he should be sure to pay this debt to the god (118a5-9). Now, through these words, Socrates suggests to his friends that he expects to journey to Hades and that he hopes to find favor with the gods there. He suggests to them that the true significance of his death is not to be found in the effect of the hemlock on his body but rather in the fate of his soul in Hades. And in this way he directs their attention away from the sight of his death and back to the arguments he has made on this day about the fate of the soul after death and about the philosophic way of living and dying. Socrates' last words suggest, then, that, in order to understand the true significance of his death, we must reflect on his speeches rather than on the death itself.

And they thereby suggest that, in order to understand whether the philosopher died and lived wisely, we must reflect on the true Socrates, the one who spoke to his friends, who, through Phaedo, spoke to Echecrates, and who, through Plato, continues to speak to us, rather than on the corpse that his friends saw once he had died.[12]

III. Conclusion

In the *Phaedo*, Socrates presents to his friends a final defense of his philosophic life (63b1-5, 63e8-64a3). In the first place, he argues that, since the wisdom the philosopher seeks is so fine and pure a thing, he cannot attain it in this life but only, if at all, in an afterlife (65a9-66e6). And he then proceeds to argue both that the soul is immortal (70c4-80e2, 102a10-107a1) and that, if the philosopher should purify his truest self—his soul— of all that is merely human and mortal, he will deserve the divine reward of pure wisdom and everlasting happiness (66e6-69d2, 80e2-84b8). On the last day of his life, then, Socrates attempts to defend the goodness, the wisdom, and the justice of his readiness, as a philosopher, to die and of his philosophic life as a whole by persuading his friends that the philosopher may reasonably hope that, when he dies, he will finally attain the wisdom he seeks, he will win for himself the greatest goods, and he will dwell with the gods forever. And the end of the dialogue suggests that Socrates succeeded in this attempt. For Phaedo concludes his account of Socrates' last conversation and death by saying, on behalf of all those present, that Socrates was the best man they had ever known or tested and that he was especially the most wise and the most just.

Yet, as we have seen, Socrates does not, in fact, show either that the individual soul is immortal or that it is possible for the philosopher to deserve divine rewards in Hades. Indeed, I have argued that Socrates himself rejects the belief in personal immortality. He rejects, in particular, the belief that our truest selves are distinct from and higher than our human and mortal selves. And consequently, he denies that any human being can deserve everlasting rewards or punishments and hence that any sensible human being will live his life hoping for such rewards or fearing such punishments. Furthermore, Socrates suggests that wisdom, or at least human wisdom, is indeed attainable in this life and hence that the goodness of the philosophic life does not, in fact, depend on the existence of an afterlife. In the *Phaedo*, then, Socrates indicates, albeit quietly, that, in his view, the philosophic life is the best way of life, not because of the rewards the divine soul of the philosopher will enjoy in Hades, but rather because of the happiness the philosopher enjoys, as a human being, in this life.

Now, if this interpretation of the dialogue is correct, we must conclude that, on the last day of his life, Socrates greatly deceived his friends. By claiming to believe in the immortality of the individual soul, he deliberately encouraged them to embrace a belief and to cherish hopes which he himself regarded as false. And he thereby exposed them, and those who might be influenced by them, to what he himself says would be the "evil" of living their lives in accordance with a false belief about the ultimate fate of the soul (see 91a1–c5). The question arises, then, how can a man who perpetrates such a great and seemingly harmful deception of his own friends be, as the conclusion of the dialogue emphatically claims he is, a just man (see also 63b5-9)?

In Socrates' defense, we begin by observing that, even before this conversation takes place, his friends already cherish in their hearts a powerful hope for immortality. That hope is implicit in their dissatisfaction with "this life" and in their longing to be cared for by the gods "always" (see 61c9-62a9, c9–e4; see also 85c1-6). It is implicit in their belief that their souls are distinct from and higher than their merely human and mortal selves (see 64c4-65a8, 69e6-7, 70a6–b1, 72e7-73a3, 81a4–11, 107a9–b3). Finally, it is implicit in their longing to attain a pure wisdom, untainted by the senses, which is unattainable in this life (see 65d4-67b6, 67e4-68b7, 69e6-7). Yet, even though Socrates' friends cherish the hope for immortality in their hearts, they are evidently not aware, to begin with, how powerful this hope of theirs is. And even though they have been trying to live the life of reason, they have evidently never subjected this, their deepest hope, to the scrutiny of reason. It seems, then, that, as the conversation begins, these men are in a kind of twilight state, ostensibly devoted to the pursuit of truth in this life while secretly longing for everlasting happiness in the afterlife.

Now, in this conversation, Socrates renders his friends' implicit hope for immortality an explicit theme of discussion. By arguing that the goal of the philosophic life can only be reached, if at all, in the afterlife, he shows them that their entire hopes for wisdom and happiness depend on the existence of an afterlife. He allows them to see and to feel for themselves just how much is at stake for them in the question of immortality. And he thereby awakens in them a desire to know the truth about this question (compare 64c2-9 with 69e5-70b4). Furthermore, by attempting to vindicate the hope for immortality through reason, he encourages them to believe that it is possible to learn the truth about the fate of the soul through reason (compare 70b1-9 with 72e3-73a3, 77c1-5). Finally, by failing in his efforts to vindicate the hope for everlasting happiness, Socrates encourages them to examine for themselves and on their own the reasonableness of this hope (see 84c4-88b8, 107b4-9). It is true that, as the conversation draws to a close, his friends appear to be largely persuaded that the individual soul is immortal and that the philosopher will win for himself the greatest goods once he has died. Yet, as they think back on this unforgettable conversation, they, or at least some of them, may come to see that Socrates has not truly vindicated their hope for immortality. As they reflect on Socrates' indications of the difficulties that beset the argument for personal immortality, they, or at least some of them, may come to see that their hopes for everlasting happiness are unreasonable. And as they reexamine Socrates' defense of his way of living and dying as a whole, they, or at least some of them, may come to see that the philosophic life is the best way of life for a human being precisely because it enables those who live it to recognize and to accept their human and mortal natures. Through this conversation, then, Socrates benefits his friends by making them fully conscious of their deepest hopes, by allowing them to see, if only they will, the unreasonableness of those hopes, and by preparing them, in this way, truly to live the life of philosophy.

Furthermore, by encouraging his friends, on the day of his death, to believe in the immortality of the soul, Socrates helps them to bear his death more easily. By reassuring them that his persecutors and all the persecutors of philosophers will suffer the greatest harm in Hades, he helps to assuage their anger and sorrow on this unhappy day. And by reassuring them that the philosophers themselves will enjoy the greatest blessings once they have died and hence are reasonably confident in the face of death, Socrates helps his friends to resist the temptation to abandon the philosophic life in the face of persecution.

Finally, by persuading his friends and through them human beings at large that he genuinely believed in the immortality of the individual soul, Socrates attempted to defuse the religious hostility to philosophy in the Greece of his day. In a world in which philosophers as such were suspected of impiety and impiety was punishable by death, Socrates sought to acquire the posthumous reputation of having been a philosopher of unassailable piety (see chapter 1). Through his speeches and his bearing on the day of his death, then, Socrates tried to protect his friends and, indeed, all friends of philosophy from the evils of persecution.

But was Socrates successful in his attempt to protect philosophers and their friends from further persecution? It is, of course, impossible for us to know with certainty what precise effect Socrates' death and Plato's account of that death had on the fate of philosophy in the ancient world. It is worth noting, however, that, some time after Plato wrote, the position of philosophers in the Greek world improved dramatically. It is true that the persecution of philosophers persisted for a time. Aristotle, Theodorus, and Stilpo were all accused of impiety by the Athenians and were forced to flee the city.[13] But these instances of hostility to philosophers are out-weighed by the overall improvement of the reputation of philosophy. Plato won enormous fame among the Greeks in his lifetime.[14] The school he founded in Athens, the Academy, attracted students from all over the an-cient world and was not closed once in the eight hundred years of its existence. During that time, it produced not only illustrious philosophers, such as Speusippus, Aristotle, and Xenocrates, but also famous statesmen, such as the Athenian Phocion, the Syracusan Dion, and the Romans Cicero and Brutus.[15]

Other philosophers, following the example of Plato, founded schools of their own which also enjoyed the good will of the Greeks.[16] Accordingly, when Aristotle's student Theophrastus was accused of impiety and a law was passed restricting the activities of philosophers in Athens, the Athe-nians shortly thereafter fined his accuser and repealed the antiphilosophic law so that Theophrastus, who had fled, would return to Athens and live there as before.[17] The Cynic Diogenes and the Stoic Zeno were honored and cherished by the Athenians.[18] And Pyrrho, whose students founded the Sceptics, was appointed the chief priest of Elis.[19]

Eventually, the philosophers won renown in the most powerful city in the ancient world, Rome. Plutarch, in his life of Marcus Cato (22), describes the welcome that the philosophers Carneades, the Academic, and Diogenes, the Stoic, received in Rome when they were sent there as ambas-sadors from Athens:[20]

> Immediately, then, the youths who most loved speeches hastened to the men and associated with them, listening to them and marveling at them. And especially the grace of Carneades, whose power was greatest and whose reputation did not fall short of his power, laid hold of great and philanthropic audiences and filled the city, like a wind, with the sound of his voice. And a report was spreading that a Greek, who was extraordinary to an astounding degree, by beguiling and subduing everyone, had cast into the young a strange *eros*, because of which they fell away from their other pleasures and pastimes and were possessed by philosophy. These things pleased the other Romans, and they saw with pleasure that their young men were receiving a Greek education and were associating with amazing men.

The reputation of philosophy grew so great there that such students of philosophy as Scipio Aemilianus Africanus, Cato the Younger, and Marcus Aurelius became its leaders.[21] Philosophy, then, which had been an activity engaged in by a small band of persecuted and despised men at the time of Socrates' death, gradually became a subject of study for preeminent states-men of the ancient world.

It is also worth noting that, in the judgment of Plutarch, it was Plato, in particular, who brought about this remarkable improvement in the status of philosophy and that he did so by giving philosophers a reputation for piety which they had lacked before. For he contends that it was Plato who removed the "slander" that philosophy was an essentially impious activity and thereby made it acceptable to "all men."[22]

If we peruse the works of Plato to see where he presents the philosopher as a pious man, we find that nowhere does he do so more persuasively than in the *Phaedo*.[23] There Socrates not only declares his belief in the immortality of the soul, in divine and incorporeal beings—the ideas, and in an afterlife in which the good will dwell with the gods and the wicked will be punished; he also appears to prove the sincerity of his belief by appearing to die fearlessly (58e3-59a1). Both the speeches and deeds of Socrates in the *Phaedo* appear to demonstrate his piety. The dialogue in which the Athenians execute Socrates for impiety is the dialogue in which Socrates appears to be most pious.

We may plausibly suggest, then, that, through his portrayal of Socrates as a pious man throughout his works but most powerfully in the *Phaedo*, Plato removed the charge of impiety against the philosophers as a whole. Although individual philosophers continued to be charged with impiety, philosophy as such ceased to be viewed as an essentially impious activity. With the threat of impiety trials no longer hanging over their heads at all times, philosophers and their students could survive unmolested and even respected in the ancient world. And Plato, whose teacher had been put to death for impiety, eventually acquired the epithet "the divine."[24]

Indeed, Plato's portrayal of the philosopher as a pious man appealed so strongly to the enduring religious passions in the human soul that, even when the religion of the pagans gave way to the new religion of the Christians, the religious reputation of Socrates and Plato, and through them of the philosophers as a whole, survived. In the second century A.D., Justin Martyr said: "And these men who lived together with the word [*logos*] are Christians, even if they were believed to be atheists, as, among the Greeks, Socrates, Heraclitus, and those similar to them. . . ." He further claimed that Christ had been known in part by Socrates.[25] Clement of Alexandria praised Socrates and Plato highly and, quoting Numenius, asked, "What, after all, is Plato but Moses in Attic?"[26] In the third century A.D., Origen lauded Socrates as a man who died "as became a philosopher" and compared his death to that of Jesus. He also expressed his agreement with Plato's doctrines of the immortality of the soul and of the preexistence of the soul.[27] Eusebius said that Plato taught that the soul is immortal as the Christians do.[28] And Gregory of Nyssa's treatise, *On the Soul and The Resurrection*, "repeatedly betrayed its ancestry in the *Phaedo*."[29]

Perhaps most significantly, St. Augustine ranked Socrates, Plato, and the Platonists above all the other pagan philosophers and claimed that none were as close to the Christians as they were. He praised them especially for believing in life after death, in the invisible and divine ideas, in an incorporeal God, and in creation, and for rejecting the materialism of other philosophers.[30] He went so far as to say that, if Plato and his followers were somehow to come back to life, "with the change of a few words and opinions they would become Christians."[31] St. Thomas Aquinas later observed that St. Augustine's work was an attempt "to follow the Platonists as far as the Catholic faith would permit."[32]

The early Christians' enthusiasm for Plato was not based essentially on their agreement with particular doctrines which they attributed to him. For there were a number of elements in Plato's writings that many early Christians attacked: his harsh view of the body, his belief in the preexistence of souls, his evident exclusion of the possibility of resurrection, and his willingness to worship a plurality of gods.[33] What drew these Christians to Plato was above all the religious image that he left of the philosopher, an image which appealed to the core of the Christians' religious beliefs and passions, but not necessarily to their particular beliefs in particular doctrines. The scholar Etienne Gilson gives a convincing account of the appeal of Plato to the early Christians in the following passage:[34]

> Platon s'est offert en allié du Christianisme sur plusieurs points importants: la doctrine d'un démiurge de l'univers; d'un Dieu providence; de l'existence d'un monde suprasensible et divin dont le monde sensible n'est que l'image; de la spiritualité de l'âme et de sa superiorité sur le corps; de l'illumination de l'âme par Dieu; de son asservissement présent au corps et de la nécessité d'une lutte pour le dominer; de l'immortalité de l'âme, enfin, et d'une vie outre-tombe où elle recevra la récompense ou le châtiment de ses actes. On pourrait d'ailleurs allonger la liste de ces affinités christiano-platoniciennes. . . . Allons plus loin: toute la doctrine de Platon était inspirée par un tel amour de la vérité et des réalités divines que tout vrai philosophe s'efforce d'atteindre, qu'on imaginerait difficilement une philosophie qui, sans être une religion soit plus près d'en être une.

Through the early Christian apologists, the Church fathers, and St. Augustine, Socrates and Plato won the admiration of Christians who came later. And as long as Socrates and Plato were admired, philosophy as such could not be condemned. Hence, important Christians such as Abelard, Roger Bacon, John of Garland, Albert the Great, Petrarch, and Marsilio Ficino gave high praise to Plato and to philosophy as a whole.[35] And when Erasmus declared, "*Sancte Socrates, ora pro nobis,*" he could appear to be only exaggerating a view of Socrates already held by Justin Martyr.[36]

This continuing admiration for Socrates and Plato by the Christians was crucial for the survival of philosophy. As a new and powerful religion that was hostile to the pagan world as a whole, Christianity might well have led to a resumption of the persecution of philosophers for impiety that Anaxagoras, Socrates, and Aristotle had suffered in early antiquity. Indeed, a strong current of hostility to philosophy persisted in the Christian world, though it never completely prevailed.[37] The early Christian Tertullian denounced Socrates and sought to arouse antiphilosophic sentiment among the pious.[38] St. Peter Damiani heaped scorn on Plato and called philosophy an invention of the devil.[39] And Luther expressed alarm at the Church's admiration for Socrates and Plato.[40] Nevertheless, the Christians as a whole professed belief in the piety of Socrates and Plato and hence gave philosophy protection. Rather than become a persecutor and possibly a destroyer of philosophy, the Christian Church became a vessel within which philosophy could endure. Although individual philosophers might be accused of heresy or atheism, philosophy itself was not accused of being an essentially impious activity. For after the death of Socrates and after the *Phaedo*, a defender of philosophy could always point to that man and to that dialogue as strong evidence that philosophers as such are not impious.

We may plausibly suggest, then, that, through his speeches and bearing on the day of his death, Socrates helped his friends and all friends of philosophy. And if it is reasonable to believe that justice consists, at least in part, in helping one's friends, we may reasonably conclude that Socrates was, indeed, a man of extraordinary justice.[41]

Notes

Introduction

1. Unless otherwise indicated, all references are to this work. The text is that of John Burnet (1967). Translations from the Greek are my own.

2. Cicero *Tusculan Disputations* 1.71.

3. Jacques Maritain 1962, 38.

4. See, for example, Plato *Gorgias* 484c4–486d1, *Republic* 487b1–e3, *Phaedo* 64a4–b6; Aristophanes *Clouds*; Plutarch *Nicias* 23.

5. Friedrich Nietzsche 1967, 89.

6. Voltaire, "Prix de la Justice et de l'humanité" (1777), article 11 in *Oeuvres*, 30:557.

7. For the comparison with Alexander, see, for example, the Emperor Julian *Letter to Themistius the Philosopher* 264b–d; Michel de Montaigne 1958, 614; Jonathan Swift, "Of Mean and Great Figures, Made by Several Persons" (1772), in *Miscellaneous and Autobiographical Pieces*, ed. H. Davis (Oxford: Basil Blackwell, 1962), 83-84; Voltaire, "Socrate," in *Dictionnaire Philosophique*, in *Oeuvres*, 20:428; Frederick the Great, Letter to Voltaire (February 16, 1774), in *Oeuvres*, 23:274. For the comparison with Cato, see, for example, Cicero *Tusculan Disputations* 1.74; Montaigne 1958, 308–310, 793; Jonathan Swift, "On the Excellency of Christianity" (1765), in *Irish Tracts and Sermons* (Oxford: Basil Blackwell, 1948), 249; Jean-Jacques Rousseau 1979b, 219. See also Plutarch *Cato* 68–70. For the comparison with Jesus, see, for example, Justin Martyr II *Apology* 10; Origen *Contra Celsium* 9.17; John Calvin, *Epistula Pauli ad Timotheum*, Bks. 1, 6, in *Corpus Reformatorum*, 52:530; Rousseau 1979a, 307–308; Johann von Goethe 1974, 236; John Stuart Mill 1975, 32–34.

8. See Plato *Phaedo* 63b5–c4, 84c5-7, 86d5–e4, 91a1–b7, 106c9–e7, 107a8–b9. See also, for example, Cicero *Tusculan Disputations* 1.49; Georg Hegel 1955, 2:43; R. Hackforth 1955, 64-65, 76, 84-86, 157, 163-66, 195–98; Paul Friedlander 1969, 3:45-49, 54, 57-60, 474; David Gallop 1975, 104–113, 134-36, 140-42, 216-222; Hans-Georg Gadamer 1980, 21-22, 25-28, 36-38; Kenneth Dorter 1982, 39-40, 43-44, 74-78, 152-161; R. S. Bluck 1982, 18-26; David Bostock 1986, 38-41, 52-59, 116-121, 187-193.

9. Bostock 1986, 191-92. See also David Keyt 1963, 167-172; Dorothy Frede 1978, 38-40.

10. Hackforth 1955, 164; see also 14, 17, 41, 91, 101, 165-66.

11. Burnet 1967, l–lv, 22, 26; A. E. Taylor 1960, 178-79, 192, 206–207; Bluck 1982, Preface, 33, 47; David White 1989, 17-23, 41-43, 127–29, 216-17.

12. Gallop 1975, 220. See also Paul Stern's helpful discussion of this point (1993, 28).

13. Gallop 1975, 222; Hackforth 1955, 165. See also Bluck 1982, 23.

14. Gallop 1975, 74.

15. The account that follows is based on what I regard as the indispensable discussions of how to read a Platonic dialogue to be found in the following works: Alfarabi 1972, 84-85; Friedrich Schleiermacher 1973, 17-18; Leo Strauss 1946, 348-352; 1978, 50-62; David Bolotin 1979, 11-12; 1987a, 39-41, 55-56; Allan Bloom 1968, xv–xix; Thomas Pangle 1980, 376; Jacob Klein 1965, 3-31. See also Stern 1993, 5-7; Friedlander 1969, 1:108-125, 137-170; Gadamer 1980, 1-6; Charles Griswold 1980, 530-546; Stanley Rosen 1987, xi–lxvii.

16. Such scholars as Burnet, Hackforth, Gallop, Bluck, Bostock, and White suggest that, at certain points in the *Phaedo*, Socrates is speaking ironically, but they never examine his irony in a systematic way. See, for example, Burnet 1967, lv–lvi, 22, 26, 103, 109; Hackforth 1955, 107, 109; Gallop 1975, 172, 174, 177; Bluck 1982, 113; Bostock 1986, 147; White 1989, 271.

17. See, for example, 91a1–c5, 107c1–d5, 118a15-17; Plato *Republic* 331c1–d3, 382c3-10, 450d10–e1.

18. See Plato *Apology of Socrates* 37e3-38a8.

19. See Plato *Republic* 336e2-337a7, *Gorgias* 489d1–e4.

20. Gregory Vlastos 1991, 23, 147-48. See also 132-156, 25-29, 37.

21. See also Plato *Lesser Hippias*.

22. Plato *Seventh Letter* 341d2–e3. See also Plato *Phaedrus* 275d4–276d5, especially 276a1–b1.

23. Schleiermacher 1973, 18.

24. See Plato *Lovers* 133d8–e1.

25. Compare 63b1-5, 91a1–c5 with Plato *Apology of Socrates* 37e3–38a8.

26. See Dorter 1982, 8-10, 20-22, 39-41, 43-44, 46, 75-78, 81, 94-97, 159-161, 180; Ronna Burger 1984, 2-3, 18-19, 33-35, 50, 110-11, 119-121, 134.

27. See Stern 1993, 22-30, 31-33, 40-43, 139-141, 162-63, 176, 179-182, 224. But see also 85, 171-72.

28. See, for example, Dorter 1982, 158-161, 179-188; Burger 1984, 185-86; Stern 1993, 4-5, 91, 130-145 (but see also 28).

Chapter 1. The Context of Socrates' Defense of Philosophy

1. Xenophon identifies Crito, Hermogenes, Simmias, Cebes, and Phaedondes as Socrates' close companions and presents Antisthenes and Apollodorus as his constant companions (*Memorabilia* 1.2.48; 3.11.17). For Socrates' association with Crito see Plato *Crito, Euthydemus, Apology of Socrates* 33d9–e1. For Critoboulos see Xenophon *Oeconomicus, Memorabilia* 2.6, *Symposium*. For Hermogenes see Plato *Cratylus*; Xenophon *Symposium, Apology of Socrates to the Jury, Memorabilia* 2.10, 4.8. For Epigenes see Xenophon *Memorabilia* 3.12. For Antisthenes see Xenophon *Symposium*. For Ctessipus see Plato *Euthydemus, Lysis*. For Menexenus see Plato *Lysis, Menexenus*. For Eucleides and Terpsion see Plato *Theatetus*. For Apollodorus see Plato *Symposium* 172a1–174a2; Xenophon *Apology of Socrates to the Jury* 28.

2. Phaedo, Eucleides, and Antisthenes respectively founded the schools of Elis, Megara, and the Cynics. Cebes, Simmias, and Aeschines reportedly composed works of philosophy. See Diogenes Laertius *Lives and Opinions of Eminent Philosophers* 1.15, 19; 2.60-64, 105-112, 121, 124-25; 6.1-19.

3. The account that follows is based both on texts which were written during the lifetimes of Socrates and Plato and also on ancient texts which were written much later. Since the accuracy of these latter texts is open to some question, I have tried to base my account as much as possible on texts written by contemporaries of Socrates and Plato. However, since such writers as Plutarch and Cicero had access to writings about the historical context of Socrates' execution which are no longer extant, and since their accounts fundamentally agree with those of such contemporaries of Socrates and Plato as Thucydides and Isocrates, I have made considerable use of their writings as well.

4. Polybius *Histories* 2.38.10ff.; Diogenes Laertius 8.39-40; Porphyry *Life of Pythagoras* 54-58; Iambilichus *Life of Pythagoras* 248ff. According to Cicero and Diogenes Laertius, Pythagoras was the first man to describe himself as a "philosopher." See Cicero *Tusculan Disputations* 5.7-9; Diogenes Laertius 1.12-13, 8.8.

5. Diogenes Laertius 9.18; Plutarch *De Stoicorum* 1051c; Diodorus Siculus *Bibliotheca Historia* 10.18.2; Diogenes Laertius 9.26; Boethius *Consolation of Philosophy* 1.3.30-43.

6. Thucydides *The War of the Peloponnesians and the Athenians* 2.39-41; Isocrates *Panegyricus* 47-50, *Antidosis* 295.

7. Burnet 1957, 254; Léon Robin 1928, 122; Plutarch *Pericles* 4.4, 5.3, 6, 8.1, 16.5-7, 32, 35.1-2, *Nicias* 23; Plato *Phaedrus* 269e1–270a8; Isocrates *Antidosis* 235-36; Diogenes Laertius 2.12-14.

8. Plutarch *Pericles* 4.1-2, *Nicias* 6.1; Isocrates *Antidosis* 235-36; Plato *Alcibiades I* 118b8–c5, *Republic* 400b1–c6, 424c5-6, *Laches* 180c5–d3; Diogenes Laertius 2.19.

9. Cicero *De Natura Deorum* 1.2, 63, 117-19; Sextus Empiricus *Against the Physicists* 1.55-57; Diogenes Laertius 9.51-52.

10. Lysias *Against Andocides* 17-18; Aristophanes *Birds* 1071–75, *Clouds* 830 and context; Cicero *De Natura Deorum* 1.2, 63, 89; Diodorus Siculus 13.6.7; Plutarch *Moralia* 1075a; Sextus Empiricus *Against the Physicists* 1.50-59. See also Eudore Derenne 1976, 64-66.

11. George Grote claims that Socrates would never have avoided persecution as long as he did in any other Greek city (1862, 6:155-56; 180-83). See also Plato *Phaedo* 64a10–b6, *Meno* 79e7-80b7, *Protagoras* 316c5-317b3, *Greater Hippias* 285b5–c2; Derenne 1976, 264-66.

12. See Plato *Parmenides*; Diogenes Laertius 9.51-52.

13. Anaxagoras probably took up residence in Athens in 462 B.C. and was prosecuted in 432. Damon was ostracized in 445 B.C. Aristophanes' *Clouds* was performed in 424 B.C. Protagoras was prosecuted in 416 B.C. Diagoras was condemned in 415 B.C. Socrates was executed in 399 B.C. For the trials of Anaxagoras, Protagoras, and Diagoras, see Derenne 1976, 13, 30-38, 51-54, 66-70. See also Edward Zeller 1980, 104-105.

14. Diogenes Laertius 2.106, 5.5-6; Aeschines *Against Timarchus* 173; Isocrates *Antidosis* 170, 173, 175-76, 215, 246-47, 270–71, 285-86, 304-305. Isocrates repeatedly echoes Plato's *Apology of Socrates* in this speech. See Plato *Phaedrus* 278e5-279b3. See also Grote 1862, 6:183; Derenne 1976, 178-181.

15. Plutarch *Pericles* 32, *Nicias* 23; Diogenes Laertius 2.12–14; Diodorus Siculus 13.6.7; Sextus Empiricus *Against the Physicists* 1.50-59; Cicero *De Natura Deorum* 1.63, 117-18; Diogenes Laertius 9.51-52; Plato *Apology of Socrates* 24b8-28a1; Xenophon *Memorabilia* 1.1; Diogenes Laertius 2.40; 5.5-6. It is possible that Xenophanes was expelled from Colophon because he said that he did not believe in the gods of Homer and Hesiod. See Diogenes Laertius 9.18; Xenophanes fragments 11, 12 Diels, Fifth Edition. See also fragments 15, 16, 19, 23-26, 32, 34D; Grote 1862, 6:68.

16. Plato *Apology of Socrates* 23c7–d7, *Laws* 966d9-967d2.

17. See W. K. C. Guthrie 1971, 62-63; Aristophanes *Clouds* 365-411, 817-831, 1227-41, 1468-1511.

18. See Lysias *Against Andocides*; Andocides *On the Mysteries* 30. Andocides was accused of impiety, and his trial took place in the same year that Socrates' trial took place. Andocides' repeated appeals to religious passion and belief indicate how pious his audience must have been (see 31-33, 113-14, 137-39).

19. See Numa Denis Fustel de Coulanges 1900, especially the introduction; Grote 1862, 5:147-48; Derenne 1976, 9-12, 254-262; J. V. Muir 1985, 193-95. See

also Aristophanes *Clouds* 395-407, 901-905, 1214-59, 1321-1477, 1506-9; Plato *Laws* 624a1-625a3, 634d7–e4, 662c5-7.

20. Thucydides 6.15, 27-32, 47-53, 60-61, 74, 88.7-93; Plutarch *Alcibiades* 18-22, 23.1-2.

21. Thucydides 7.50ff.; Plutarch *Nicias* 23-30.

22. Xenophon *Hellenica* 1.6.24–1.7.35; Diodorus Siculus 13.31. See Fustel de Coulanges 1900, 11-12; Montaigne 1958, 12-13.

23. There were cases in which the Athenians and other Greeks were willing to take even more extreme measures to appease the gods. Several decades before Socrates' trial, on the eve of the battle of Salamis, the Athenians performed human sacrifices at the behest of their seers (Plutarch *Themistocles* 13, *Pelopidas* 21). And a few decades after Socrates' trial the Thebans seriously considered performing human sacrifices on the eve of the battle of Leuctra (Plutarch *Pelopidas* 21-22).

24. See Lysias *Against Andocides* 1-2, 13-14, 19-34, 53; Antiphon *Tetralogy* 1.1.10, *Murder of Herodes* 81-83. See also Derenne 1976, 254-58.

25. But see Plato *Phaedo* 96a6ff.

26. See Diogenes Laertius 1.23; Aristophanes *Clouds* 395-407, 901-905; Lysias *Against Andocides* 19-32; Cicero *De Natura Deorum* 1.1-4, 117-120; Plutarch *Pericles* 6, 35.1-2, *Nicias* 23.

27. See Aristophanes *Clouds* 366-402, 889-1104, 1140-62; Plato *Republic* 358e1-367e5, especially 365b4–e1.

28. Guthrie 1950, 340, 351; see also 132-33, 136-37, 144. For the relevant fragments of the Pre-Socratic philosophers, see Xenophanes 11-12, 14-16, 23-26, 32, 34D; Heraclitus 5, 14-15, 27, 30, 32, 40-42, 80, 96, 102, 132D; Epicharmus 1, 64D; Empedocles 17, 21, 28, 131-34D; Anaxagoras 19D; Diogenes of Apollonia 5D; Democritus 297D; Protagoras 1, 4D; Thrasymachus 10D. See also Aristophanes *Clouds* 365-402, 1321-1511; Plato *Laws* 889e3-890b2.

29. Robin says: "By taking flight he [Anaxagoras] escaped the dangerous consequences of a trial for impiety—a menace which was henceforward to hang over the heads of all philosophers in Athens" (1928, 122). See also Grote 1888, 1:252, 388-390.

30. Burnet 1962, 182-89.

31. Taylor 1960, 157-60; 1924, 109-110, 143; Stone 1989, 237–247. See also Arnold Toynbee's claim that "It was Politics, not Religion, that cost Socrates his life" (1939, 7:472), and G. M. A. Grube's astonishing claim that "Plato had no experience of a persecuting religion" (1980, 175). For what may be the first expression of the opinion that Socrates was executed primarily for political reasons, see Voltaire, "Des sectes des Grecs," in *Essai sur les moeurs et l'esprit des nations* (1767), chap. 26, in *Oeuvres* 11:77. See also "Des Grecs, de Socrate et de la double doctrine," in *Dieu et les hommes* (1769), chap. 12, in *Oeuvres* 28:153.

32. Burnet 1962, 182-83.

33. Burnet 1962, 117.

34. But consider Cicero *De Natura Deorum* 1.3-4.

35. Burnet 1962, 187-88.

36. Burnet 1962, 186; see 209-211, 218-19, 221, 294-301. See also Plato *Euthyphro* 5c4-8, 12e1-4, 15e5-16a4.

37. Plato *Apology of Socrates* 23c7–d7, *Laws* 966d9-967d2.

38. Thucydides 6.27-29, 53, 60-61; Plutarch *Alcibiades* 18-22; Critias fragment 25D; Sextus Empiricus *Against the Physicists* 1.54 and context.

39. See Guthrie 1971, 62-63; Grote 1862, 6:155, 160, 181-83. See also Grote 1862, 5:147-48; Fustel de Coulanges 1900, 420; Derenne 1976, 254-262; E. R. Dodds 1951, 189-191; Muir 1985, 193-95.

40. Burnet 1962, 76; Lysias *Against Andocides* 17-18; Diodorus Siculus 12.6.7; Cicero *De Natura Deorum* 1.2, 63, 117-18; Sextus Empiricus *Against the Physicists* 1.50-54. See also Derenne 1976, 64-66; Dodds 1951, 189, 201.

41. Burnet 1962, 76; Plato *Apology of Socrates* 26b8-e5, *Laws* 967b4–d2 and *Phaedo* 97b8-c2; Plutarch *Nicias* 23, *Pericles* 32; Diogenes Laertius 2.12-14. See also Derenne 1976, 23-26, 41.

42. Burnet 1962, 117; Cicero *De Natura Deorum* 1.63; Sextus Empiricus *Against the Physicists* 1.56-57; Diogenes Laertius 9.51-52. See also Cicero *De Natura Deorum* 1.2, 117-18; Plutarch *Nicias* 23; Derenne 1976, 45-55.

43. See Derenne 1976, 9-12, 14-16, 21-25, 254-264 and, above all, his excellent discussion on 217-223.

44. See Aristophanes *Clouds* 1464-1509; Plato *Laws* 887c7-888a2.

45. Burnet's discussions of Greek piety stand in marked contrast to the extraordinarily careful and sensitive discussions of that subject by Grote, Fustel de Coulanges, and Derenne. Compare Burnet 1962, 117-18, 182-83, 189-190 with Grote 1862, 5:147-49, 151; 6:68, 155, 181-83; Fustel de Coulanges 1900, especially 420; Derenne 1976, 9-12, 14-16, 21-25, 217-223, 254-264.

46. See Plato *Republic* 487b1–e3; compare 516e3-517a7 with Plato *Phaedo* 64a4–b6. See also Plato *Theatetus* 173c6-175b7, *Lovers* 132b8-10, *Seventh Letter* 328d4–e5.

47. See Plato *Gorgias* 484c4-486d1.

48. See Plato *Gorgias* 484c4-486d1, especially 486b4–c2, 521b2-522c6. See also Plato *Apology of Socrates* 28b3-5.

49. See Plato *Crito* 45b2-5. For their association with Socrates see also Xenophon *Memorabilia* 1.2.48, 3.11.17.

50. The word *philosophy* does not occur in Plato's *Crito*. Compare also 50a6-54d1 with Plato *Apology of Socrates* 29c5–d5.

Chapter 2. The Opening of the Dialogue

1. For the Athenians' desire to silence Socrates, see Plato *Apology of Socrates* 29b9-30c1, 30e1-31a7, 37e3-4, 39c3–d5.

2. See 60d5ff., 89b4–c4, 115b5–c1, 116a4-5. See also Plato *Theatetus* 142c5-143c5.

3. Compare 115c6–d2 with 58d5-6; Plato *Symposium* 215d3-216c3.

4. See 88c8–d6, 58d5-9, 59a7–c3, 60a2. According to Diogenes Laertius, Echecrates was a follower of the Pythagoreans (8.46).

5. See Klein 1965, 147-48.

6. Compare 116a4-7, 117c5–d1, 118a15-17 with 59a1–b1. See also 68a3-7; Plato *Republic* 603e3-604a9.

Chapter 3. The Opening of Socrates' Last Conversation

1. See Plato *Apology of Socrates* 18a7–e4, 20c4-24b1, 28a4–b2, 37e3–38a8; see also 33c4-34b2.

2. While commentators generally acknowledge that Socrates is here defending the philosophic way of living and dying, they tend to overlook the fact that his defense is directed specifically against the repetition by Cebes and Simmias of the Athenians' impiety charge against him. See Hackforth 1955, 3, 41, 57; Gallop 1975, 86; Bluck 1982, 5, 46-47; Bostock 1986, 21; Gadamer 1980, 23-25; White 1989, 37-38. See also Burger 1984, 33-35. Dorter and Stern do point out that Socrates is responding here to the impiety charge, but I believe that Dorter and even Stern tend to underestimate the degree to which Socrates takes this charge seriously (Dorter 1982, 20-22; Stern 1993, 24-30; but see 21).

3. See Plato *Apology of Socrates* 31b1-5. See also Xenophon *Symposium* 2.9-10 and especially 9.7, where Xenophon does not include Socrates among the married men. But consider Plato *Phaedo* 60a1-2.

4. See 116a5-7, 117c5–e4; Plato *Crito* 43c5-8, 44b5–c5.

5. As Burnet says, "There is no hint in the *Phaedo*, or anywhere else in Plato, that Xanthippe was a shrew" (1967, 12). Xanthippe's reputation as a shrew appears to be based on certain passages in Xenophon. See *Symposium* 2.10; *Memorabilia* 2.2.7-8 (but see also 9-11). For a witty survey of scholarly opinions of Xanthippe, see Guthrie 1971, 65-66.

6. Burnet argues that, since Socrates' youngest child is brought back to him later on (see 60a1-2, 116a7–b5), it is "surely impossible to believe . . . that Xanthippe is not included among" the women of his household who see him before his execution and therefore "we can find no fault with the behaviour of Socrates in the matter" (1967, 144, 12). But even if Burnet is correct, since Socrates does not assure his wife here that he will see her once more before his death and since he does not even speak to her at all, it is hard to see how his words here can be justly described as "kindly and considerate" (13)

7. In this way, the Platonic Socrates' dismissal of Xanthippe here for suggesting that death is bad may resemble the Aristophanic Socrates' similarly harsh dismissal of Strepsiades in the *Clouds* for suggesting that death, in certain circumstances, may be desirable (776-790). On the other hand, Socrates may dismiss Xanthippe here because, in her way, she sees all too clearly, and more clearly than his companions will, that he is not happy on this day. See 58e3 where Phaedo says to Echecrates, "For Socrates *appeared to me* to be happy" and also 90e4-91b7.

8. Plato *Apology of Socrates* 19d8-20c1, *Phaedrus* 267a2-5.

9. See Plato *Republic* 595a1-608b2, especially 607a5–e2.

10. See White 1989, 30-31; Nietzsche 1967, 92-93; Bolotin 1987a, 41; Stern 1993, 20.

11. Aristotle *The Regime of Athens* 1; Plato *Phaedo* 58a10–b4.

12. See Plato *Apology of Socrates* 33c4-7.

13. See, for example, Plato *Apology of Socrates* 33c4-7; Moses Maimonides, *The Guide of the Perplexed* 2.44.

14. Consider, for example, *Deuteronomy* 13:1-5.

15. See also Aristotle *Nicomachean Ethics* 1138a3-14.

16. See Plato *Euthyphro* 12c10–d7.

17. Plato *Apology of Socrates* 38a1-8.

18. Gadamer contends that Cebes and Simmias "represent the modern scientific enlightenment" and goes so far as to claim that "the truth of the religious tradition has paled to such an extent for Cebes that the fate of the soul in the beyond is no longer of any concern to him" (1980, 23-25).

19. Gallop suggests that Socrates here "implies that his own death will be self-inflicted" (1975, 85).

20. See 98e2-99a4; Plato *Crito* 50e2-54e2, especially 54b2–d1.

21. See Plato *Crito* 43b10–c4, 53a8-54a1, *Apology of Socrates* 38c1-7; compare 31c4-32a3 with 40a2–c3.

22. See Plato *Apology of Socrates* 25c5-26a7.

23. I therefore do not agree with Burger's claim that Socrates "manages now to avoid any attempt to defend himself against the apparently justifiable charge of impiety" (1984, 34). Indeed, by apparently taking it for granted here that Socrates is guilty of impiety, Burger sets aside what I believe to be the central issue of the dialogue. Compare also 217 with Plato *Euthyphro* 12d1-6.

Chapter 4. Socrates' Defense of the Philosopher's Readiness to Die

1. See Hackforth 1955, 3, 171.

2. See Plato *Philebus* 49d6-8. See also Stern 1993, 33.

3. But consider 118a15-17; see also present work, chapter 12, section 3.

4. See Plato *Apology of Socrates* 20d6–e3, 21b4-5, d2-7, 22b8–e5, 23a5–b4, 29a4–b6, 42a2-5. But see also 29b6-7, 38a1-8.

5. See Bolotin 1987b, 184-190; see also 190-92.

6. See 65b1-4; Burnet 1967, 31. See also Plato *Republic* 380d1-383c7.

7. As Gallop says, "It is not merely that they [the senses] misrepresent the physical world, but that they never present anything else. They hamper the soul's access to the real objects of its understanding, the 'Forms'.... They give no indication that there are any such objects and strongly suggest that there are not. Clear philosophic understanding can therefore be achieved only when normal sensory awareness is suspended" (1975, 91-92). It seems to me more reasonable, however, to identify this view with Simmias rather than with Socrates since, as Gallop himself acknowledges (121, 172, 222), Socrates distances himself from this view at various points in the dialogue (for example, 60b3–c7, 73c1-74a8, 89e5-90b3, 107b4-9). See also White 1989, 46.

8. As Gallop observes, "it might be supposed that their existence has to be accepted purely on faith. The Theory [of separate forms] is, indeed, everywhere assumed rather than proved" (1975, 95). He also says, "It is, however, nowhere defended but is simply accepted without argument by all parties" (97). Yet, here, too, it seems to me more reasonable to identify this "faith" with the interlocutors rather than with Socrates. See, for example, 76d7-9, 100b3-7, 107b4-10. Gallop himself acknowledges that Socrates thought that the "Theory offers only a provisional solution, which is itself in need of further exploration" (172; see 222). Furthermore, Burnet suggests that the theory of separate forms is "essentially Pythagorean," and we learn in the dialogue that Simmias and Cebes studied with the Pythagorean Philolaus. See 1967, xliii–xlvi, 19; Diogenes Laertius 8.84. Burnet also suggests that Plato was aware that the theory required revision (124), and Grube contends, in the light of the *Parmenides* and the *Sophist*, that Plato became aware that the theory is problematic, but only after having written the *Phaedo* (1980, 32-42, 48). Indeed, Bostock suggests that Plato eventually abandoned the

theory of separate forms (1986, 201-207). Yet, Plato dramatically situates the *Parmenides* (in which the young Socrates hears Parmenides' critique of the theory of separate forms) and the *Sophist* (in which Socrates witnesses the Eleatic Stranger's critique of this theory shortly before his trial) prior in time to the *Phaedo* and thereby clearly suggests that the Socrates of his *Phaedo* was at least aware of the problems that beset the theory of separate forms. See Plato *Parmenides* 128e5-135d6, *Theatetus* 210d1-4, *Sophist* 216a1-4, 246b6ff.

9. See also Gallop 1975, 141; Strauss 1978, 120-21.

10. See Bolotin 1987a, 44-45.

11. It seems to me that Burger and Stern are too quick to describe this argument as "ironic." See Burger 1984, 38-50, especially 44, 50; Stern 1993, 36-43, especially 36. I think that it is only by considering more fully than they do the power of this important argument that one can see clearly and appreciate fully the grave difficulties that beset it.

12. See Paul *Epistle to the Romans* 7:14-25.

13. Compare 66b1-7, e2-4 with Plato *Symposium* 199e6-200b3, 204a1-7.

14. See Stern 1993, 44-45.

15. See Bolotin 1987a, 47-48.

16. Hackforth (1955, 49) and Gallop (1975, 88) note that in other dialogues Socrates is not so harsh on the body.

17. Taylor claims that "Socrates, like all great religious teachers, rests his hopes for the unseen future in the last resort on the goodness of God. . . ." (1960, 179; see also 192).

Chapter 5. The First Argument for the Immortality of the Soul

1. For a somewhat different account of the contrast between Cebes and Simmias, see Stern 1993, 47-48.

2. 70b5-9. See also Plato *Apology of Socrates* 39e1ff.

3. See Aristophanes *Clouds* 245-6, 365-411, 1224-42, 1458-80.

4. See Bolotin 1987a, 45-46; Stern 1993, 28; Gallop 1975, 220.

5. 70c4-8. See Xenophanes, fragment 7D; Diogenes Laertius 8.4-5; Plato *Meno* 81a10-c7, *Republic* 614b2-621b7, *Phaedo* 81d6-82c1.

6. See Burger 1984, 55.

7. In other words, Socrates does not attempt to show here that being alive and being dead are contradictories rather than contraries. On this point see Bostock

1986, 47-53; Stern 1993, 55; Burger 1984, 59-60; Dorter 1982, 37-39; Gallop 1975, 107-108.

8. See Stern 1993, 50-51; Burger 1984, 65-66.

9. Stern, Gallop, and Bostock identify this specific problem with the argument but they do not, in my view, recognize that the argument itself seems to point to the conclusion that we are mortal. See Stern 1993, 53-61 (but consider 56); Gallop 1975, 110; Bostock 1986, 42. See also T. M. Robinson 1969, 124-25; Hackforth 1955, 195. Burger, on the other hand, does allude to this feature of the argument (1984, 59, 234-35).

10. See Bostock 1986, 52-53.

11. Plato *Laws* 808b3–c2. Compare also Plato *Apology of Socrates* 30e1-31a7, 38a1-8 with 40c5–e4.

12. I therefore disagree with Bostock's claim that Plato "has not really seen the problems that this [namely, personal survival] involves" (1986, 39).

13. See Plato *Symposium* 206a3-12, 206e8-207a4.

14. Bostock alludes to this aspect of the argument (1986, 58).

15. In this way, Socrates attempts to counteract what Stern calls the "self-forgetting" inclination of Cebes (1993, 78, 144, 164).

16. See Gadamer 1980, 25-26.

Chapter 6. The Argument That Learning is Recollection

1. See Plato *Meno* 80d1-81e2, 86b1–c2.

2. See Burger 1984, 70.

3. See Plato *Phaedo* 73a7-b2, *Meno* 81c5–d5.

4. See Plato *Meno* 86a6-9.

5. For a different formulation of this point, see Burger 1984, 80.

6. See Plato *Meno* 81e5-86c8. For brief comparisons of the accounts of recollection in the two dialogues, see Gallop 1975, 115; Burger 1984, 238.

7. See K. M. W. Shipton's extremely valuable comparison of Simmias' and Socrates' views of knowledge (1979). It seems to me, however, that Shipton overstates the parallelism between their views and that he fails to notice that Socrates first challenges Simmias' skepticism in this section of the dialogue and therefore long before his account of his second sailing (see 34-40, 41-44).

8. Klein suggests that "It is *the action of learning* which conveys the truth about it. The answer to the question about the possibility of learning is not a 'theory of knowledge' or an 'epistemology' but the very *effort* to learn" (1965, 171-72).

9. Compare 74a9-75d6 with 76a9–b12. Hackforth and Gallop notice the contradiction between these two passages but do not recognize how Socrates' pedagogical purpose here accounts for this contradiction. See Hackforth 1955, 76; Gallop 1975, 120. For a somewhat different interpretation of Socrates' pedagogical purpose here, see Stern 1993, 62, 69-73.

10. See Michael Davis 1980, 569. See also Gallop 1975, 121.

11. For a fuller discussion of this point, see Bolotin 1979, 155-59.

12. For the importance of the distinction between understanding the forms or ideas as common properties of perceptible things and understanding them as separate, imperceptible beings, see Hegel 1955, 2:29-31; Strauss 1978, 118-121; Gallop 1975, 95-97, 127-28; Bluck 1982, 174-187; Bostock 1986, 94-101, 194-213. See also Plato *Parmenides* 128e5-135d6, especially 130b1-10, 133a8–b3, 134e10-135d1. Gallop says that "It is this 'separation' of Forms from sensible objects that distinguishes the fully-fledged Theory found in the *Phaedo*. Nowhere is the contrast between Forms and sensible things drawn more sharply than here" (94). But he also notices that the forms sometimes function in the dialogue as common properties or "universals" (96, 127).

13. See Dorter 1982, 56; Bostock 1986, 86-87.

14. For a helpful account of what it means to know the "equal itself," see J. B. Gosling 1965, especially 160-61. See also Bostock 1986, 69-94.

15. Dorter notices this point but not Socrates' later humbling of Simmias (1982, 61). Burger, too, does not, in my view, give sufficient weight to this aspect of the discussion (1984, 78-80).

16. See Stern 1993, 71.

17. I therefore disagree with Burger that Simmias' perplexity here is "justifiable" (1984, 79-80). For different interpretations of this key passage, see Dorter 1982, 63; Stern 1993, 69.

18. Stern seems to allude to this point (1993, 73).

19. See Stern 1993, 74. According to one manuscript authority (W), Cebes here exhorts Socrates alone to attempt to persuade the child within them not to fear death. I find the other manuscript authorities (B,T) on this passage more plausible, however, because their reading is more consistent with Cebes' attempt to distinguish the childish fear within himself and Simmias from their true selves. For an explanation of the different manuscript authorities of the *Phaedo*, see Burnet 1967, lvii-lix.

Chapter 7. The Third Argument for the Immortality of the Soul

1. See Burnet 1967, 70; Hackforth 1955, 85-86; Gallop 1975, 142; Stern 1993, 75, 81; Bostock 1986, 119-120. It seems to me that these commentators overlook

the extent to which this argument points to the conclusion that the soul is mortal. Burger, however, alludes to this aspect of the argument (1984, 92-93).

2. See Stern 1993, 75; compare with Gallop 1975, 137.

3. See Stern 1993, 75-77; Burger 1984, 87-89.

4. Dorter goes so far as to suggest that "this argument, though the least rigorous, may be the most persuasive. Perhaps the most significant and fundamental reason why people have continued to believe in the non-finality of death and their personal immortality is the sense of something eternal within us" (1982, 76). But the fact that this argument provokes such powerful objections from Simmias and Cebes would seem to suggest that Dorter overstates its persuasiveness. See also Plato *Phaedo* 80b8-10.

5. See Stern 1993, 79-80; Hackforth 1955, 85-86.

6. The reason that Socrates and Cebes agree so easily that the body is not a purely visible being may be that here, at least, they tend to regard the body as the seat of passions which are not themselves visible (see, for example, 80e2-81c3). This may explain why Socrates speaks of the corpse as simply or purely visible (compare 80c2-4 with 79b4-6). See Burger 1984, 90, 242.

7. See Stern 1993, 79-80; Gallop 1975, 140.

8. Bostock remarks, "Indeed, one wonders why Plato dared to make this comparison at all, for it is obvious that the soul is a changing thing, and in this respect is like the body and *not* like the forms" (1986, 119). See also Gallop 1975, 140-41.

9. See Lucretius *De Rerum Natura* 3.476-486.

10. See Plato *Euthyphro* 3a8–b4.

11. See 88e4-89a7, 94c9–e6. See also Plato *Republic* 380d1-383c7.

12. Gallop notices Socrates' identification of the forms with the gods, but he does not consider the questions this raises about the nature of divine beings (1975, 141, 143).

13. See Xenophon *Apology of Socrates to the Jury* 27. See also Lucretius *De Rerum Natura* 3.931-951; Montaigne 1958, 64-67.

14. See Plato *Symposium* 205e7-206a13, 206e8-207a4.

15. I consequently disagree with the suggestion of Dorter and Burger that Socrates does not fear death. See, for example, Dorter 1982, 159; Burger 1984, 94, 111, 119-121 (but see 107).

16. I do not, then, agree with Gadamer's claim that "the point of the demonstrations . . . is that they refute doubts and not that they justify belief" (1980, 37). See especially Plato *Phaedo* 85e3-88b8.

17. See, for example, 58a10–b4, 60e1-7, 62b6-63c7, 69c3-7. See also Plato *Republic* 380d1-383c7.

18. Dorter suggests that the ensuing section is a "noble lie" (1982, 81), Burger suggests that it is "mythological" (1984, 86), and Hackforth (1955, 81) and Gallop (1975, 137) suggest that it is merely speculative. Stern says that Socrates now "moves from discursive argument to mythic presentation" and argues that he proceeds to sharpen the choice between reason and belief (1993, 81-84). I believe that Socrates here rationally investigates the pious belief in "a providential view of the whole" and therewith the pious belief in immortality. I view this section, then, as a continuation and even the culmination of the preceding argument.

19. See Stern 1993, 82; Bolotin 1987a, 48.

20. See Bostock 1986, 32-35; Bolotin 1987a, 49-51; Stern 1993, 45-46, 97, 178, 204. Gallop considers this point when discussing 69a6–c3, 82c1-8, and 114d8-115a1, but he repeatedly rejects it on the grounds that "the spirit of the present passage [69a6–c3], and of the dialogue as a whole, is against this interpretation" (1975, 103; see 144, 224).

21. See Stern 1993, 81.

22. As Schleiermacher says, "it must have been the Philosopher's chief object to conduct every investigation in such a manner from the beginning onwards, as that he might reckon upon the reader's either being driven to an inward and self-originated creation of the thought in view, or submitting to surrender himself most decisively to the feeling of not having discovered or understood anything. To this end, then, it is requisite that the final object of the investigation be not directly enunciated and laid down in words, a process which might very easily serve to entangle many persons who are glad to rest content, provided only that they are in possession of the final result, but that the mind be reduced to the necessity of seeking, and put in the way by which it might find it. The first is done by the mind's being brought to so distinct a consciousness of its own state of ignorance, that it is impossible it should willingly continue therein. The other is effected either by an enigma being woven out of contradictions, to which the only possible solution is to be found in the thought in view, and often several hints thrown out in a way apparently utterly foreign and accidental which can only be found and understood by one who does really investigate with an activity of his own. . . . These are something like the arts by which Plato succeeds with almost every one in either attaining to what he wishes, or, at least, avoiding what he fears" (1973, 17-18).

23. See Bolotin 1987a, 51.

24. Homer *Odyssey* 2.87-128, 19.130-56.

25. For my account of Socrates' irony, see the Introduction.

26. Plato *Apology of Socrates* 38a1-8.

27. See Plato *Republic* 382c6-10.

28. See Plato *Republic* 518b6-d8.

29. See Stern 1993, 28-30, 41-43.

30. See Stern 1993, 91.

31. See, for example, Plato *Apology of Socrates* 32c3–d8.

32. See Plato *Apology of Socrates* 38c1-7, *Crito* 43b10–c3, 53d7–e3. Compare Plato *Apology of Socrates* 31c4-32a3 with 40a2–c3; 23b7–c1, 31b5–c3 with Plato *Republic* 328d7-329e5. See also Xenophon *Apology of Socrates to the Jury* 1-9, and *Memorabilia* 4.8.1, 4-8.

33. See, for example, Homer *Iliad* 24.525-533. Consider also *Isaiah* 55:8-9, *Exodus* 3:13-14, *Genesis* 22:1-12; *Matthew* 20:1-16.

34. For what follows, I am especially indebted to David Bolotin (1987a, especially 52-53).

35. I therefore do not agree with Stern's contention that Socratic rationalism "rests on the human wisdom *that is knowledge of ignorance*" (1993, 137 [my emphasis]; see 130-145, 178-182 [but see 28]). This point marks what I regard as the most significant substantive difference between Stern's interpretation of Socrates' defense of rationalism in the dialogue and my own.

36. Compare 118a5-8 with Plato *Republic* 330d1-331b7, especially 331b1-5. But see also *Phaedo* 84d9–e2, 91a1-3. Consider also chapter 12, 198–99.

Chapter 8. The Objections of Simmias and Cebes to the Argument for Immortality

1. I do not, then, agree with the suggestion of Hackforth (1955, 101) and Gallop (1975, 146) that Plato's Socrates shares Simmias' attitude toward life and philosophy. Consider also Shipton 1979, 41-44 and note 7, chapter 6 of the present work.

2. Shipton characterizes Simmias' view of human reason as one of "religious caution" (1979, 41; see 36, 42-43).

3. As Bluck (1982, 22, 86) and Gallop (1975, 147, 149) note, Socrates never answers this objection to the argument.

4. See Stern 1993, 87-88.

5. Gallop observes that, if Cebes' argument here is correct, "the soul's immortality is not only proven, but is actually disproved." He also points out that Cebes' argument is "never refuted" by Socrates or explicitly "recanted" by Cebes and that, even though Socrates will argue that the soul is imperishable, he "never disputes the theory as a model for understanding the relation between body and soul" (1975, 151). For Gallop's appraisal of Socrates' argument that the soul is imperishable, see 216-222.

6. See Plato *Republic* 369d1–e1.

7. See Bolotin 1987a, 52; Stern 1993, 88-89.

Chapter 9. Socrates' Warning Against Misology

1. See the excellent discussions of this point by Bolotin (1987a, 54-55) and Stern (1993, 92-93). Compare Plato *Phaedo* 88c6-7, 90c1-6 with d6-7; see Plato *Theatetus* 152a1-4, 160c7–e2, 178b2-7, 183a4-7.

2. In other words, Socrates here strengthens the very "faith" in personal immortality which, according to Hackforth, he will appeal to in the final argument for immortality (1955, 164).

3. See Bolotin 1987a, 52-53. This interpretation explains what Bostock calls "Cebes' disappointing reply" to the final argument (1986, 191).

4. See Plato *Lesser Hippias* 365d6-368b1.

5. Consider St. Augustine's account of human friendship in chapters 4-9 of Book IV of his *Confessions*.

6. See 62c9–e4, 81a4-11. See also Strauss 1966, 80-83.

7. Commentators tend to overlook this point. Indeed, Hackforth, Bluck, and Gallop virtually ignore the account of misanthropy, and Bostock simply skips Socrates' account of both misanthropy, and misology. See Hackforth 1955, 110; Bluck 1982, 92; Gallop 1975, 153-54; Bostock 1986, ix, 15.

8. See Burger 1984, 116.

9. See Stern 1993, 95-96.

10. See Stern 1993, 24-25, 42.

11. It seems to me, then, that Hackforth's characterization of misology as "intellectual apathy," "intellectual defeatism," and "indifference to truth and knowledge" is too mild (1955, 105, 110).

12. Burger emphasizes the hope for perfect wisdom rather than the hope for immortality as the cause of misology (1984, 117-19).

13. My discussion of this passage, in particular, owes a great deal to Bolotin's discussion of it (1987a, 49-53).

14. Compare 90e4-91b7 with 63e8-64a2, 69c3–e2, 80e1-81a10; Plato *Republic* 330d1-331b7, 331d6-9.

15. I disagree, then, with Burger's claim that Socrates is here warning his friends against self-interest (1984, 119-121). See Stern 1993, 97.

Chapter 10. Socrates' Response to Simmias' Argument Against Immortality

1. See note 3, chapter 8.

2. See Burger 1984, 126; Stern 1993, 99.

3. For accounts of the structure of this discussion, see Dorter 1982, 99; Gallop 1975, 157-58; Bostock 1986, 126-27.

4. See Bostock 1986, 122-125. For Bostock's defense of Simmias' "materialist" account of the soul, see 125-134. See also Dorter 1982, 99-108.

5. See also Plato *Republic* 430c8–e4ff.

6. See Hackforth 1955, 120; Burger 1984, 128-29.

7. See also Plato *Republic* 611a10–b8. I disagree, then, with Stern's suggestion that here "Socrates considers the character of the soul itself *rather than* its immortality" (1993, 97; my emphasis).

8. See Burger 1984, 131.

9. Homer *Odyssey* 20.17-18.

10. See Hackforth 1955, 117; Gallop 1975, 166-67; Burger 1984, 132; Bostock 1986, 131-32; Stern 1993, 101-102.

Chapter 11. Socrates' Response to Cebes' Argument Against Immortality

1. See, for example, Keyt 1963, 169-171. Even Frede, who attempts to defend this argument against its many critics, concludes only that it is "formally correct" and concedes that it is based on the mere assumption that the soul is a "separable substance" (1978, 32-33, 39).

2. As Gadamer says, "But there could hardly have ever been an interpreter of Plato who could not see that this proof of the ontological relationship of idea, life, and soul, is incapable of demonstrating anything more than the character of the universal *eide*, Life and Soul, and that it most certainly cannot allay the fears which the specific individual soul has of being destroyed, fears which pervade its self-understanding" (1980, 36). Dorter does suggest that the dialogue demonstrates the immortality of "a world-soul or principle of energy" to which all individuals belong and consequently claims that "the Platonic Socrates believed that death was not to be feared and that there is a meaningful sense in which we may be said to be immortal, but I doubt that he regarded immortality as personal in a way acceptable to popular religious imagination" (1982, 43-44, 159; see also 70-71, 157). But, as Bostock points out, "it is clearly no comfort to *me*, when faced with death, to be told to cheer up because the *form* of soul will not perish. What is of concern to me

is my individual soul, and that must be what the argument is meant to be about" (1986, 187).

3. Compare Plato *Apology of Socrates* 38a1-8 with 39e1-40e4.

4. Commentators tend to overlook the extent to which Socrates is addressing Cebes' specific doubts about the philosophic life in this section of the dialogue. See, for example, Gallop 1975, 168-171; Bostock 1986, 134-35.

5. Compare 96c2-7 with Plato *Apology of Socrates* 20c4-23c1, *Alcibiades I* 117d7-118c2.

6. See Montaigne 1958, 306-308.

7. For discussions of this phrase see Shipton 1979, 50; White 1989, 164-65; Stern 1993, 206-207.

8. See Stern 1993, 120-21; see also Shipton 1979, 41-44.

9. See Plato *Parmenides* 130c1–e4.

10. It seems to me that Gallop (1975, 172) and Hackforth (1955, 124) do not fully appreciate this point because they assume too quickly that Socrates' claim that he was "blinded" is "ironical." For helpful discussions of this point, see Davis 1980, 563-64; Dorter 1982, 130-31; Stern 1993, 110-13.

11. See also Burger 1984, 126.

12. See Klein 1965, 50; Strauss 1978, 120-21.

13. See Klein 1965, 133-36; Dorter 1982, 124; Stern 1993, 119–120, 128. Consider also Bluck 1982, 44, 207-209.

14. For this reason, I am inclined to disagree with Taylor's suggestion that "Plato did cling to the notion of the final cause as the true cause, and that the method of the *Phaedo* was intended to be a more laborious method of arriving at the final cause of any phenomenon. . . . " (1969, 53). I do not mean to imply, however, that Socrates ever turned away from investigating teleological (or theological) accounts of the world. See Gallop 1975, 176-77. For others who hold Taylor's view, see Shipton 1979, 33–34, 40; Dorter 1982, 120-24; Bluck 1982, 15; White 1989, 165-67. For the opposing view, see Vlastos 1978, 138-39; Hackforth 1955, 132; Burger 1984, 254; Stern 1993, 209.

15. Compare Plato *Apology of Socrates* 19b2–d8 with *Phaedo* 96aff., especially b8–c1, 97d5-98a6.

16. See Plato *Apology of Socrates* 26d1-5; Aristophanes *Clouds*.

17. For a different interpretation of Socrates' reference to his trial here, see Stern 1993, 115-17, 138. I believe that Stern does not emphasize sufficiently the extent to which Socrates' second sailing reflects his awareness of the theoretical challenge piety, in particular, poses to the philosophic life.

18. See Plato *Republic* 595a1-596e3; compare 596c2-9 with d3–e3.

19. See Hackforth 1955, 143-44; Stern 1993, 122.

20. See Keyt 1963, 168-69; John Brentlinger 1972, 68.

21. I therefore do not agree with the view that Socrates' second sailing marks a rejection of the senses and a turn toward the *separate* ideas or forms. For this view see, for example, Hackforth 1955, 136-144; Vlastos 1978, 139-143; Gallop 1975, 169, 178-184; Shipton 1979, 42-43. For a qualified statement of this view, see Bostock 1986, 157-162. Bostock notes that, in the *Parmenides*, Plato raises several objections to the theory of the forms as we find it in the *Phaedo*" and consequently suggests that "Plato henceforth abandoned the whole notion of forms as standard examples" in favor of the view that forms are common properties of things or immanent (1986, 182-83, 201-207). Grube observes that the *Parmenides* contains a "severe criticism" of the theory of separate forms and admits that Plato never fully answered it but he denies that Plato abandoned this theory (1980, 32-36; see also Hackforth 1955, 143-44; Gallop 1975, 182-83, 189). Burnet suggests, however, that the *Phaedo* and the *Parmenides* "confirm each other in the most remarkable way" (1967, 103). I suggest that in the *Phaedo* itself Socrates calls into question the theory of separate forms and favors the view that the forms are common properties of things and hence are immanent. For a similar view see, for example, Stern 1993, 120-27, 134-37; Burger 1984, 144-160.

22. I disagree, then, with Hackforth's claim that "There is then a sense in which the Forms are hypothetically existent, but it is not a sense which implies doubt on the part of one affirming their existence" (1955, 143). See also Gallop 1975, 179.

23. See Vlastos 1978, 141-42.

24. See Gallop 1975, 97, 191, 222. Gallop remarks that "Socrates' puzzlement is no doubt meant to be infectious. A reader who first has to puzzle over the nature of his puzzles will come to feel them as his own" (172; see also 74).

25. Consider Gallop 1975, 96-97.

26. See Keyt 1963, 170-71.

27. On this point see Burnet 1967, 115; D. O'Brien 1967, 1968, 199-200; Gallop 1975, 192.

28. See Stern 1993, 161-62; Burger 1984, 180-86. Dorter does claim that, according to Socrates, the whole is eternal (1982, 159-160). See also Gallop 1975, 219-221. But consider Stern's response to Dorter (220).

29. See Frede 1978, 33.

30. As Keyt says, even if we grant that what is "immortal" must be indestructible, "What follows is not that the soul is indestructible but that the ensouled body, the entire man, is indestructible" (1963, 170-71).

31. I consequently agree with Frede's contention that Socrates does not simply take it for granted that "deathlessness also means indestructibility" (1978, 31).

32. I suggest, then, that it is Cebes and not, as Keyt maintains, Socrates, who commits "the fallacy of equivocation" (1963, 170-71). But once Cebes commits this fallacy, Socrates does refrain from correcting it. As Friedlander suggests, "The Philosopher does not disturb the faith according to which the soul passing through death's gate enters into a world of splendor and magnificent sights" (1969, 3:60; but see Plato *Phaedo* 107b4-9).

33. See Bostock 1986, 187.

34. As Shipton suggests, Socrates is here "gently rebuking Simmias' distrust—both that of 85cff. and of 107b" (1979, 43).

Chapter 12. The Ending of the Dialogue

1. See White 1989, 138.

2. For this reason, it seems to me that Gallop is too quick to dismiss the details of the myth on the grounds that such myths "do not lend themselves to logical analysis" (1975, 224). As I will argue below, a detailed analysis of the myth calls into question Gallop's assertion that, "by contrasting our earth with 'the true earth' above, it symbolizes the distinction between the sensible world and the world of the Forms" (222).

3. For a discussion of the significance of Socrates' use of the term *idea* here, see Stern 1993, 166-68.

4. Compare 111b6–c1, 108e4-109a7 with 111e6-112a5 and Homer *Iliad* 8.13-27, especially 21-27. See also Plato *Phaedo* 107a9-b3.

5. See, for example, Plato *Gorgias* 476d5-481b1, *Lovers* 137b7–d14, *Republic* 335b2–e5, 380a5–c3. See also Plato *Crito* 49a4-e4; compare with *Phaedo* 114a7–b6.

6. See Plato *Gorgias* 486a5–c3; see also 521b4–d3; Plato *Apology of Socrates* 28b3-5.

7. See Burger 1984, 201-202; Dorter 1982, 172.

8. See Plato *Crito* 45c8–d6, 54a1–b1.

9. See Plato *Laws* 721b6–c8, *Symposium* 207c8-208e5; but see 209c2–e4.

10. It is helpful, in this context, to consider the example of Achilles, who loved Patroclus as much as life itself and who continued to love his friend's corpse, to speak to it, and to embrace it even after his friend had died. See Homer *Iliad* 18.80-82, 234-38, 314-355, especially 333-342, 19.4-5, 23-27, 209-213, 314-333, 23.6-183, 217-225.

11. See also Plato *Crito* 44c3–d5.

12. For other interpretations of Socrates' last words, see, for example, Nietzsche 1968, 473; Burger 1984, 215-16; Joseph Cropsey 1986, 173-74; Stern 1993, 177-78, 224. Consider also chapter 7, 113.

13. See Diogenes Laertius 5.5-6; 2.101-2; 2.116; Derenne 1976, 188-194, 202-212. See also Diogenes Laertius 3.23-24; Grote 1888, 260.

14. See Diogenes Laertius 3.23-25; Grote 1888, 246, 255, 261; Plutarch *Dion* 10-11.

15. See Friedlander 1969, 1:91-92; Grote 1888, 254-56, 261, 265-67; Burnet 1962, 213-14; Taylor 1924, 6-7; Plutarch *Phocion* 4, 5.2, 14.4, 38.2, *Dion* 1-2, 4, 10-11, 17-18.1, 22, *Cicero* 3-4, 32.6, *Brutus* 2, 24.1-2.

16. See Grote 1888, 266.

17. See Diogenes Laertius 5.37-39.

18. Diogenes Laertius 6.43, 7.6, 9-12, 29-30.

19. Diogenes Laertius 9.64, 69-70.

20. Plutarch also explains in this passage that Marcus Cato was so alarmed by the long visit and the growing fame of the philosophers that he sought to remove them from the city on some pretext. Even though he appears to have been alone in his hostility to the philosophers, his authority was so great that he persuaded the senate to settle the Athenians' petition so that the ambassadors would leave Rome and return to Athens.

21. See Cicero *De Republica* 3.5-6, 4.4-5 (see also 1.34; *Tusculan Disputations* 1.79); Plutarch *Cato the Younger* 4, 6.1-3, 10, 65.5, 66-70. Consider also E. K. Rand 1943, 9-30. He suggests that ". . . Plato . . . was, invisibly but potently, one of the builders of Rome" (30).

22. See Plutarch *Nicias* 23.

23. See also, for example, Plato *Republic* 613e6-621d3, *Gorgias* 523a1-527a8, *Meno* 81a5–e3, *Phaedrus* 245b7-257a2, *Apology of Socrates* 39e1-41c7, *Crito* 54b2–c8, *Laws* 886e6ff. Compare also Plato *Apology of Socrates* 18b4–c3, 23d2-7, with *Timaeus* 27a3-6, c1–d4, 29a2-6, 29e1-30c1, 39e3-42d2, 46e6-47c4, 52d3–e6, 90b1–d7. Plato also defended the piety of philosophy by reinterpreting the traditional religion of the Greeks so as to render it compatible with the rationalism of the philosopher. See Plato *Republic* 377b11–383c7, *Cratylus* 395d7-410e1.

24. See Cicero *De Legibus* 3.1; *De Natura Deorum* 2.32.

25. Justin Martyr I *Apology* 46.3; II *Apology* 10.8. Justin also compares the execution of Socrates for impiety with the persecution of the Christians (I *Apology* 5). For his praise of Plato and Socrates, see also I *Apology* 3, 18, 20, 59-60; II *Apology* 12-13. According to Werner Jaeger, "The parallel of Socrates and Jesus

runs through the entire work" (1961, 118; see also 28-29, 34-35; Etienne Gilson 1944, 16-21). Jaroslav Pelikan observes that "A comparison between the suffering of Christ and that of Socrates seems to have become a common idea in Christian apologetics. . . ." (1971, 58).

26. Clement *Stromata* 1.22. 150; see also 6.17.159.8-9; 5.5. 29.3-4. Consider as well Jean Daniélou 1961, 50-67. Gilson paraphrases Clement as saying, "Les deux maîtres par excellence seront Pythagore, homme illuminé de Dieu, et Platon, dont toute la philosophie se tourne à la piété" (1944, 51-52).

27. Origen *Contra Celsium* 9.17, 5.56; compare Pelikan 1971, 48, with Plato *Phaedo* 72e3-77b1, 105c9-107a1. See also Jaeger 1961, 65, 68, 136.

28. Gilson 1944, 60-61.

29. Pelikan 1971, 50-51; see also Jaeger 1961, 80-81, 86-100.

30. See St. Augustine *City of God* 8.1, 3-8, 11; 10.1-2; 11.21; 12.25, 28, *Confessions* 7.9-10, 20.

31. St. Augustine *De Vera Religione* 4.7.

32. As quoted by Gilson (1944, 137).

33. See St. Augustine *City of God* 8.12-13; 10.30-31; 13.16; 14.5; 22.11, 25. Augustine criticizes the Platonists for censuring the body as evil and for creating a cult of the soul. Compare 14.5 with Plato *Phaedo* 64c4-69e5, especially 66b3-67b6, 78b4-84b8. For the difficulty the Christians had in reconciling the biblical doctrine of resurrection with the doctrine of the immortality of the soul, see Pelikan 1971, 51-52; Gilson 1944, 103-104.

34. Gilson 1944, 93-94. For the influence of Plato and Platonism on the Christians as a whole, see 268; Taylor 1924, 17-24; Jaeger 1947, 2; 1961, 44-46; 1943, 2:77-78; Raymond Klibansky 1939. Consider also Nietzsche 1989, 2.

35. For Abelard see *Theologia "Summi Boni"*, edited by H. Ostlender (Munster, 1939), 25; Gilson 1944, 342. For Roger Bacon, John of Garland, and Albert the Great, see Gilson, 401-402, 409, 512. For Petrarch see *The Triumph of Fame*, Pt. 3, translated by Hugh Boyd in *The Sonnets, Triumphs, and Other Poems of Petrarch* (London, 1883), 391; Gilson 1944, 723, 725. For Marsilio Ficino see *Opera Omnia* (Basel, 1562), 25, 267, 868; Klibansky 1939, 35-36, 42-43. For other Christians who praise Socrates and Plato, namely, St. Johannes Bonaventura, St. Thomas Aquinas, Jean de Meun, John Duns Scotus, Ulrich Zwingli, John Calvin, Erasmus, Robert Barclay, Søren Kirekegaard, and Karl Barth, see H. Spiegelberg 1964, 51-54, 60-62, 66, 70-71, 273, 291-306.

36. Erasmus, *Convivium Religiosum* in *Opera* (1703), I, 683. See Gilson 1944, 21; Jaeger 1961, 100-102. But see also Martin Luther's attack on Erasmus for praising Socrates in *Werke* (Weimar, 1833), 11.350; 43.614.

37. See Gilson 1944, 755.

38. See Tertullian *Apology* 46, *A Treatise on the Soul*, II, in *The Anti-Nicene Fathers* (Grand Rapids, 1950), 3.51, 181-2; Gilson 1944, 97-99; Jaeger 1961, 33, 122.

39. Gilson 1944, 236-38.

40. Luther, 11.292, 350; 43.614; 56.157. For other Christians who criticize Socrates, see Spiegelberg 1964, 44-48, 66.

41. See Plato *Cleitophon* 410a7–b2, *Republic* 335a6–e5. See also Plato *Euthyphro* 12d1-6.

Selected Bibliography

Alfarabi. 1972. "Plato's Laws." Translated by Muhsin Mahdi. In *Medieval Political Philosophy*. Edited by Ralph Lerner and Muhsin Mahdi. Ithaca: Cornell University Press.

Bloom, Allan. 1968. *The Republic of Plato*. New York: Basic Books.

Bluck, R. S. 1982. *Plato's Phaedo*. Indianapolis: Library of Liberal Arts.

Bolotin, David. 1979. *Plato's Dialogue on Friendship*. Ithaca: Cornell University Press.

———. 1987a. "The Life of Philosophy and the Immortality of the Soul: An Introduction to Plato's *Phaedo*." *Ancient Philosophy* 7:39–56.

———. 1987b. "The *Theatetus* and the Possibility of False Opinion." *Interpretation* 15(May and September):179–193.

Bostock, David. 1986. *Plato's Phaedo*. Oxford: Clarendon Press.

Brentlinger, John. 1972. "Incomplete Predicates and the Two-World Theory of the *Phaedo*." *Phronesis*, 61–79.

Burger, Ronna. 1984. *The Phaedo: A Platonic Labyrinth*. New Haven: Yale University Press.

Burnet, John. [1930] 1957. *Early Greek Philosophy*. Reprint. New York: Meridian Books.

———. [1914] 1962. *Greek Philosophy, Part I: Thales to Plato*. Reprint. London: Macmillan and Co.

———. [1911] 1967. *Plato's Phaedo*. Reprint. Oxford: Clarendon Press.

Cropsey, Joseph. 1986. "The Dramatic End of Plato's Socrates." *Interpretation* 14(May and September):155–175.

Daniélou, Jean. 1961. *Message Evangélique et Culture Hellenistique*. Paris: Bibliothèque de Théologie.

Davis, Michael. 1980. "Socrates' Pre-Socratism: Some Remarks on the Structure of Plato's *Phaedo*." *Review of Metaphysics* 33:559–577.

Derenne, Eudore. [1930] 1976. *Les Procès D'Impiété Intentés aux Philosophes à Athènes au Vme et au IVme Siècles avant J-C*. Reprint. New York: Arno Press.

Dodds, E. R. 1951. *The Greeks and the Irrational*. Berkeley: University of California Press.

Dorter, Kenneth. 1982. *Plato's Phaedo: An Interpretation*. Toronto: University of Toronto Press.

Frede, Dorothy. 1978. "The Final Proof of the Immortality of the Soul in Plato's *Phaedo* 102a–107a." *Phronesis* 23: 27–41.

Friedlander, Paul. 1969. *Plato*. 3 vols. Translated by H. Meyerhoff. Princeton: Princeton University Press.

Fustel de Coulanges, Numa Denis. 1900. *La Cité Antique*. Paris: Libraire Hachette.

Gadamer, Hans-Georg. 1980. *Dialogue and Dialectic: Eight Hermeneutical Studies on Plato*. Translated by P. Christopher Smith. New Haven: Yale University Press.

Gallop, David. 1975. *Plato's Phaedo*. Oxford: Clarendon Press.

Gilson, Etienne. 1944. *La Philosophie au Moyen Age*. Paris: R. Bussière.

Goethe, Johann Wolfgang von. 1974. *The Autobiography of Johann Wolfgang von Goethe*. Translated by J. Oxenford. Chicago: University of Chicago Press.

Gosling, J. B. 1965. "Similarity in *Phaedo* 73b seq.." *Phronesis* 10:151–161.

Griswold, Charles, Jr. 1980. "Style and Philosophy: The Case of Plato's Dialogues." *Monist* 63:530–546.

Grote, George. 1862. *A History of Greece*, vols. 5–6. London: John Murray.

———. 1888. *Plato and the Other Companions of Socrates*. vol. 1. London: John Murray.

Grube, G. M. A. [1935] 1980. *Plato's Thought*. Reprint. Indianapolis, IN: Hackett Publishing Company.

Guthrie, W. K. C. 1950. *The Greeks and Their Gods*. Boston: Beacon Press.

———. 1971. *Socrates*. Cambridge: Cambridge University Press.

Hackforth, R. 1955. *Plato's Phaedo*. Cambridge: Cambridge University Press.

Hegel, Georg. 1955. *Lectures on the History of Philosophy*. vols. 1–2. Translated by E. S. Haldane and F. Simson. New Jersey: Humanities Press.

Jaeger, Werner. 1943. *Paideia: The Ideals of Greek Culture*. 2 vols. New York: Oxford University Press.

————. 1947. *The Theology of the Early Greek Philosophers*. Translated by E. Robinson. Oxford: Clarendon Press.

————. 1961. *Early Christianity and Greek Paideia*. Cambridge: Belknap Press of Harvard University Press.

Keyt, David. 1963. "The Fallacies in *Phaedo* 102a–107b." *Phronesis* 8:167–172.

Klein, Jacob. 1965. *A Commentary on Plato's Meno*. Chapel Hill: University of North Carolina Press.

Klibansky, Raymond. 1939. *The Continuity of the Platonic Tradition During the Middle Ages*. London: Warburg Institute.

Maritain, Jacques. 1962. *An Introduction to Philosophy*. Translated by E. I. Watkins. New York: Sheed and Ward.

Mill, John Stuart. 1975. "On Liberty." In *Three Essays*. Oxford: Oxford University Press.

Montaigne, Michel. 1958. *The Complete Essays of Montaigne*. Translated by Donald Frame. Stanford: Stanford University Press.

Muir, J. V. 1985. "Religion and the New Education: The Challenge of the Sophists." In *Greek Religion and Society*. Edited by P. E. Easterling and J. V. Muir. Cambridge: Cambridge University Press, 191–218.

Nietzsche, Friedrich. 1967. *The Birth of Tragedy*. Translated by Walter Kaufmann. New York: Vintage Books.

————. 1968. *Twilight of the Idols*. Translated by Walter Kaufmann. In *The Portable Nietzsche*. New York: Viking Press.

————. 1989. *Beyond Good and Evil*. Translated by Walter Kaufmann. New York: Vintage Books.

O'Brien, D. 1967, 1968. "The Last Argument of Plato's *Phaedo*." *Classical Quarterly* 17–18:198–231, 95–106.

Pangle, Thomas. 1980. *The Laws of Plato*. New York: Basic Books.

Pelikan, Jaroslav. 1971. *The Emergence of the Catholic Tradition*. Chicago: University of Chicago Press.

Rand, E. K. 1943. *The Building of Eternal Rome*. Cambridge: Harvard University Press.

Robin, Léon. 1928. *Greek Thought and the Origins of the Scientific Spirit*. Translated by M. R. Dobie. New York: Alfred A. Knopf.

Robinson, T. M. 1969. "*Phaedo* 70c: An Error and an Explanation." *Dialogue* 8(June):124–25.

Rosen, Stanley. 1987. *Plato's Symposium*. 2nd Ed. New Haven:Yale University Press.

Rousseau, Jean-Jacques. 1979a. *Emile*. Translated by Allan Bloom. New York: Basic Books.

———. 1979b. *Political Economy*. In *On the Social Contract, with Geneva Manuscript and Political Economy*. Translated by Judith Masters. New York: St. Martin's Press.

Schleiermacher, Friedrich. 1973. *Introductions to the Dialogues of Plato*. Translated by William Dobson. New York: Arno Press.

Shipton, K. M. W. 1979. "A good second-best: *Phaedo* 99bff." *Phronesis* 24:33–54.

Spiegelberg, H., ed. 1964. *The Socratic Enigma*. Indianapolis: Bobbs-Merrill.

Stern, Paul. 1993. *Socratic Rationalism and Political Philosophy*. State University of New York Press.

Stone, I. F. 1989. *The Trial of Socrates*. London: Pan Books.

Strauss, Leo. 1946. "On a New Interpretation of Plato's Political Philosophy." *Social Research* 13 (September):326–67.

———. 1966. *Socrates and Aristophanes*. New York: Basic Books.

———. 1978. *The City and Man*. Chicago: The University of Chicago Press.

Taylor, A. E. 1924. *Platonism and Its Influence*. Boston: Marshall Jones Co.

———. 1960. *Plato: The Man and His Work*. 7th ed. London: Methuen and Co.

Taylor, C. C. W. 1969. "Forms as Causes in the *Phaedo*." *Mind* 73:45–59.

Toynbee, Arnold. 1939. *A Study of History*. vol. 7. New York and London.

Vlastos, Gregory. 1978. "Reasons and Causes in the *Phaedo*." In *Plato: A Collection of Critical Essays I*. Edited by Gregory Vlastos. Notre Dame: University of Notre Dame Press.

———. 1991. *Socrates, Ironist and Moral Philosopher*. Cornell: Cornell University Press.

White, David. 1989. *Myth and Metaphysics in Plato's Phaedo*. Selinsgrove, PA: Susquehanna University Press.

Zeller, Eduard. 1980. *Outlines of the History of Greek Philosophy*. Revised by Wilhelm Nestle. Translated by L. R. Palmer. New York: Dover Publications.

Index

Abelard, 204, 228n. 35
Achilles, 226n. 10
Aeschines (character in *Phaedo*), 209n. 2
Aeschines (orator), 210n. 14
Aesop, 22–23
Albert the Great, 204, 228n. 35
Alcibiades, 5, 11, 13, 14
Alexander the Great, 2, 207n. 7
Alfarabi, 208n. 15
Anaxagoras, 10, 11, 12, 14, 166–170,
    172–73, 205, 210n. 13, 211nn. 28, 29
Andocides, 210n. 18
Antiphon, 211n. 24
Antisthenes, 209nn. 1, 2
Apollodorus, 209n. 1
Aristophanes, 62, 207n. 4, 210nn. 10, 13,
    17, 211nn. 19, 26, 27, 28, 212n. 44,
    214n. 7, 216n. 3, 224n. 16
Aristotle, 10, 11, 201, 202, 205, 214nn. 11,
    15
Augustine, Saint, 204, 222n. 5, 228nn. 30,
    31, 33

Bacon, Roger, 204, 228n. 35
Barclay, Robert, 228n. 35
Barth, Karl, 228n. 35
Bloom, Allan, 208n. 15
Bluck, R. S., 4, 207n. 8, 208nn. 11, 13, 16,
    213n. 2, 218n. 12, 221n. 3, 222n. 7,
    224nn. 13, 14
Boethius, 209n. 5
Bolotin, David, 7, 208n. 15, 214n. 10, 215n.
    5, 216nn. 10, 15, 4, 218n. 11, 220nn. 19,
    20, 23, 221n. 34, 222nn. 7, 1, 3, 13
Bostock, David, 3, 207n. 8, 208nn. 9, 16,
    213n. 2, 215n. 8, 216n. 7, 217nn. 9, 10,
    12, 14, 218nn. 12, 13, 14, 1, 219n. 8,

220n. 20, 222nn. 3, 7, 223nn. 3, 4, 10, 2,
    224n. 4, 225n. 21, 226n. 33
Brentlinger, John, 225n. 20
Brutus, 202
Burger, Ronna, 7, 208n. 26, 209n. 28,
    213n. 2, 215n. 23, 216nn. 11, 6, 217nn.
    7, 8, 9, 2, 5, 6, 218nn. 15, 17, 219nn. 1,
    3, 6, 15, 220n. 18, 222nn. 8, 12, 15,
    223nn. 2, 6, 8, 10, 224nn. 11, 14, 225nn.
    21, 28, 226n. 7, 227n. 12
Burnet, John, 4, 13–15, 207n. 1, 208nn. 11,
    16, 209n. 7, 211n. 30, 212nn. 32, 33, 35,
    36, 40, 41, 42, 45, 213n. 5, 214n. 6,
    215nn. 6, 8, 218nn. 19, 1, 225nn. 21, 27,
    227n. 15

Calvin, John, 207n. 7, 228n. 35
Carneades, 202
Cato the Younger, 2, 202, 207n. 7
Cephalus, 113
Cicero, 1, 202, 207nn. 2, 7, 8, 209nn. 3, 4,
    210nn. 9, 10, 15, 211n. 26, 212nn. 34,
    40, 42, 227nn. 21, 24
Clement of Alexandria, 203, 228n. 26
Critias, 13, 14, 212n. 38
Crito, 16, 22, 113, 193–96, 198, 209n. 1
Critoboulos, 209n. 1
Cropsey, Joseph, 227n. 12
Ctessipus, 209n. 1

Damon, 10, 210n. 13
Daniélou, Jean, 228n. 26
Davis, Michael, 218n. 10, 224n. 10
Democritus, 10, 211n. 28
Derenne, Eudore, 210nn. 10, 11, 13, 14,
    19, 211n. 24, 212nn. 39, 40, 41, 42, 43,
    45, 227n. 13

235